CORRECTIONAL OFFICER RESOURCE GUIDE

Third Edition

edited by Don Bales

American Correctional Association
4380 Forbes Boulevard
Lanham, MD 20706-4322

Copyright 1997 by the American Correctional Association. All rights reserved. The reproduction, distribution, or inclusion in other publications of materials in this book is prohibited without prior written permission from the American Correctional Association. No part of this book may be reproduced by any electronic means including information storage and retrieval systems without permission in writing from the publisher.

Reginald A. Wilkinson, President
James A. Gondles, Jr., Executive Director
Gabriella M. Daley, Director, Communications and Publications
Leslie A. Maxam, Assistant Director, Communications and Publications
Alice Fins, Publications Managing Editor
Michael Kelly, Associate Editor
Dana M. Murray, Graphics and Production Manager
Cover Design by Quintina Kornegay

ISBN 1-56991-064-2

This publication may be ordered from:

American Correctional Association
4380 Forbes Boulevard
Lanham, Maryland 20706-4322
1-800-222-5646

For information on publications and videos available from ACA, contact our World Wide Web home page at: http://www.corrections.com/aca.

Printed in the United States of America by McArdle Printing Company, Upper Marlboro, Md.

Library of Congress Cataloging-in-Publication Data

    Correctional officer resource guide / edited by Don Bales. — 3rd ed.
        p.   cm.
    ISBN 1-56991-064-2 (pbk.)
    1. Corrections—Handbooks, manuals, etc. 2. Correctional personnel—
Handbooks, manuals, etc. 3. Correctional personnel--Training of—
Handbooks, manuals, etc. I. Bales, Don L., 1933-   .
HV8670.C76 1997
365—dc21

                                                                                  97-9814
                                                                                     CIP

Contents

Preface by James A. Gondles, Jr. iv
Acknowledgments v
Introduction vii
   1. An Overview of the Criminal Justice System and the
      Role of the Correctional Officer 1
   2. Officers' Responsibilities and Training 9
   3. Corrections and the Law *by Craig Hemmens, J.D., Ph.D.* 15
   4. Inmate Supervision and Discipline 23
   5. Security and Control 37
   6. Firearms, Gas, and Use of Force 51
   7. Emergency Plans and Procedures 61
   8. Food Service 75
   9. Sanitation and Hygiene 83
  10. Health Care 89
  11. Inmates with Mental Illness *by John L. Gannon, Ph.D.* 103
  12. Reception, Orientation, and Classification of Inmates 111
  13. Programming and Related Services 117
  14. Parole and Release *by Edward M. Read, LCSW, NCAC II* 131
  15. Public Relations and Citizen Involvement 135
Job Titles 141
Glossary 143
Index 155
ACA Code of Ethics 161

Preface

This revised edition of the *Correctional Officer Resource Guide* will enable new correctional officers and their supervisors to understand the vital role of this position within the institution. The objective is to provide a clear guide to the duties and responsibilities of the correctional officer and his or her relationship with others on the staff and in the community.

Certainly, there will be differences in policies and procedures among various institutions. This book is intended to provide a broad overview of the role of the correctional officer. As such, it may be usefully employed in college courses as well as in staff training programs. It should also be a part of each high school's and library's career corner. It provides information that should enable individuals who want to know if a career in corrections is for them an opportunity to learn about the role of those on the first rung in a corrections career. Certainly, if information in this publication conflicts with local policies and practices, correctional officers should follow the rules of their institution.

We are indebted to the conscientious attention to the content of this publication from a wide range of individuals, but most especially Don Bales, who spearheaded the editorial effort. Additionally, in particular we thank Craig Hemmens, J.D., Ph.D., for his chapter on law, Dr. John Gannon for the chapter on mental health, and Edward Read, LCSW, NCAC II, for the chapter on parole and release. Many other individuals took time to review chapters and suggest changes. We are grateful for their help, as well. We asked several of our affiliate organizations to review specific chapters and are pleased that they could provide this service. What this great outpouring of help reveals is a vibrant association membership that is willing to help increase the professionalization of the new members of our chosen field.

At the end of each chapter and throughout the chapters, reference is made to the standards of the American Correctional Association. These standards are guidelines for the efficient and humane operation of institutions. Many states have adopted them, and in other states, they have been mandated by the courts to ensure the safe and effective operation of correctional institutions. There are over eighteen separate sets of standards for a wide range of institutions. The standards referenced in this book refer to those contained in *Standards for Adult Correctional Institutions*.

These standards specifically state how things are to be handled in the following categories: administration and management, physical plant, institutional operations, institutional services, and inmate programs. Copies of this publication and the *Standards Supplement* that updates the standards are available from the American Correctional Association.

We invite those reading this book to call the American Correctional Association—1-800-ACA-JOIN, or contact us on the Internet at http://www.corrections.com/aca, so that you can continue to increase your professionalization through participation in seminars, conferences, and a wide range of professional literature, including our award-winning magazine, *Corrections Today*. Members also may take advantage of correspondence courses and even receive college credit for some courses. More important, by joining the association representing your profession, you are announcing that you are a professional and wish to join with others to increase the integrity and respect for correctional officers.

James A. Gondles, Jr.
Executive Director

Acknowledgments

The following people have reviewed and or made significant contributions to this publication. We thank them for their contribution to the profession.

- Helen Campbell Altmeyer, Assistant United States Attorney, U.S. Department of Justice, Northern District of West Virginia
- Don Bales, Consultant, Gerrardstown, West Virginia, formerly Officer Major and Shift Commander, Maryland Department of Corrections
- Eleanor (Ellie) G. Bowles, R.N., Regional Contract Administrator, Maryland Division of Corrections, Western Maryland Region
- Chaplin Clarence Earl Brubaker, Roxbury Correctional Institution, Hagerstown, Maryland
- Ronald Daniel Bucher, Volunteer Activities Coordinator III, Roxbury Correctional Institution, Hagerstown, Maryland
- Mary Beth Chunn, Director, Community Relations, Corrections Corporation of America, Nashville, Tennessee
- John H. Clark, M.D., Chief Physician III, Los Angeles County Sheriff's Department
- Carl B. Clements, Professor, Department of Psychology, University of Alabama, Tuscalosa, Alabama
- William C. Collins, Attorney at Law, Olympia, Washington
- Patricia K. Cushwa, Commissioner, Maryland Parole Commission, Baltimore, Maryland
- Karen Ann Elliott, Correctional Case Management Supervisor, Roxbury Correctional Institution, Hagerstown, Maryland
- Robert M. Freeman, Assistant Professor, Department of Criminal Justice, Shippensburg University, Camp Hill, Pennsylvania
- John L. Gannon, Ph.D., Director, Central Coast Consultancy, Pismo Beach, California
- Robert D. Hannigan, Warden, Hutchinson Correctional Facility, Hutchinson, Kansas
- Richard E. Hawkins, Correctional Principle, Roxbury Correctional Institution, Hagerstown, Maryland
- Gail Heller, President, Choices, Columbus, Ohio
- Craig Hemmens, J.D., Ph.D., Assistant Professor of Criminal Justice, Boise State University, Boise, Idaho
- Dr. Patrick Henry, Associate Professor of Sociology, Eckerd College, Lakeland, Florida
- Lavinia Johnson, President, American Correctional Food Services Association, Richmond, Virginia
- Justin Jones, Regional Director, Oklahoma Department of Corrections, Northeast Region, Tulsa, Oklahoma
- Peggy G. Kanche, Executive Director, First Corrections Corporation, First Arizona Youth Academy, Phoenix, Arizona
- William Louis Keller, Jr., Correctional Dietary Supervisor, Roxbury Correctional Institution, Hagerstown, Maryland
- Paul F. Kradel, Ed.D., Chief Psychologist, Roxbury Correctional Institution, Hagerstown, Maryland
- Joseph J. Marchese, President, International Association of Correctional Training Personnel, Chicago, Illinois
- Robert L. Matthews, Regional Director/Southeast Region, Federal Bureau of Prisons, Atlanta, Georgia
- Duncan Mills, Central Classification Board Member, Virginia Department of Corrections, Richmond, Virginia
- Kenneth B. Moritsugu, M.D., Assistant Surgeon General, Medical Director, Health Services Division, Federal Bureau of Prisons, Washington, D.C.
- Edward M. Read, LCSW, NCAC II, U.S. Probation Officer, Washington, D.C.
- John Roberts, Chief of Communications and Archives, Bureau of Prisons, Washington, D.C.
- Dennis Sherman, Education Director, Highland Residential Center, Highland, New York
- John Slansky, Warden, Lovelock Correctional Center, Carson City, Nevada
- Jan Sorenson, R.N., Regional Health Systems Administrator, Federal Bureau of Prisons, Mid-Atlantic Regional Office, Atlanta, Georgia
- J. Michael Stouffer, Assistant Warden, Maryland Correctional Training Center, Hagerstown, Maryland
- Dorothy Strawsburg, LCSW-C, Western Regional Social Services Supervisor, Maryland Division of Corrections, Western Maryland Correctional Complex, Cumberland, Maryland
- Michael James Walsh, Correctional Dietary Manager-General, Roxbury Correctional Institution, Hagerstown, Maryland
- Karen Wesloh, Executive Director, American Correctional Food Services Association, St. Louis Park, Minnesota
- Maceo M. Williams, Commissioner, Maryland Parole Commission, Baltimore, Maryland

The Many Faces of Corrections

Photos courtesy (left to right): Maryland Correctional Institution, Hagerstown; photos 2 and 4 Montgomery County, Maryland, Detention Center; photo 3, California Department of Corrections; photo 5, Prince George's County, Maryland, Department of Corrections; photo 6, Montgomery County, Maryland, Department of Corrections; photo 7, ACA.

Introduction

Correctional operations in America are shaped by a changing balance in our society—the balance between the public's right to be free from crime and inmates' rights as they are constantly redefined by the courts. Over time, the balances shift, and corrections must shift with them.

In recent years, the shift has been tied to increased incarceration. In the late 1980s and early 1990s, prison populations soared due, in part, to increased drug trafficking, heightened enforcement efforts, and the "get tough" on crime attitude resulting in various changes in laws and mandatory sentencing rules. In 1995 and 1996, there was a reduction in the quantity of crimes committed, but prisons now house inmates with longer sentences. Crowding is still an issue. Even though fewer inmates are coming into the system, they are staying longer.

Legislators' interpretation of public feelings about crime and punishment are dictating prison, rather than community corrections, as an option more often. As a result, during the past decade, the nation's adult prison population has more then doubled; by the end of 1995, it had reached more than 1,633,331 (Bureau of Justice Statistics 1997).

This population increase has not been matched by the necessary prison construction and expansion. Thus, crowding in correctional institutions is now a major concern. In many prisons, two or more inmates are forced to live in cells designed for only one; others live in crowded double-bunked dormitories, or in hallways, recreation halls, day rooms, gymnasiums, and other areas not designed as living quarters.

As correctional institutions become more crowded, many inmates who should be confined in single cells because of their violent backgrounds are housed, instead, in dormitories. This dramatically increases the chance for problems. Under such conditions, the other physical limits of an institution become more pronounced.

CHART 1: Adult Inmate Population in the United States: 1985-1995

	1985	1995	Percentage Increase	Percentage Held
State Prisons	452,372	1,026,037	127	63
Federal Prisons	37,669	100,250	166	6
Local Jails	254,986	507,044	99	31
Totals	745,027	1,633,331	119	100

Source: Bureau of Justice Statistics, 1997

Support facilities which have not been enlarged, such as gymnasiums, kitchens, dining rooms, industrial and vocational areas, academic classrooms, and medical and mental health facilities, are severely stressed. In many cases, program resources are inadequate for the increased numbers of inmates they must serve. Perhaps, most important, due to budget constraints, there has been an increase in inmate/staff ratios. This has resulted in less supervision, reduced security, and increased stress in many institutions.

Inmates in prison today contribute to the problem. American correctional institutions are populated primarily by young, unmarried males. Although they increased 2 percent in 1992-1993, female inmates still make up only 5.4 percent of the entire inmate population in the United States (ACA 1995). Inmates are mainly from the lower social and economic strata of society. Both the women and men are frequently the products of broken homes, poorly educated, and possess unstable work histories.

At the end of 1995, the state prison population was 1,026,037.

With the rapid growth in the prison population, crowding becomes a too common occurrence.

State Prison Population
(in percentage)

	Male	Female
White*	40.4	2.7
Black*	52.1	3.3
All Others	1.4	.1

*includes Hispanics
Source: *Correctional Populations in the United States, 1995*. Bureau of Justice Statistics, May 1997.

In the Federal Bureau of Prisons, as of September 1995: the total population was 100,958, 92.5 percent male and 7.5 percent female. Ethnicity was Hispanic 27.2 percent and Non Hispanic 72.8 percent. By race, white 60.4 percent, black 36.6 percent, and other 3 percent (U.S. Department of Justice 1995).

Typical inmates are apt to have a prior criminal record, low self-esteem, and be uncommitted to any major goals in life. Material failure in a culture firmly oriented toward material success is the most common denominator among them.

Correctional institutions also incarcerate a disproportionate share of individuals who are mentally deficient, emotionally unstable, or prone to violent and other socially deviant behavior. In addition, some special groups within the general prison population, for a variety of reasons, are especially prone to causing problems.

Prison gangs, which have become more widespread in recent years, often are formed along racial or ethnic lines, and are increasingly sophisticated, as they align themselves with outside religious or political groups. Revolutionary organizations, with their terrorist tactics, have continued to be active in some institutions; their influence, as well as that of prison gangs, occasionally has become a threat to ex-inmates and their families, as well as to correctional staff. Dealing with these various types of inmates is a challenge.

The other visible sign of a shifting balance has been in the legal area. Throughout the last several decades, police and corrections practices have been under close review by state and federal courts. The right to privacy, search and seizure practices, prearraignment procedures, and investigative techniques employed by law enforcement agencies were questioned and, at times, redefined by the legal process. In 1996, there were fresh videotaped acts of excessive force, used by police, for the courts to review.

Today, corrections is attracting a great deal of interest and concern that had been given in the past to law enforcement. Many correctional agencies themselves are acknowledging problems and attempting systemwide improvements by adopting standards, either from the American Correctional Association or from other sources.

Standards are guidelines established as a basis of comparison in measuring or judging the adequacy of programs, facilities, or activities. These guidelines can be very formal and supported by the force of law (as in Maryland), or can be rather informal with only moderate social pressure to comply. Standards are important for many reasons, such as maintaining and supporting

Introduction

quality, encouraging improvement, and providing both a means to recognize excellence and to identify and possibly eliminate inferior programs. Correctional standards have been developed by many groups including the United Nations, the American Medical Association, the United States Department of Justice, and many state and local governmental agencies.

The most comprehensive and widely recognized set of standards that apply to correctional institutions have been developed by the Commission of Accreditation for Corrections (CAC), now a part of the American Correctional Association (ACA). In 1967, the Ford Foundation provided a grant to ACA to develop a self-evaluation procedure for corrections (Gettinger 1982). Then, in 1974, the ACA, with a grant from the Law Enforcement Assistance Administration, established the Commission on Accreditation for Corrections, which was charged with the responsibility of developing comprehensive national standards for corrections (Keve 1996). The first set of standards was published in 1977; later, revised editions have been published. There are more than twenty-five sets of standards for various types of institutions from adult local detention facilities, boot camps, and adult correctional institutions to several for juvenile institutions. The standards have been divided into four categories: mandatory, essential, important, and desirable. These descriptive categories let the correctional agency personnel know what emphasis should be placed on each area of the standards. The standards are recognized as minimum guidelines an agency should attempt to meet. It is the hope of most professionals that eventually all correctional institutions not only will meet but exceed these guidelines. There are measures now underway to make all the standards performance based.

Finally, the involvement of the courts, communities, and other decision makers also influences the daily activities of the correctional employee. Chapter 3, "Corrections and the Law," is a must read for all correctional officers. Assistant United States Attorney Helen Campbell Altmeyer states, "I have reviewed the ACA 'Corrections and the Law.' I believe that it is right on point and, in fact, if the suggestions contained in it had been followed by the correctional officers I have been called upon to represent, I do not believe they would have been sued."

Many correctional systems are operating under some type of court order or supervision. Fifteen states have emergency-release programs that mandate release of incarcerated inmates when a court-imposed total prison population cap is reached. Others are managed by court-appointed "Special Masters."

Other corrections' departments formally have agreed to make specific changes to avoid further court cases. However, in systems throughout the country, inmates are suing individual institutional staff for alleged violations of their rights.

The Americans with Disabilities Act (ADA) requires making institutions barrier free and accessible for those in wheelchairs or those with other types of disabilities including vision and hearing impairments, and other problems. By 1996, most states made necessary changes and offered staff training so that staff can comply with the ADA. In other cases, the changes are being made as a result of inmate litigation. Taken together, the impact that these legal forces are having on prisons is very significant.

American Correctional Association auditors question staff during an accreditation audit.

The institutional world, with its many varieties of inmates and inmate groups, is often very strange to new correctional staff. The changing demands of the legal system are equally difficult to understand and master. It is important that officers know how to do the technical part of their job well, understand the nature of the inmate population, develop the skills to accurately assess inmate behavior, and be able to react quickly and appropriately to situations. At the same time, they have to maintain a high level of professional conduct that is consistent with the courts' demands.

An additional burden on the new as well seasoned correctional officers is the escalation of juvenile crime. A number of states have changed the age at which a juvenile may be tried as an adult. More juveniles now are being sent to adult correctional institutions, creating a need for special programs targeted at these youthful offenders and special training for those who interact with them. The

Correctional Officer Resource Guide

Correctional officer helps a special needs inmate in keeping with the Americans with Disability Act regulations.

The Correctional Officer

Well-informed, properly supervised correctional personnel form the foundation for an effective, proactive security program, one that can prevent many prison problems. Since correctional officers, along with inmate work supervisors, have the most contacts with inmates, their knowledge and competence in security techniques, their powers of observation, and their insight into inmate behavior are of great importance. In addition, since inmates rely on officers for supervision, direction, and information, correctional officers must be well informed about the institution's policies, programs, and procedures.

At one time, some people thought the way to be a successful correctional officer was through muscle and the sheer weight of unquestioned authority. However, today's correctional setting requires far more. Detailed written regulations, post orders, and policy manuals are replacing hunches and instincts as a basis for action. Technology now plays an important part in security. Officers constantly must be aware of new inmate rights and staff responsibilities because their decisions increasingly are subject to review by the courts, correctional administrators, legislators, and the general public. These are some of the reasons why standards of professional conduct have been developed and continually are being refined. They provide the necessary guidance to agencies in setting up their institutional operations and supervising their staff.

Training is critical in maintaining a professional work force. Correctional officers who are thoroughly trained in technical, interpersonal, and helping skills can handle responsibilities and emergencies calmly. They are more likely to respond quickly and efficiently to urgent situations. Training, that includes emergency

Administrative officer of the Fairfax County, Virginia, Sheriff's Department reviews the policies and procedures manual.

results of the latest survey by the American Correctional Association show approximately 50 percent more juveniles from 1992 through 1995 are being incarcerated in adult facilities, and twice as many black male juveniles as white male juveniles are being incarcerated. The figures for female juvenile offenders are approximately the same.

The ACA survey further indicates that juveniles tend to be impulsive and do not think of future consequences. They have little or no respect for authority, have poor work habits, low self-esteem, and have inadequate academic or vocational skills. In general, they are less mature than the rest of the inmate population, and their behavior can be unpredictable and violent. They exhibit predatory behaviors toward other juveniles as well as the general population (Myers 1996).

drills, combined with experience, will help staff react appropriately to the many types of problems and issues that they will confront in their day-to-day duties.

This publication cannot describe an entire training program for correctional officers. Most agencies have a predetermined training program, either on the shift, at the local institution, or at a central training academy, and each employee should take full advantage of all agency resources. However, if the following topics are not covered in the agency's training program, then additional study would be helpful for the individual officer in dealing with inmates:

- *Communicating your idea*—Relating your ideas in a clear manner is essential. Being a straight talker earns the correctional officer a reputation for being someone to be trusted. People tend to listen to those they trust. Thus, simply by communicating in a straightforward, honest manner, correctional officers can achieve control over many situations. They can be in charge of potentially violent or even explosive situations and accomplish their objectives without the need for the use of force.

- *Understanding minorities*—The disproportionately large percentage of minorities and the relatively high number of white correctional officers in any institution often lead to severe problems and tensions. Staff should develop an understanding of cultural, social, and ethnic differences within their inmate populations, as reflected in language, appearances, gestures, and value systems. Hostility between inmates of different races is common in today's correctional institutions. Thus, a correctional officer's career development should include courses on human behavior, interpersonal relationships, group dynamics, and the effects of cultural differences on behavior.

- *Understanding inmate rights*—State and federal court decisions increasingly have extended offenders' constitutional rights, providing them expanded civil rights, due process, and equal protection under the law. An awareness of the rights of those confined, as well as the rights and responsibilities of correctional staff, will reduce the possibility of tension in the correctional facility.

- *Understanding the mentally and physically disabled inmates*—In a normal adult institution, the mentally and physically disabled are 1 percent or less of the total population. State correctional commissioners see that the disabled are distributed throughout their system so that the individual institutions are in compliance with the Americans with

An administrative officer completes his report.

Careworker at the Jessup, Maryland, Reception and Diagnostic Center communicates with youths in his care.

Control room officers monitor all sites within and outside the institution.

Disabilities Act. Correctional officers need more than common sense to deal with inmates with special needs.

The basic tasks required of correctional officers have not changed over the years—security inspections, inmate searches, countless head counts, observation and supervision of groups, and marksmanship. Additionally, the correctional officer needs to know how to use new technologies, including being able to make extensive use of computers. However, the same interpersonal skills and humane attitudes that made good correctional officers in the past make good correctional officers today. Even if there were no intervention by court officials, no public demand for accountability, no greater recognition of the rights of the confined, and no changing prison population, good correctional practice still would focus our attention on the basics of security and supervision and emphasize humane performance of these duties.

The American Correctional Association offers some excellent resource materials to help you become more confident and proficient in your new career. Please call ACA at (800) 222-5646 to get a copy of the latest publications catalog. Each chapter lists publications and products available from ACA that will provide resources for your professional benefit. ACA also is on the Internet at http://www.corrections.com/aca.

BIBLIOGRAPHY

American Correctional Association. 1994. *Vital Statistics*. Lanham, Maryland: American Correctional Association.

Bureau of Justice Statistics, January 1997. "Prison and Jail Inmates at Midyear 1996."

———. May 1997. *Correctional Populations in the United States, 1995.*

Commission on Accreditation for Corrections. 1978. *Accreditation: Blueprint for Corrections*. Rockville, Maryland: Commission on Accreditation for Corrections.

Gettinger, Stephen. 1982. "Accreditation on Trial." *Corrections Magazine*. 8:1. February.

Keve, Paul, W. 1996. *Measuring Excellence: The History of Correctional Standards and Accreditation*. Lanham, Maryland: American Correctional Association.

Myers, Lawrence G. March 1996. Juveniles Who Commit Serious, Violent Offenses Survey. Lanham, Maryland: American Correctional Association.

U.S. Department of Justice. 1995. *State of the Bureau 1995*. Washington, D.C.: Bureau of Prisons.

1

An Overview of the Criminal Justice System and the Role of the Correctional Officer

The criminal justice system in the United States involves a number of very different organizations carrying out the process of identifying, arresting, detaining, accusing, trying, convicting, and punishing people who have broken the law at the city, county, state, and federal level.

Components of the Criminal Justice System

The four primary components of the criminal justice system are law enforcement, the prosecution, the courts, and corrections.

Law Enforcement

Law enforcement agencies primarily are responsible for crime prevention, investigation of criminal activities, and apprehension of offenders; they generally ensure public order. State and federal law enforcement agencies, in particular, also have the responsibility for enforcement of regulatory provisions of the law, in addition to the criminal code. In larger jurisdictions, good community relations are emphasized as an aid in crime prevention.

From time to time, the line correctional officer will interface with county, state, and federal law enforcement personnel (U.S. Marshals, Federal Bureau of Investigation, Immigration and Naturalization Service, Secret Service, State Police, and others). It is important to use positive interpersonal skills and maintain professional relations with these outside agencies and others with whom you interact.

Prosecution

The prosecutory agencies, typically the Offices of the District/States Attorney at the state and local levels, or the Office of the U.S. Attorney at the federal level, are involved in the criminal justice process from arrest to pronouncement of the sentence. These agencies are responsible for determining the actual nature of criminal or regulatory complaints first identified by enforcement agencies. They determine how the law may apply to the particular set of facts, and the likelihood that successful prosecution will result if the case is pursued.

Prosecutors represent the government in the preparation and presentation of the case to the courts. Where appropriate, they conduct plea negotiations, where the offender agrees to plead guilty before trial, usually in exchange for the recommendation of a lesser sentence, and they also present the evidence if the case goes to trial. The prosecutor can make recommendations to the court on the sentence to be imposed on the offender.

Courts

The structure of the criminal court depends on the jurisdiction involved. The function of the criminal court may be restricted to processing or judging matters involving minor criminal offenses, traffic violations, and other local ordinance violations.

Correctional Officer Resource Guide

Correctional officers pay homage to fallen comrades at the Peace Officers' Memorial in Washington, D.C., during Correctional Peace Officers' Week.

In the case of state and federal courts, the criminal courts may act on all cases relating to state laws or federal codes. The court system also includes appeals and supreme courts, which hear appeals from the lower courts. The U.S. Supreme Court is the final level of appeal (court of last resort) for all cases, although very few cases ever reach this level.

Corrections

The corrections part of the criminal justice system generally refers to three major functions: confinement, probation, and parole. Corrections is responsible for carrying out the sentences that the court imposes.

Probation

Probation is a diversion from incarceration. It is a sentence that permits the offender to remain in the community under certain specified conditions. The offender is assisted and supervised in the community by a probation officer. If an offender violates any conditions of probation, the court may choose to revoke the probation and place the offender in confinement as specified in the original sentence. Probation also may be imposed without a finding of guilt, usually in the case of a first offender with a minor crime. Upon completion of this type of probation in a satisfactory manner, the offender will have no record of conviction. If offenders violate the conditions of probation, they may be brought to trial, reconvicted, and possibly confined in a correctional institution.

Confinement facilities include the following: jails, prison camps, correctional institutions, and prisons or penitentiaries. In many cases, confinement facilities may include halfway houses, restitution centers, and other facilities with similar programs.

Jails tend to be managed by the local government, with the sheriff or other local official as the primary administrator. The role of the jail is to hold pretrial and presentence detainees, and those convicted and sentenced to relatively short terms (often a year or under). Sometimes, work- and study-release programs are operated out of jails. In these cases, inmates live in the jail but are permitted to leave for school or work during the day.

Halfway houses are also a form of confinement, generally used for minimum-security inmates about to complete their sentences. These centers usually are located near or in the community where the inmate is about to be released. They provide housing, job placement assistance, drug and alcohol counseling, and other services. They generally help the inmate make the sometimes difficult and stressful change from institutional life to the free world. Halfway houses sometimes are used instead of short periods of regular prison or jail confinement, when an offender needs the types of services the halfway house staff can provide.

Prison camps of various types, correctional institutions, prisons, and penitentiaries are used for the longer-term confinement of convicted offenders. Depending on the type of inmate, they can range in security from those with very few controls, to a very severely controlled environment where inmates are locked in cells up to twenty-three hours a day. They usually are operated through a state corrections department headed by an administrator appointed by a member of the governor's cabinet, such as the secretary of public safety. Federal prisons primarily confine offenders convicted of violating federal laws, and are operated by the Federal Bureau of Prisons, an agency of the U.S. Department of Justice.

Parole

Parole is a method of selectively releasing inmates from prison and providing them community supervision with a combination of certain reporting requirements, personal restrictions, and guidance. Parole usually operates through an appointed board or commission. The correctional institution's connection with the parole process is explained further in Chapter 14.

The Correctional Setting

Before the development of prisons in the United States during the late 1700s, corrections consisted of punishments ranging from verbal disapproval to public hanging, depending on the severity of the offense. Jails were used to house inmates before punishment, but there were no prisons or other long-term correctional facilities as we now know them. Prisons were established to carry out the courts' judgment for punishment. Long-term confinement, rather than physical punishment, torture, or death, was viewed as a more humane means of satisfying society's need for punishment and crime prevention.

Early in American prison history, the element of "reform" was introduced. This is reflected in some of the early terminology—penitentiaries were established to provide inmates an opportunity to reflect back on and repent of their sins. Reformatories were created to provide vocational training and education, particularly for reforming younger offenders. Later, rehabilitation and treatment became a part of the overall correctional vocabulary. This was based on the theory that offenders could be "cured" of criminal tendencies. This led to the introduction of academic and vocational programs, psychological diagnosis, and other "treatment" programs, such as counseling and group therapy. This "medical model" borrowed heavily from the mental health field, but is no longer widely accepted as a practical reality.

In America of the late 1990s, public sentiments against crime, the growth of drug abuse and related trafficking, and many other attitude changes are in the forefront of another series of shifts. For example, the use of community programs is being recognized as necessary and effective, but it is difficult to find neighborhoods that are willing to have such programs near homes and schools. This has led to the not in my backyard (NIMBY) syndrome. New technologies and new trends in labor management and human resources development challenge modern administrators in their day-to-day work.

Scarce resources finally are being found for correctional construction, but bricks and mortar will not solve the problem, and the public has not grasped the long-term costs of building, maintaining, and staffing correctional facilities. See Chapter 15 on the role of the correctional officer in informing the community of the cost of incarceration.

Even so, today, correctional administrators are seeking a more balanced view of corrections—one that attempts to provide for:

- incapacitation (preventing a specific offender from committing more crimes while in prison)
- deterrence (setting an example with one offender that will prevent others from committing crimes)
- retribution (punishment)
- treatment (providing inmates, who wish to change, with the opportunity to do so)

Investigative officer meets with representative of the Murray County, Georgia, Sheriff's Department to discuss a warrant.

This balance, while having positive effects, also can result in confusion for many as to the proper role of corrections and how its goals should be met. The challenge for each agency is to provide its staff with a clear view of the particular balance that its specific public, legal, and political setting demands.

Court Intervention

The relatively recent pattern of court intervention into the area of inmate rights and institutional management also has had an impact on the manner in which correctional programs and facilities are operated. For many years, the courts traditionally had taken a "hands-off" approach to corrections. In *Ruffin v. Commonwealth,* 1871, a Virginia court decided the status of the inmate. "A convicted felon is one whom the law in its humanity punishes by confinement in the penitentiary instead of death . . . . For the time being, during his term of service in the penitentiary, he is a slave of penal servitude to the State . . . . for the time being, the slave of the State."

A change to "hands on" began in the 1960s, focusing on prison conditions. In *Cooper v. Pate* (1964), the Supreme Court reversed a circuit court decision dismissing a Muslim inmate's petition that he was denied access to the *Koran* and opportunities to worship. The Court recognized that inmates of the Muslim faith had the right to sue prison officials for religious discrimination under Title 42, Section 1983, United States Code (Civil Rights Act of 1871). Court intervention began to occur more frequently after the Supreme Court extended constitutional rights to minority groups, and a riot at the Attica (New York) prison in 1971 brought recognition by the courts that inmates were persons and entitled to basic constitutional rights. Since then, a whole body of correctional case law has developed, affecting every phase of corrections. Entire state systems have been declared unconstitutional. Correctional administrators and officers also have been defendants in civil suits, in which inmates claimed the employees were liable for paying damages personally for their actions as prison employees.

As a result of this changing legal climate, prisons have had to make numerous changes. Some of them have resulted in abandoning long-standing policies and procedures to ensure the protection of inmates' individual rights, including following the standards promulgated by the American Correctional Association. Other changes have included the hiring of many more staff, or providing significantly more resources to prison administrators to insure unconstitutional conditions do not continue. Thus, the courts have made a tremendous impact on the correctional setting in recent years.

Of all the individuals among the components of the criminal justice system, correctional officers have perhaps the most unique vantage point from which to observe the effectiveness and consequences of changes in prison management and sentencing policies.

The Correctional Officer's Role in the Correctional System

Is a career in corrections for you? Will corrections downsize? The number of incarcerated individuals in the United States has grown beyond 1.5 million and is increasing every year. This increase, along with individuals who obtain alternatives to incarceration (such as probation, parole, or aftercare), guarantees the continuing need for jobs in corrections.

By far, the most available job in this field is that of correctional officer or, as they are called in facilities for juveniles, "careworkers." These individuals are employed in prisons, jails, and other correctional facilities. Expansion and construction of new correctional facilities, as well as the adoption of mandatory sentencing guidelines calling for longer sentences and reduced parole, are expected to increase the demand for correctional officers much faster than the average for all occupations.

Courtesy Capitol Communication Systems, Inc.

In the early penitentiaries, the prisoners wore striped uniforms and marched in lockstep.

According to the United States Bureau of Labor Statistics, the correctional officer is one of the twenty fastest-growing occupations in the United States. The numbers of correctional officers needed are expected to increase by more than 50 percent by 2005.

What sort of pay can you expect as a correctional officer? In California, the average salary for a correctional officer is around $55,000. In New Jersey, beginning correctional officers earn around $30,000. The median range for entry-level correctional officer is $18,589 - $25,000. After one year, it ranges from $20,148 - $28,260. Most correctional officers receive health benefits and other benefits including vacation, sick leave, and pensions. In addition, many agencies offer educational assistance.

With additional education, training, and experience, correctional officers can advance to supervisory, administrative, or counseling positions. Many institutions require experience as a correctional officer as a minimum qualification for a higher position. The promotional policies of many departments of corrections and institutions give priority to those already in the system.

As with any profession, education is a major factor for a successful career in corrections. While many entry-level positions require a high-school education or its equivalent, increasingly, employers are looking for individuals with postsecondary education in psychology, sociology, criminal justice, and related fields. Because almost all facets of corrections deal in some way with assisting, observing, and reporting on offenders, developing solid oral and written communication skills is crucial.

"Education is the key to getting through the door," says Samuel Saxton, director of the Prince George's County, Maryland, Department of Corrections and E. R. Cass Award winner, and your education "should be geared toward experience you will need on the job." Saxton identified four disciplines that will help corrections employees succeed: budget preparation, computer technology, business, and social psychology.

Working in corrections does not necessarily mean a job with the federal, state, or local government. With the increasing costs of incarceration, many governments are turning to the private sector. More than ninety correctional facilities in the United States are operated by private-sector companies. The largest of these companies, Nashville-based Corrections Corporation of America, has more than 6,000 employees in the United States and other countries.

However, studies have shown that one of the primary incentives for becoming a correctional officer is the security that civil service provides. In addition, since most correctional facilities are located in rural areas, work at the prison is often better than other available employment options, and the salary often can be supplemented by part-time farming or other enterprises.

Courtesy U.S. Bureau of Prisons
Perimeter security involves communication between officers and the control center.

An increasing number of women are entering and gaining upper-level positions in corrections—including the current Attorney General of the United States (Janet Reno), and Director of the Federal Bureau of Prisons, Kathleen M. Hawk, and their numbers are growing yearly.

Longtime correctional experts recommend that all individuals, but especially women and minorities new to corrections, should participate in educational or professional development opportunities. These will provide job experience that prepares them so they are ready when opportunities for promotion arise. These experts suggest that they actively should seek a mentor who can guide their career, and they should network extensively by joining professional organizations, the American Correctional Association (ACA), American Jail Association (AJA), the International Association of Correctional Officers (IACO), to name a few.

An increasing number of women officers work in male institutions. Just as female police officers often have found themselves excluded from certain assignments and from being fully a part of the social group that constitutes the force, some women in corrections feel discriminated against. In a study of women officers in two prisons for men, Lynn Zimmer found that their

Communication between officers and inmates keeps down tension.

male counterparts were opposed to sexual integration of the correctional officer force.[1] Male officers argued that women could not handle the violence and confrontations with inmates that occur in prisons. In reality, however, women officers had less trouble with the inmates than their male counterparts had.

In some states, male prisoners raised the issue of privacy when female officers were assigned to cell block duty; courts have upheld objections with regard to women supervising inmate shower and toilet facilities. This problem has been overcome by a mid-chest to a mid-thigh screen for showers, and an order to inmates not to leave their cells without clothing. The toilet problem was resolved by requiring the female officer to warn the block or tier she was supervising before making routine security rounds.

It is through the work of correctional officers that management controls and operates the prison community. In many ways, the correctional officer is the extension of the warden or managing officer in carrying out orders and rules.

Members of the custody department comprise about 75 percent of all prison employees at institutions. The correctional officer's work is absolutely essential to the operation of the prison or jail. Although the nature of work performed varies based on the individual assignment and the particular institution, there are duty assignments that can be identified.

Lucien X. Lombardo identified seven general categories of work assignments held by correctional officers:

- Cell block officers—oversee housing units
- Work detail supervisors—enforce work assignments
- Industrial shop and school officers—maintain order and security in these areas
- Yard officers—patrol the yard and watch for trouble
- Administrative building assignment officers—enforce building security; receive public (little contact with inmates)
- Wall post officers—secure the perimeter (little contact with inmates)
- Relief officers—work whenever and wherever needed.[2]

In some correctional institutions, it is standard operating procedure to rotate officers through new duty assignments. These reassignments serve to reduce boredom with familiar tasks. Correctional officers are, in a sense, also prisoners. "I am doing my time eight hours a day, five days a week, for twenty years." (State custody staff usually have a twenty-year retirement plan).

The correctional officer, as other correctional workers, often must function with conflicting goals. The correctional officer's primary responsibility is maintaining order and preventing escapes. There are, however, numerous secondary goals ranging from meeting various production quotas, to assisting troubled inmates, to dealing with the general public—including attorneys, vendors, the commissioner, the governor, volunteers, the FBI, Immigration and Naturalization Service, U.S. Marshal's Service, local police agencies, and emergency services including ambulance, and fire department.

If you are working a wall post, your goals are clear and relatively easy to meet. You must prevent escapes and monitor activity near and within the institutional compound. Most correctional officers have far more complex tasks.

Institutions operate around the clock. Correctional officers usually will be assigned to one of three operational shifts, and may be responsible for supervising fifty or more inmates at a time.

A candid, tongue in cheek, job description for a position as a correctional officer could read something like this: Excellent employment opportunity for men and women who are willing to work eight-hour shifts at varying times (early morning, afternoon, and late nights) on a rotating basis. Applicants must enforce numerous rules with few guidelines. They must be willing to risk physical harm, psychological harassment, and endure the threat of inmate lawsuits, which could involve civil liability. They must be willing to spend eight hours each day among people who do not like them. They will not be allowed to fraternize with these people, but are expected to control as well as help them. Applicants must accept that they have little or no input into the rules that they will be asked to enforce, nor will they be privy to the policy rationale for these rules. They should realize that management probably will not listen to their complaints.

Despite this, correctional facilities could not function without correctional officers, and many correctional officers truly enjoy the work that they do. Then, too, times are changing, and often upper-level management is realizing that correctional officers see and hear what they do not, and do have something of value to add to the operation of the institution.

Each security shift has different secondary tasks to perform that keep correctional officers busy from the beginning to the end of each shift. The midnight shift poses some problems. Usually the smallest (in number), the shift is in a caretaker mode. However, the inmate population do not all sleep. This is the time for problems that have festered all day to explode in the individual cells. It is also time for reaction to medication taken or not taken to surface.

The inmates complain about problems that occurred on one of the other shifts. They did not get the mail or package they expected to receive. Many inmates have had time to think about the mail or visit they did get that day, and simply need someone who will listen to them. Although not listed in the usual job description, the correctional officer's responsibilities far exceed turning a key, firing a gun, searching for contraband, and keeping good order and discipline in the institution.

The correctional officer must be a good communicator, a people person. Even when the correctional officers know that the inmates they supervise are not in prison for "spitting on the sidewalk," and the "first offender" is incarcerated because the courts finally got tired of giving him or her a break, the correctional officer cannot turn away, but must be a firm, fair, impartial, and caring individual time after time, remembering the mission of the correctional officer is public safety.

We live in a litigious society, and inmates are no exception. In 1995, the number of civil cases filed by prisoners in United States District Courts totaled 63,550 on the following issues: motions to vacate sentences, 5,988; habeas corpuses, 14,975; mandamus and other releases, 908; civil rights, 41,679.[3]

Who defends the correctional officer? For the fifty states, the correctional officer usually is defended by an attorney from the office of the state's Attorney General. For the Federal Bureau, it is an assistant United States Attorney. For the jails, the correctional officer is defended by whomever the sheriff or the jail administrator chooses or retains. For those situations, when representation is not provided by any level of government, the officers must look out for themselves.

Legal defense programs for correctional officers can take many forms. Officers are encouraged to ask their union or classified employee association representative about legal coverage provided by membership, or by paying additional fees to your union or employee association to be covered for your personal legal matters.

Less than 1 percent of lawsuits against a correctional employee threaten the employee's personal finances. Although offenders may file many suits, an overwhelming majority of such suits are resolved in favor of the defendant-correctional employee, usually without even going to trial. It is equally important to recognize that suits are serious matters and should not be taken lightly. The employee who is sued needs to make prompt contact with legal counsel and work closely with counsel through the defense of the case.

Summary

Correctional officers play a key role in effective institutional operations, and it is necessary that they understand the criminal justice setting of which they are a part. This includes knowledge of the entire criminal justice system, as well as the role of corrections as a component of that system.

BIBLIOGRAPHY

American Correctional Association. 1992. *The Effective Correctional Officer*. Lanham, Maryland: American Correctional Association.

Bayse, Daniel J. 1995. *Working in Jails and Prisons: Becoming Part of the Team*. Lanham, Maryland: American Correctional Association.

Collins, William C. 1997. *Correctional Law for the Correctional Officer*, Second Edition. Lanham, Maryland: American Correctional Association.

Cornelius, Gary F. 1994. *Stressed Out! Strategies for Living and Working with Stress in Corrections*. Lanham, Maryland: American Correctional Association.

Morton, Joann B., ed. 1991. *Change, Challenge and Choices: Women's Role in Modern Corrections*. Lanham, Maryland: American Correctional Association.

Roberts, John W. 1997. *Reform and Retribution: An Illustrated History of the American Prison*. Lanham, Maryland: American Correctional Association.

Stinchcomb, Jeanne, B. 1995. *Managing Stress: Performing Under Pressure* (a correspondence course equivalent to forty hours of inservice training). Lanham, Maryland: American Correctional Association.

ENDNOTES

[1] Lynn E. Zimmer, 1986. *Women Guarding Men*. Chicago: University of Chicago Press.

[2] Lucien X. Lombardo. 1989. *Guards Imprisoned*, Second Edition. Cincinnati: Anderson Publishing Co.

[3] Judicial Business of the United States Courts. *Report of the Director*. Leonidas Ralph Mecham. 1996.

2
Officers' Responsibilities and Training

Today's corrections professionals increasingly face career challenges. With corrections resources dwindling and public fervor over crime growing, correctional officers face the challenge of providing inmates with a safe environment, humane supervision, and the opportunity for positive change. Although inmates, obviously, have failed to respond to previous social interventions, new information and tested program techniques are becoming more available. And with ever-increasing knowledge and the ability to adapt to its use, today's corrections professionals can help to change inmates' lives for the better.

The position of correctional officer, itself, is very challenging. With numerous competencies required, including providing security, emergency medical care, and interpersonal communications, the position goes beyond the publicly acknowledged and limiting term "guard." Because the public understands only this one duty of the correctional officer, new recruits may be surprised at the range of responsibility needed to perform well in this job. As the discipline of corrections increases, in its skill and knowledge, even experienced officers will find opportunities to learn and new ways to apply this knowledge in the field.

After hundreds of years of American prison operations, even the basic purpose of corrections is still under debate. The public has changed its goals for corrections many times over the years. And during all this change and upheaval, correctional officers have had to be responsible for those individuals under their supervision.

In the midst of such change, staff members are trained in methods they will use throughout their careers, institutions are built that will last for decades, and specific management systems are developed that last for many years. Despite these fixed quantities, correctional officers must adapt to changes in public feelings and in laws that concern incarcerated individuals.

Indeed, correctional staff still must perform their duties, despite surges of public controversy, lack of operational funds, few salary raises, occasional hostility, and the indifference and even disrespect of many Americans regarding the penal system. These factors make it hard for beginning correctional officers to understand exactly their new career.

One thing is certain—on a day-to-day basis, correctional staff must manage their institution's security and inmate supervision in a competent and humane way, because human lives depend on it. Outlining how that is done is the subject of this chapter, and indeed, the entire *Guide*.

The Role of Corrections and Correctional Officers

Defining the role of the correctional officer actually starts with the mission of corrections. While different correctional organizations have quite different missions, for those with a confinement component, the one common factor is to carry out the courts' judgments and protect the public by confining convicted offenders. Correctional staff do not judge which offenders are so dangerous, violent, or troublesome as to require imprisonment. They do not decide what accountability or deterrence requires in the way of a prison term for a specific offender. Corrections' first job is to accept the courts' judgments and confine inmates for the legal term of their sentences.

Sergeant Joyce Kucharski, MP and K-9 Holly, winners of the 1992 Top Drug Dog Inside and Top Drug Dog Outside for the Maryland Department of Corrections.

While other roles, such as providing treatment, clearly also are important, maintaining security is the first priority in any institution and the prime responsibility of correctional officers. Most of the other chapters in this book tell how this and other major responsibilities are accomplished.

In many systems, there is an emphasis on the "correctional worker" concept, where every employee is a correctional officer first and a specialist in his or her field second. There is great merit to this approach, because it raises the security consciousness of all employees, and increases institutional security far more than if only the uniformed correctional force is involved. Indeed, a great deal of the information in this *Guide* applies to everyone who works in an institution. But correctional officers most directly are involved in maintaining security as a primary duty, and for that reason, these remarks are directed to them.

In addition to their primary security role, correctional officers probably are the most important employees in inmates' lives. In most institutions, officers supervise inmates as they eat, sleep, work, and exercise; control their movement; protect them; maintain security; and, at times, isolate or segregate those who are a threat to themselves or to others. Officers see inmates' subtle actions, reactions, and interactions—the slight behavior changes that can signal an inmate's personal problems progress toward positive change or an impending riot.

Training

To carry out their security and supervision responsibilities, officers need to understand their agency's correctional philosophy and their institution's policy/regulations and procedures. They must be security technicians—expert in their search, supervision, and inmate management skills. They must know the limits of their responsibility and authority, as well as know how to work as team members with other staff, both correctional and noncorrectional. They must understand the judicial and legislative decisions that affect what they do. Finally, they must take responsibility for assuring that they act in a professional manner. To know all of these important facts, the correctional officer should receive information and training from a well-developed training program.

Poorly trained officers with no prior experience are a threat to themselves, other staff, and inmates. New officers without adequate training have little idea of the proper role or job responsibilities of correctional officers. And yet, most new correctional staff have no prior experience in working with inmates, and few have any training that applies to the prison setting. Outside of the recent surge in private institutions, there is no position in the private sector comparable to that of the correctional officer; yet, as a line employee, he or she is expected to have the skills of a supervisor.

That is why training is so critical. In fact, the American Correctional Association has established a standard that all new officers should receive forty hours of orientation and training before they receive an independent assignment. At a minimum, this training can be used to familiarize new staff members with the purpose, goals, policies, and procedures of the institution and parent agency; working conditions and regulations; responsibilities; inmate rights; emergency procedures; and an overview of their institution and the correctional field.

In many agencies, staff receive more training in line with American Correctional Association standards: an additional 120 hours of training during their first year of employment and 40 hours of training each following year. Courses typically cover the following information:

- Security procedures
- Supervision of inmates
- Use-of-force regulations and procedures
- Report writing
- Rules and regulations for inmates
- Inmates' rights and responsibilities

Officers' Responsibilities and Training

- Fire and emergency procedures
- Firearms training
- Tool control
- Key control
- Interpersonal relations
- Con games (games criminals play)
- Social/cultural lifestyles of the inmate population
- Communication skills
- Toxic/caustic material control
- First aid
- Civil liability for officers

Training also has the potential to help staff to:
- Advance in rank and salary
- Achieve personal development
- Develop ease in handling work assignments
- Develop sound judgment
- Acquire knowledge of occupational hazards
- Improve working conditions
- Increase dignity and pride in employment, in other words, to develop a professional attitude
- Understand and practice the institution's philosophy and policies

- Improve job satisfaction

Specific skill training for correctional officers often is provided on an ongoing basis. Goals of such training include the following:

- To provide a safe environment for staff and inmates
- To further improve the technical skills of correctional officers who must supervise inmates and implement the security program
- To give management skills to correctional officers who must supervise special needs inmates
- To increase the effectiveness of correctional officers and thereby obtain greater efficiency and economy in operations
- To provide correctional officers with the improved ability to recognize, understand, and solve the problems that occur in the correctional institution
- To offer correctional officers improved job satisfaction and career services
- To build self-esteem in officers
- To provide an environment conducive to positive change
- To provide maximum protection to the public

Top left: Being physically fit enables cadets, shown here, and correctional officers to perform more efficiently. Bottom right: Firearms training enables correctional officers to learn needed skills.

Correctional Officer Resource Guide

Standard Responsibilities of All Officers

There are twenty standard responsibilities of all officers, regardless of assignment or rank. All officers will do the following things:

1. Report to work promptly. If they cannot report to work, they will notify the shift sergeant as soon as possible, but at least one hour prior to the scheduled reporting time. They will not report to work if impaired by the use of alcohol or controlled substances.

2. Report to the institution promptly when recalled to work overtime or to respond to an emergency situation. They will report any change of address or telephone number to the shift sergeant and to the personnel officer.

3. Wear and maintain their uniforms according to the professional standards of the institution. They will not wear their uniforms in bars or gaming establishments, except when assigned to do so.

4. Secure their vehicles in the parking lot by rolling up the windows and locking the doors. They will not carry weapons, ammunition, or alcohol in their vehicles when at the institution.

5. Bring to work only those items which are absolutely necessary. They will not bring large sums of money, magazines, books, newspapers, personal radios, weapons, knives, alcohol, or controlled substances into the institution.

6. Report to the shift sergeant prior to the beginning of the shift any incapacity, which might affect or limit their ability to perform an assignment.

7. Respect and follow the chain of command established by post orders and procedures.

8. Remain at their assigned posts and perform their duties thoroughly and professionally until relieved or given orders to close the post. They will maintain the sanitation and cleanliness of their posts.

9. Report and document in writing to the shift sergeant any evidence of tampering, damage, or malfunction of any piece of equipment, tool, or weapon at any posts. They will not attempt to adjust or repair any item.

10. Address all other officers professionally and, when appropriate, by rank. They will not use profanity or make ethnic or sexual remarks or references.

11. Use the institutional communications system—radios, telephones, and intercoms—professionally and for official purposes only. They will not make personal telephone calls while on duty.

12. Not read, listen to radios, or watch television while on duty. They will not engage in any activity which directs their attention away from their specific assignments.

13. Notify the shift sergeant immediately if they become sleepy, and request a temporary relief or reassignment.

14. Request the assistance of the shift sergeant when uncertain of what action to take in any situation.

15. Address inmates professionally. They will not use nicknames and will not use profanity or make ethnic or sexual remarks or references.

16. Not develop personal relationships or give special privileges to inmates. They will never discuss personal matters or other staff members with inmates. They will never discuss the affairs of any inmate with any other inmate. They will never contact an inmate's family, friends, or visitors, and immediately will report and document in writing to the associate warden of operations any contact initiated by the family, friends, or visitors of an inmate.

17. Not give anything to, nor accept anything whatsoever from an inmate. They will immediately report and document in writing to the shift sergeant any attempt by an inmate to give them anything.

18. Document to the shift sergeant, lieutenant, and associate warden of operations, any relationship, friendship, or acquaintanceship with any inmate which existed prior to the inmate's incarceration.

19. Report and document in writing to the shift sergeant any unusual inmate activities.

20. Report and document in writing to the shift sergeant any changes in appearance or behavior by inmates.

Source: Joseph Marchese, President, International Association of Correctional Training Personnel

Officers' Responsibilities and Training

Understanding the concerns of inmates enables a correctional officer to find peaceful solutions.

The American Correctional Association (ACA) offers a wide range of professional development material and opportunities for training. ACA offers correspondence courses on such topics as correctional supervision, legal issues for correctional staff, working with manipulative inmates, working with special needs offenders, suicide prevention in custody, and others. ACA also publishes a wide range of books on topics of professional interest. Some of these are cited in each chapter's bibliography. In addition, ACA hosts professional development seminars around the country and offers many workshops and programs during its two annual conferences in January and in August. By attending ACA conferences, attendees may earn continuing education credits.

Summary

The professional officer in today's correctional environment must have a wide variety of skills. A comprehensive, well-organized training program is essential to developing an effective work force. However, officers should appreciate that training only provides solid information. Officers must then use this information to adapt to change their own institutional environment.

In addition to the institutional training program (which in many agencies is set up using American Correctional Association standards), correctional officers also should consider obtaining training to improve their skills from outside sources, such as professional associations (which offer a wide range of administration of justice programs), as well as community colleges and universities.

APPLICABLE ACA STANDARDS
Training and Staff Development 3-4070 - 3-4091

BIBLIOGRAPHY

Bayse, Daniel. 1995. *Working in Jails and Prisons: Becoming Part of the Team.* Lanham, Maryland: American Correctional Association.

Roberts, John. 1997. *Reform and Retribution: An Illustrated History of American Prisons.* Lanham, Maryland: American Correctional Association.

3

Corrections and the Law

by Craig Hemmens, J.D., Ph.D.*

An important part of the job for correctional staff at every level is knowing, enforcing, and obeying the law. This includes respecting the constitutional rights of inmates. While inmates lose many of their rights when they are incarcerated, they do not lose them all. It is vital that correctional staff be aware of what rights inmates retain. Failure to respect the rights of inmates may result in civil and/or criminal liability for the institution as well as the correctional officer.

While there is a possible legal consequence to virtually every aspect of correctional institutions, being aware of the legal issues that affect correctional operations will reduce the likelihood of litigation. Correctional officers cannot be expected to be legal experts, but they can be, and are expected to be familiar with the general legal principles which affect corrections. Correctional staff who are well trained, act professionally, use good judgment, and follow the policies set forth by the institution's administration should be able to avoid any serious legal problems.

This chapter provides an overview of correctional law, highlighting the major legal issues, the legal remedies available to inmates, the sources of civil and criminal liability for correctional staff, and recent developments in correctional law which are likely to have a major impact on the operation of correctional institutions.

Background

Until recently, inmates had few rights. Once incarcerated, individuals lost almost all their rights and found themselves at the mercy of correctional personnel. Those convicted of crimes were seen by courts as little more than "slaves of the state." Most states had "civil death" statutes which stripped inmates of most of their civil rights, such as the right to vote or hold elective office. This loss of rights was justified as a part of the punishment for committing a crime.

Courts took what was referred to as a "hands-off" approach to the rights of prisoners, choosing not to become involved with the affairs of corrections agencies. Courts reasoned that correctional administrators were better equipped to deal with prisoners than judges, and that judicial involvement, through the hearing of inmate complaints, would weaken the operation and security of correctional institutions.

By the 1940s, courts began paying closer attention to the rights of prisoners as part of a growing trend towards increased protection of individual rights. In 1941, the Supreme Court held that inmates had a right to unrestricted access to federal courts. This decision signaled the beginning of the end of the "hands-off" doctrine and the beginning of the era of judicial intervention in corrections. In 1944, a federal district court expanded the scope of habeas corpus to include lawsuits filed by inmates which challenged the conditions of their confinement.

During the 1960s, the United States Supreme Court extended a number of constitutional rights to inmates. These included the right to due process, the right to exercise their religious beliefs, and the right to communicate with people outside the institution. Courts began to allow inmates to file lawsuits alleging not just the denial of individual rights, but also lawsuits involving the conditions of their confinement. In 1976, the Supreme Court held that correctional administrators could be held liable for injury to an inmate if the administrators displayed "deliberate indifference" to the situation.

* This chapter is based in part on original material written by by William C. Collins, J.D.

Correctional Officer Resource Guide

The U.S. Supreme Court provides the final decision on inmates' litigation and the rights of correctional officers.

What Regulates An Institution's Operation?

The operation of correctional institutions is based on several sources, including the United States and state constitutions; state statutes; administrative regulations such as fire, safety, and health codes; and internal agency regulations or policies. In addition, court decisions in past lawsuits provide some guidance for correctional agencies.

Correctional staff must be aware of the state and federal laws and administrative regulations which govern their actions. This information most often is given to staff during training, and through internal communications such as newsletters and memorandums. Agency policy is perhaps the most practical and useful source of information for correctional staff. Policy is often very specific and provides staff with clear guidelines as to proper conduct. Agency policy also generally is provided during training and through internal communications.

Perhaps the single most important and most difficult to understand source of information on how to operate a correctional institution within the bounds of the law are court decisions, or case law. During the past thirty-five years, the courts have reviewed thousands of challenges to actions by correctional staff based on the claim that these actions in some way violated the constitutional rights of inmates. Consequently, correctional staff must be familiar with the principles set forth by the courts in these cases, and they also must stay abreast of new developments in correctional law. This does not mean correctional staff are expected to know the case law, but staff should be aware that case law is reflected in the policies of the institution, and that these policies therefore must be followed carefully.

Commonly Litigated Aspects of Institutional Operations

Inmates often file lawsuits against correctional staff, either as individuals or as part of the agency structure. These lawsuits may be filed in good faith by inmates who honestly believe their rights have been violated, or they may be filed in an attempt to harass staff or prevent them from doing their jobs. Regardless of the reason for the lawsuit, it should be taken seriously by staff. Many disputes can be settled without resorting to the courts, either informally or through the institution's grievance procedure. But sometimes, lawsuits cannot be avoided.

Correctional staff have a legal duty to protect inmates, within certain limits. Whether a staff member is liable for an injury to an inmate often depends on whether the officer's conduct involved a failure to fulfill this duty to protect. Courts generally use a "reasonableness" test to determine if correctional staff acted properly in performing their duties. This means a court will look at the facts of the case and decide whether the actions of the correctional officer were those that a reasonable person would have taken under the circumstances.

Other lawsuits involve not what is done to an inmate, but *how* something is done to an inmate. This is the legal principle of "due process." According to this principle, an inmate may not be deprived of his or her rights by the state unless the state follows certain procedures. Common situations in corrections involve how disciplinary proceedings are carried out, and how parole is determined.

Depending on the nature of the complaint, an inmate can sue either the state, the correctional agency, the head of the agency, or the correctional officer who allegedly caused the injury to the inmate. Lawsuits against individual correctional officers are not unusual, and staff can be held liable both civilly and criminally for injury to an inmate, if the courts determine the officer acted unreasonably, or with "deliberate indifference."

There are three bases for inmate lawsuits. These include the United States Constitution and state constitutions, federal statutes, and state tort law. Each of these is discussed briefly.

Federal Constitutional Lawsuits

The courts have attempted to balance the individual rights of inmates and the authority of correctional administrators. These rights include the First Amendment rights of speech, association, and religious freedom, the Fourth Amendment prohibition of unreasonable searches and seizures, the Fourteenth Amendment rights of due process and equal protection, the Sixth Amendment right to counsel, and the Eighth Amendment prohibition on cruel and unusual punishment and the right to treatment.

Right to Treatment

While a right to treatment is not mentioned in the text of the Constitution, courts have made it clear that inmates do enjoy such a right. This treatment need not be the best that science has to offer—rather, it is enough if the state provides reasonable care. The state may not be held liable for mere negligent treatment. Liability attaches only if there is evidence akin to recklessness or intentional disregard for the client. Furthermore, the Supreme Court recently held that an institutionalized person does not have an absolute right to refuse treatment.

The rationale behind mandating a right to treatment for incarcerated persons is that because the state has restricted their liberty, they are unable to obtain medical services on their own initiative. Thus, the state must accept responsibility for their medical well-being. Correctional staff are not required to do more than is possible, given the limited resources of the institution. Access to health care is a frequently litigated issue and is likely to become even more common, as the inmate population ages and more inmates come into the institution in poor health.

The Eighth Amendment and "Cruel and Unusual" Punishment

The Eighth Amendment prohibits "cruel and unusual" punishment. Exactly what is cruel and unusual has changed as society has evolved. The Supreme Court has applied the standard to a variety of situations in corrections, including the death penalty, corporal punishment, and the use of force.

In general, every prisoner has the right to be free of both offensive bodily contact and the fear of offensive bodily contact. Correctional staff are permitted to use reasonable force to enforce discipline and protect themselves and others. The key here is that the force must be reasonable under the circumstances. Thus, correctional staff may be justified in using extreme force, even deadly force, if the situation warrants it. While correctional staff are allowed to use force when necessary to enforce

A correctional officer checks out legal issues in his institution's law library.

prison regulations, courts have backed away from earlier decisions which upheld the practice of corporal punishment, or the use of physical force to punish inmates for rule violations. While the Supreme Court never has prohibited the practice, a number of lower courts have declared corporal punishment unconstitutional.

In addition, the Supreme Court recently has held that correctional personnel may be liable for failing to prevent harm to an inmate by another inmate, but only if it can be demonstrated that their conduct displayed "deliberate indifference" to the safety of the inmate. An emerging area of liability is the duty to protect incarcerated inmates from themselves and each other. This traditionally has arisen in the context of inmate-on-inmate assaults, but the current AIDS crisis has had an impact on this area. While the Supreme Court recently has reiterated its support for the "deliberate indifference" standard, and as the spread of communicable diseases such as AIDS and tuberculosis increases in prison, more lawsuits are being filed challenging correctional policies regarding segregation, treatment, and disclosure of information on AIDS-infected inmates.

Correctional Officer Resource Guide

A probation officer swears in before the court prior to a violation hearing.

Fourth Amendment Rights of Inmates

The right of an individual to be free of unreasonable searches and seizures provided in the Fourth Amendment obviously has limited application to the correctional setting. Inmates frequently file lawsuits alleging a violation of their Fourth Amendment rights, but these suits are rarely successful. Inmates are subject to searches of their person, belongings, and cell without warrant or even probable cause. Courts recognize that the unique security needs of the institution outweigh the individual rights of the inmate. So long as correctional staff are not acting maliciously or unprofessionally in searching an inmate, no liability will attach.

Fourteenth Amendment Rights of Inmates

The Fourteenth Amendment prohibits the taking of life, liberty, or property without due process of law. What this means for corrections is that there are certain rights which cannot be taken from an inmate without having a hearing or some other formal procedure, so as to protect the inmate's right to "due process." An area of correctional administration which has received a good deal of attention from the courts is the process by which inmates are disciplined. The courts require correctional administrators to provide "due process of law" to inmates involved in disciplinary proceedings. This means that before punishment can be meted out, certain procedures must be followed to ensure inmates are being treated fairly. These procedures include: (1) providing the inmate with written notice of the charges against him or her; (2) offering an opportunity for the inmate to present evidence and witnesses in his or her defense; (3) allowing the assistance of staff or a fellow prisoner, if necessary under the circumstances; and (4) providing a written statement by the disciplinary board explaining its findings. The policies and procedures of every correctional institution should provide clear guidelines as to what is required.

The Fourteenth Amendment also requires equal protection under the law. This means that different treatment of two individuals who are in similar circumstances is prohibited, unless there is some justification. Common claims involve treating male and female inmates differently. It is important to remember that equal protection does not require that every inmate be treated the same, but that differential treatment must be based on some reason which is acceptable to the courts.

Access to the Courts

Access to the courts was one of the very first constitutional rights that the Supreme Court extended to inmates. According to the Court, access to the court system is a basic requirement of due process, as provided by the Fourteenth Amendment. The question that courts have struggled with is what constitutes "access"? Prison officials may restrict the amount of legal materials possessed by an inmate, or the time and place for legal assistance, so long as such limitations are reasonable. Improper restriction of access to court, legal counsel, or legal materials is a clear constitutional violation.

The Supreme Court has held that a correctional institution has a duty to provide inmates with access to legal resources. These legal resources typically include a law library in the institution, permission to keep personal legal materials in one's cell, the ability to mail and receive uncensored letters to and from their attorneys, and the right to private visits with their attorneys. Even inmates in segregation have a right to these activities, although access may be limited somewhat in the interests of institutional security.

In 1996, the Prison Litigation Reform Act (PLRA) was enacted. This act is expected to have a significant impact on corrections litigation, as it places several restrictions on inmate litigation. The act requires a number of changes in how inmate lawsuits are handled, including: (1) that an inmate exhaust all available administrative remedies before filing a Section 1983 action; (2) that frivolous or malicious lawsuits could be dismissed without requiring exhaustion of administrative remedies; and (3) that court orders for relief are to be limited to correct only the rights of the particular plaintiff-inmate.

First Amendment Rights of Inmates

The First Amendment includes several separate individual rights, including freedom of religion, speech, and the press. The Supreme Court has held that inmates have only those First Amendment rights that are consistent with the legitimate penological objectives of institutional administration.

Inmates most often claim a violation of the First Amendment when they believe their right to exercise their beliefs has been restricted improperly. The Supreme Court has held that correctional staff have the right to regulate religious activity to promote valid interests such as security, discipline, limited resources, and inmate and correctional officer safety. Lower courts generally have deferred to the wisdom of correctional administrators when limitations on religious freedom are based on such grounds. More difficult questions are what constitutes a "religion," or "religious activity."

The Religious Freedom Restoration Act of 1993 (42 U.S.C. 2000bb) has several implications for corrections. This act now forms the basis for most inmate lawsuits involving restrictions on religious beliefs and practices. The RFRA states that the government can restrict a person's exercise of religion only if it demonstrates both "a compelling state interest" and shows that the application of the burden on religious freedom is the "least restrictive means" of furthering the compelling state interest. The constitutionality of the RFRA currently is being challenged, but unless it is voided by the Supreme Court, the act makes it much more difficult for corrections staff to limit an inmate's exercise of his or her religious freedom.

Inmates often file lawsuits alleging First Amendment violations based on restrictions that the institution places on their correspondence. Courts have allowed institutions to inspect and censor mail to and from inmates, and to limit the types of periodicals inmates can receive, so long as the restriction rationally is related to a legitimate penological objective, such as institutional security.

Federal Statutes

In addition to possible constitutional grounds for a lawsuit, cases can be filed based on an allegation of a violation of federal law. The applicable federal statutes include the Federal Tort Claims Act of 1946 and the Federal Civil Rights Act of 1871 (42 U.S.C. Section 1983). The Federal Tort Claims Act of 1946 waives the sovereign immunity of the federal government in a number of areas, and 42 U.S.C. Section 1983 provides a federal law remedy for injury caused by state actors. In 1964, the Supreme Court held that state inmates can bring suit under Section 1983. Such suits must involve

Being sued for actions arising out of the course of employment is, unfortunately, an occupational hazard for persons working in corrections.

Courtesy Capitol Communication Systems, Inc.

the conditions of confinement, however. If an inmate wishes to challenge the fact or length of his or her custody, habeas corpus is the proper action.

Inmates frequently use the Federal Civil Rights Act of 1871 when they believe there has been a violation of their constitutional rights. For an inmate to succeed under a Section 1983 claim, they must show that the correctional officer acted "under color of law," meaning that the injury was a result of misconduct by a state agent acting in his or her role as a state agent. In addition, the injury must involve a constitutional or federally protected right. The law permits inmates, in appropriate cases, to receive financial damages from those convicted of violating their rights. Liability does not attach on the basis of mere negligence, however—there must be evidence of intentional injury, or "deliberate indifference" to the situation which caused the injury. The liability of a defendant in a Section 1983 action must be personal. There is no basis for respondeat superior liability. Under respondeat superior, an employer may be held liable for the torts of an employee, if these torts are committed in the scope of employment.

Fortunately, Section 1983 claims are rarely successful. The cases where an inmate succeeds in a lawsuit often involve the improper use of force by correctional staff, or the malicious, intentional deprivation of an inmate's constitutional rights.

State Law

Inmates also may look to state tort law as a basis for a lawsuit. State tort law varies a great deal from state to state; consequently, correctional staff must be familiar with the law in their jurisdiction. A tort is a civil wrong. There are three conditions which must exist for a tort to be proven. (1) First, it must be shown that the defendant owed a duty to the plaintiff. (2) Second, there must be a breach of that duty. In legal terminology, there are three forms that this breach of duty may take in regards to

The correctional officer who is a defendant in a suit should have no hesitation in asking his or her lawyer about the status of the case.

state agents. If a staff member takes an improper action, it is termed *misfeasance*. If the caseworker takes no action, it is referred to as *nonfeasance*. If the caseworker takes a required action but performs it inappropriately, it is termed *malfeasance*. (3) The third condition for a tort is a demonstration that the injury suffered by the plaintiff, in fact, was caused by the defendant's breach of duty. Proximate cause is a legal creation intended to limit liability for damages to consequences which are reasonably foreseeable and related to the defendant's conduct.

It is also important to note that in extreme cases, correctional staff have been prosecuted under state criminal laws for their actions in the correctional setting. While these instances are rare, correctional staff should be aware that they are responsible for their actions, not only to the inmate, but to the state. Furthermore, violation of an inmate's civil rights is a federal offense.

Immunity

According to the doctrine of sovereign immunity, the state cannot be sued for civil damages as a result of its actions unless it consents to the suit. Most states have some statutory provision waiving their sovereign immunity in certain circumstances. This allows lawsuits to be brought in state court relying on state tort law. A tort is a "private or civil wrong or injury other than beach of contract, for which the court will provide a remedy in the form of an action for damages" (Black 1983).

While the federal and state governments all provide for waiver of their sovereign immunity in some circumstances, this waiver is far from complete. There are three forms of immunity defenses invoked in liability suits: absolute, qualified, and quasijudicial immunity. Under absolute immunity, a lawsuit is dismissed without delving into the merits of the claim itself. Absolute immunity generally applies only to officials in the judicial or legislative branches of government. Where absolute immunity protects officials completely, regardless of motive or intent, qualified immunity protects an official only if the official acted in "good faith." This form of immunity generally applies only to members of the executive branch of government. Quasijudicial immunity applies to officials who perform both judicial and executive functions. Under this form of immunity, official duties which are essentially nondiscretionary are not protected from liability, while those official duties which are judicial in nature and involve the exercise of discretion are accorded protection from liability.

The importance of the doctrine of sovereign immunity is that it allows a plaintiff to sue not merely the individual correctional officer for damages, but to sue the government, as the employer of the individual, under the doctrine of respondeat superior.

Generally speaking, for liability to attach, there must be not only a waiver of sovereign immunity, but proof of inappropriate conduct by the correctional officer. In tort law, there are several levels of conduct for which liability may be imposed: strict liability, negligence, and recklessness. In strict liability, liability attaches irrespective of the knowledge of the defendant. This rarely applies to correctional personnel. Usually, negligence is not enough to impose liability, either. Rather, there must be a showing of recklessness—conduct which displays both serious risk-taking and an awareness of the likelihood of harm. This is similar to the "deliberate indifference" standard enunciated by the Supreme Court.

All correctional agencies provide legal support to their staff who are sued in the course of their official duties. It is the responsibility of the staff member to inform the agency when he or she is sued. Virtually all state agencies have a policy of providing legal support for, and reimbursing an employee for adverse court judgments resulting from official duties. This is not absolute, however, as agencies may refuse to support an employee who has acted in violation of official policy.

Reducing Litigation

After reading this chapter, one might think that every dispute between inmates and correctional staff results in a lawsuit. This is not the case, however. There are several ways to reduce the likelihood of litigation. These include the fostering of professionalism among correctional staff and the use of common sense in dealing with inmates. Perhaps the most effective means of reducing litigation is the use of internal grievance procedures. The Prison Litigation Reform Act of 1996 requires that inmates exhaust administrative remedies before filing lawsuits, and the Supreme Court repeatedly has endorsed the use of formalized grievance procedures as a means of protecting the constitutional rights of inmates.

In a properly administered grievance system, an inmate's formal, written complaint is reviewed and investigated at the institution by a person not involved with the original action. The inmate is provided with a formal, written response to the grievance. Grievance hearings even may be held. Correctional staff who do their job properly have little to fear from inmates filing a grievance against them. These informal methods of adjusting problems are good management.

Because it is likely that any review of an event, whether by a grievance committee or a court, will occur long after the event itself, a report should be written whenever an unusual incident occurs. Many institutions require correctional staff to document any unusual contact with an inmate as a matter of course. The report is crucial, because it will serve, along with the inmate grievance form, as the basis for the investigation. Thus, clear, concise, and accurate report writing is very important. The report should contain any relevant information, such as "who, what, where, when, why, and how."

Summary

Correctional law has changed dramatically over the past thirty-five years, and it continues to change. While correctional staff cannot be expected to know every nuance of the law, or to cite cases, it is vital that correctional staff be familiar with the general principles of law, as well as any new developments in the area. This information should be provided by the correctional institution, in a form which is easily understood by correctional staff. Correctional staff who understand the legal issues involved will be far more effective in their daily work, and better equipped to advance in their careers. In addition, it will ensure the correctional staff members that they do not incur personal liability.

APPLICABLE ACA STANDARDS

Inmates' Rights: 3-4262 - 3-4271, 3-4387, 3-4395

BIBLIOGRAPHY

Collins, W. 1997. *Correctional Law for the Correctional Officer,* Second Edition. Lanham, Maryland: American Correctional Association.

4

Inmate Supervision and Discipline

Correctional officers are key figures in managing a well-run institution. To be effective, they must have a command of policies and procedures, know and effectively use the many security and supervision techniques employed in modern prisons and other secure facilities, and, at the same time, treat inmates in a fair, humane way.

Supervision is more than simply visual observation; line staff and supervisors must be involved actively in every aspect of the facility's operation. They actively must control inmates and their activities every moment of the day. This involves issuing orders, performing counts, working towers, mastering surveillance technology, maintaining personal contact with inmates, and much more. Although it seems inconsistent at first, supervising inmates inside the facility is actually the key to perimeter security, because if inmates are not adequately controlled inside the perimeter, they eventually will be able to find ways to escape, no matter how secure the institution.

Interacting with Inmates

The degree of supervision required by inmates varies according to their security classification (maximum, medium, minimum). The principles behind classification are discussed in later chapters in this *Guide*, but generally speaking, inmates with similar security and supervision needs are housed in the same institution.

A good classification system provides for a regular review of inmates' cases, so that staff can move those who need more or less security to the proper location. As a rule, as inmates move closer to the end of their sentences, they can be moved to lower (lesser) security settings. However, every system always has a few high-security inmates whose custody or supervision levels should not be reduced at any point in their sentences.

Corrections is a very intense people business. In starting their career, correctional officers, and indeed all correctional workers, would do well to assess their attitudes toward others, and particularly toward inmates as human beings.

Some people, because of their negative attitudes, cannot work with any degree of success in an institution. This includes people who have a high degree of racial hatred toward specific racial or religious groups. Without the proper attitude, it is almost impossible to do a good job for the institution, or to deal effectively with inmates.

If an officer does not have some degree of personal concern about inmates as human beings, then no amount of training, education, or supervision will make it possible for that correctional officer to supervise effectively and assist inmates. If you are a good people person, working with others in your local community, you need not change your attitude when the sally port gate closes behind you, and you are at work.

Impartial Rule Enforcement

It is important that officers not let their personal beliefs and feelings affect their interactions with inmates. Impartial rule enforcement is the best way to gain inmates' compliance. Officers can get more cooperation if they convey their authority through fair actions and neutral attitudes, rather than through overbearing, heavy-handed tactics.

Given that every inmate is a unique person, it stands to reason that inmates will respond differently to the same treatment. However, fair, impartial treatment is one of the cornerstones of prison life. Inequality is almost certain to create serious problems.

Some decisions can and should be individualized and spelled out in policy. In other instances, what to do is not immediately clear. Sometimes, experience is the

Pat search of newly committed inmate at the West Virginia Central Regional Jail.

best teacher; a new officer should rely on more experienced staff and supervisors for advice in questionable instances. When in doubt, ask a question. There is no such thing as a dumb question in corrections.

New institutional designs have improved officers' ability to supervise inmates directly. Smaller housing units, interior layouts that provide easy visibility into all parts of the unit, and other design features all make it easier for an officer to maintain contact with inmates, and thus know what is going on in the unit. This type of design reflects a personal staff contact philosophy; employees interact with inmates, move freely throughout the unit and shakedown rooms, and generally are involved personally in unit operations.

However, some designs in recent years have provided less staff contact with inmates, instead of more. Units with a remote supervision design often are characterized by electromechanically operated doors activated by a unit control center, where the assigned officer stays locked in all day, having very little contact with the inmates, except by an intercommunication system. Housing areas with these designs are sometimes staffed with an officer "on the floor" also, but when this is done, there is the management drawback of requiring twice as many employees for the same size inmate population. The advantage, however, of these designs is said to be in the area of staff safety. The disadvantages stem from employees having far less normal interaction with inmates; staff may require personal body alarms; staff search inmates and their cells less often. This organization requires staff that work extremely well together, but generally the staff knows less about what is going on in the unit.

Considerable debate in recent years has concerned the relative merits of these two design philosophies. To the degree that it favors normal interaction with inmates and more direct supervision and search activity, direct supervision designs are felt to be more advantageous in most institutions. For those few units, and even fewer total institutions, where ultra-high security needs may dictate a unit control center, the indirect contact strategy may have merit. But even in those locations, staff still must be in contact with inmates, if only for conducting searches, applying restraints, and performing other direct contact functions. In short, an inmate housing unit must be supervised through direct, hands-on techniques if it is to remain secure and safe.

Issuing Orders

Officers often must make inmates do things they do not want to do, and inmate reactions to orders sometimes are threatening. Correctional officers need to remember the inmates' names. "Hey you! Do this," just does not get the job done. Calling inmates by their names when giving an order makes it more personal, and if it is done properly, the inmate knows you know who he or she is.

As difficult as it may be when confronted by hostile or defiant inmates, correctional officers must maintain self-control and a professional attitude, while insisting on compliance. All inmates know they eventually will have to comply with the order or face segregation time. Generally, inmates can tell who is a new correctional officer, and many will test a new officer's self-control. If the inmate cannot be persuaded to comply with an order, then assistance should be called. A show of force is next to the last resort, and is usually very effective in dealing with a defiant inmate.

To give orders and instructions successfully, avoid vague or inappropriate words, confusing instructions, or incomplete information. Keep it simple. If an officer permits the inmate to not follow an order, then the basic elements of control in the institution begin to break down. Refusing an order can result in a direct confrontation, in which case it can be dealt with directly. In other cases, the refusal may be through passive or obstructive activity, in which the inmate works slowly or in a way that actually sabotages the job. Officers must intervene in those instances also. Know your inmates!

Some inmates legitimately may be unable to comply with an order on a matter that is essentially discretionary. Officers need to be flexible and especially alert to medical or mental health problems that can prevent a specific inmate from doing something. Again, ask questions: a health care professional is usually only a phone call away. In medical cases, the medical staff may issue special orders, such as feed in the cell, lower bunk only, use a bed board, a "fifth feeding" meal, or some other variation of normal operations. One may ask, "Well, isn't that treating inmates unequally—isn't that unfair?" Yes, it is treating them unequally, but it is fair.

In optional or judgment call areas, other inmates will understand an officer granting a variation in a routine order if there is a legitimate reason. Most inmates are locked up because they did a dumb thing on the street, but they are not stupid, and as long as the variation does not violate basic institutional procedures or security, most inmates will not object to this variation.

Observing Inmates

Individual and group activities, and the patterns and habits they represent, can be important indicators of an institution's mood or of illegal activity. Staff observation practices should include not only obvious duties such as breaking up fights and searching inmates and their cells, but also awareness of the subtle day-to-day changes in an institution, a unit, or individual inmates.

When an inmate who has previously been sullen and secretive begins to act friendly and cooperative, officers should be suspicious, and investigate immediately, reporting the change to a supervisor. Inmates who are anxious, who withdraw from group activities, who become careless about their personal appearance, or show other clear behavior changes are also a concern. However, changes in an inmate's behavior are not necessarily negative, and making judgments on which changes are a cause for concern becomes easier with time and experience. Again, know your inmates.

Of the inmates you supervise, you need to know who the organizers are, those who engage in strong-arm activities, the weapon makers, and the gang leaders. If a serious incident occurs, and you witness it, you will be better able to identify the inmates involved. Learn as many nicknames as you can and be able to match them with the inmate.

Supervision in Housing Units

Consistent supervision is essential for the safe and orderly operation of any correctional institution, and there is perhaps no place where that is more true than in the housing unit. An officer's poor judgment, lack of consistency, favoritism, or undue severity can change a quiet, peaceful housing unit into a dangerous place.

Officers' observation of inmate behavior in the housing area can lead to the discovery of escape plots, contraband, and other serious security concerns. Security inspections and routine but unpredictable shakedowns of cells and common areas are critical to this process. Observing changes in behavior, attitude, and friends of inmates, and other factors also can be important. These changes may signal an inmate under pressure for sex, one who has just started using drugs, one who is deep in debt, an escape plot in the works, or any number of other problems.

Signs of Trouble

Certain inmate behaviors may be a sign of impending trouble such as the tension that precedes a riot. Disturbances can be prevented if staff observe and report changes in the following routines:

- Separation by racial or ethnic groups
- Purchases of foodstuffs at canteens or commissaries
- Transfer requests
- Requests for protective custody
- Staff requests for sick leave
- Inmates spending excessive time in cell
- Inmate groupings with point men facing away from the group
- Increasing numbers of disciplinary cases
- Increasing numbers of voluntary lockups
- Inmate-employee confrontations
- Direct and indirect inmate intimidation of officers
- Threats against officers—written and verbal
- Increased sick calls from inmates
- Inmate violence against other inmates
- Increased numbers of weapons found in shakedowns
- Harsh stares from inmates
- Drop in attendance at movies or other popular functions
- Unusual and/or subdued actions by inmate groups
- Reluctance on the part of inmates to communicate with staff
- Inmates avoiding eye contact with staff
- Inmates making excessive and/or specific demands
- Appearance of inflammatory and rebellious materials
- Warning to "friendly" officers to take sick leave or vacation
- Employee demands for safety
- Staff resignations
- Letters and/or phone calls from concerned inmate families demanding protection for inmates
- Unusual numbers of telephone inquiries about prison conditions
- Unusual interest from the media
- Outside agitation by lawyers or activists

A work detail supervisor discusses the job performed by an inmate. A clean and orderly institution has fewer security problems.

Enforcing daily routines is very important for the smooth management of the housing area. These routines include wake-up, cell cleaning, cleaning of common areas, enforcement of noise-level restrictions and personal property limits, and many other routines. They also ordinarily include enforcing rules restricting inmate visits from other housing units, top tier not visiting with the bottom or from tier to tier in the same unit; searches of incoming inmates; searches of all materials, carts, toolboxes, and other items moving into the unit; and general traffic control.

Know your inmates. Unit managers must insist that line staff learn to recognize the inmates they supervise by name. Know who belongs in what cell in what bed. If you have twenty-four cells and all have two beds in them, it is important to know, at count time, that the right inmate is in the right bed.

During the day, most inmates are released from their cell blocks or dormitories to go to work or to participate in treatment programs. While responsible for the general accountability of the remaining inmates, the housing unit officer also is responsible for supervising inmates who clean and maintain the unit. This maintenance may be performed on a rotating basis, but a fixed set of tasks should be accomplished on a regular schedule. Each inmate on the work detail must be assigned a specific task/area of responsibility, be told what the finished task should look like, and be held accountable for completion within reasonable time parameters.

These standards of what constitute properly completed work must not vary from day to day, and staff should remember that inmates never will do a better job than staff insist that they do. The unit manager must insist that all correctional staff understand what constitutes clean. If low standards are acceptable, the institution will deteriorate. Jobs should be organized in correct operational sequence; cleaning materials and equipment must be properly used, stored, and accounted for at the conclusion of work.

Correctional officers should inspect daily for signs of unsafe or deteriorating facilities, including cracked paint, broken windows, and faulty plumbing, as well as evidence of tampered bars and locking devices, which could result in escape or injury either to inmates or to employees. These sanitation, maintenance, and security inspections are very important for keeping the institution running in a safe and secure fashion. As indicated next, record keeping is important. A written record of the daily bar check is a must.

Post Orders, Logs, and Records

Unit logs or shift turnover logs should be maintained and reflect events on every shift. They should include inmate transfers in and out, results of security equipment inventories, records of major maintenance, medical or security issues and to whom they have been reported, and any details or concerns regarding the group as a whole or individual inmates in particular. These records are important for maintaining continuity and staff safety from shift to shift.

Potential problem inmates, especially those in segregation/special management units, must be tracked. For example, if an inmate said he would kill the next officer who entered his cell, the oncoming shift responsible for

A bar check is a central part of a security routine.

Inmate Supervision and Discipline

the bar check would not want to walk into the cell without being forewarned.

Each unit should have a set of post orders (updated annually) that chronologically describes the major duties of each post in that unit and that also contains certain topical information. In addition, post orders typically have sections with portions of major policies that affect the post's operation. These might include placing sections of the hostage or use-of-force policies in the post orders of a high-security unit, or portions of the inmate accountability policy in the post orders of all housing units.

Bed books (a list of who is in each bed from when to when), picture cards (identification cards), and other inmate records, including information on the basic sentence and cell search, should be maintained in the unit to enable staff to correctly and quickly identify all inmates in the unit and their living areas, whether these are cells or dormitory bunks. A picture card system (maintained in the unit or in master control), enables staff to quickly determine who may be missing in an escape attempt or when facing other major problems.

Information Issues

Reliable information, systematically collected and analyzed, helps in regularly supervising and managing the institution, and can prevent riots or other disturbances. Collecting intelligence data is a daily operation and includes receiving input from all personnel and information gathered by supervisors.

Interaction with inmates in a calm, reasoned manner relieves inmates' stress.

Staff observation practices should include not only obvious duties such as breaking up fights and searching inmates and their cells, but also being aware of the subtle day-to-day changes in an institution, a unit, or individual inmates. You must learn to be as perceptive as the inmates you supervise.

Information gathered by supervisory, commissary, medical, program, and line staff are channeled to one place, usually under the supervision of an investigative or intelligence supervisor. That employee analyzes the information, determines its significance, and briefs top staff and possibly other institutions, if they are affected. Such information may concern the inmate population's mood and other important details. The use of computers enhances this operation.

To gather this information, sound relationships must be maintained with inmates so that they are willing to communicate their problems and concerns. This is where the contact supervision strategy is valuable, because if staff are regularly interacting with inmates, this information almost naturally will flow to them.

If used responsibly and with proper verification, inmates are good sources of information, despite the inmate code of "don't snitch." To a great degree, this is because most of them want to do their time without problems, and in a well-managed, safe institution. Riots, escapes, and other disruptions in the facility's routine may result in lost visits, reduced industrial wages, and other lost privileges, and may put the inmates at physical risk. So, most inmates have an interest in seeing that the institution runs smoothly. Often, inmates will see that

Verifying information is an important aspect of a correctional officer's job.

Courtesy U.S. Bureau of Prisons

While inmates are enjoying their free time, a correctional officer must remain alert.

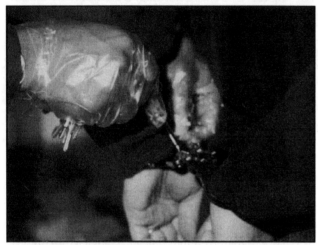
A correctional officer protects himself by wearing disposable gloves while locking an inmate in restraints.

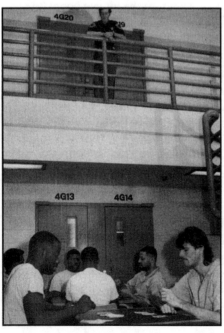
A correctional officer observes inmates from a balcony. He must be alert at all times.

Photos courtesy Capitol Communication Systems, Inc.

staff know in advance about impending problems. This occurs so long as the channels of communication are open and natural, as they are in an institution where staff are visible, active, and involved.

On the other hand, inmates who serve as regular informants with personal gain as a motive not only are despised by other inmates, but using them extensively can be disastrous. During the 1980 riot in Santa Fe, New Mexico, numerous informants were murdered by fellow inmates.

Information is a two-way street, however, and both inmates and staff must receive official information about programs and policies, particularly when changes are to be made or new policies instituted. Post orders—instructions about various job duties and policies—should be on all posts throughout the institution for regular review by staff and supervisors. Staff bulletin boards, roll calls, institution newsletters, and other communication devices also are important.

To prevent dangerous gaps in communication, officers should brief each other during shift changes. The relieving officer should be made aware of the current situation when coming on duty. The personal information passed on from one officer to another should be supplemented by carefully kept unit logs and other records on the post.

Likewise, inmates should be kept up-to-date on facts. When they lack good information from reliable staff sources, rumors and misinformation spread throughout the institution, which can lead to unrest and disorder. Newsletters, bulletin boards, and unit meetings can be good means to provide this information to the population.

Supervising Inmates at Work

Correctional officers often are involved in supervising inmates on job assignments such as the kitchen, shops, and farm and camp details. These duties, of course, vary from job to job, but the following principles apply in almost all cases.

- Every inmate leaving the institution must be properly identified, and the releasing documents properly authenticated. Whenever possible, staff escorting an inmate outside the institution should have an opportunity to review the inmate's file to learn any relevant background information, such as a history of escapes, medical problems, or assaults.

- Escorting officers should have a picture identification card of the inmate they are escorting, and that picture should have security and/or medical alerts attached.

- Inmates leaving the institution on escorted trips should be strip searched by the escorting staff; it is not wise to trust another employee's search of an inmate when personal safety is at stake.

- Restraints should be inspected carefully before applying them, and regularly reinspected while on the inmate to detect any signs of tampering.
- Inmates under escort never should be permitted to come in direct contact with an armed staff member.
- Inmates should not be permitted to come in contact with the public.

Sexual Behavior in the Correctional Setting

Inmate sexual activity is a particularly important supervision issue, even though sex is not permitted in the correctional setting, except for a few family visiting programs. Many inmates are sexually preoccupied as a direct result of their deprivation of relationships. Many inmates are young adults, and their sexual drive is an extremely strong factor in their behavior. Staff need to understand this aspect of inmate behavior and prepare themselves to deal with it appropriately.

The lack of heterosexual relations can cause different types of behavior. Masturbation is not unusual in the correctional setting. To the extent allowed by institution regulations, there may be pinups, photos, and written material with sexual overtones. Also, staff members of the opposite sex receive a great deal of attention; this attention may be in the form of direct or indirect propositions or sexual comments.

Formerly, the only work women correctional officers performed was to function as matrons in female correctional institutions. In recent years, many of the barriers to employing women as correctional officers in all-male institutions have been dropped. In a number of prisons, women regularly serve as line correctional officers. Women traditionally were excluded from correctional officer positions to protect inmate privacy, for the safety of the women, and because of fears that women would be unable to control inmates. Despite some court action that has upheld the right to exclude women from contact positions in certain types of correctional facilities (*Dothard v. Rawlinson,* 433 U.S. 321), an increasing number of women are employed as line correctional officers throughout the country. Many of the traditional assumptions and fears about women as correctional officers were not based on fact, but rather on myths and misconceptions.

Women who are correctional officers may work in either male institutions or female institutions, as may men.

The addition of female correctional officers to all-male institutions often has positive outcomes in terms of normalizing the prison experience. Seeing women in the prison can lend an air of naturalness and reality to the prison community. The positive effects the female correctional officers can have on an institution may help to alter the public image of both the institution and correctional officers.

Correctional officers should be careful to not share personal incidents with inmates because such information may be used against them in the future.

Heterosexual Activity

Heterosexual activity is a problem in those few institutions where male and female inmates are confined in the same location, or when staff members of the opposite gender are involved. Staff must be careful to provide the highest possible level of supervision to inmates in institutions where both sexes are confined. Supervision of mixed groups, and of areas where inmates might hide, are major tasks. The potential problems associated with these programs often are said to be offset by the improved atmosphere of the institution and the less dehumanized environment. However, due to detrimental effects on women inmates, few of these co-correctional institutions remain.

Obviously, staff-inmate sexual activity is completely forbidden in all institutions. Yet, with the assignment of staff of both genders to institutions housing the opposite sex, this may be a problem. No staff member should initiate, or allow to start, any personal or intimate relationship with an inmate. Staff need to take care of how they respond to unwanted overtures.

Inmates interpret responses the way they desire. For example, an inmate might say to one of the female treatment staff, "I would like to take you out some time." If she responds that she cannot go because it is against institution policy, the inmate may reason that she wants to go—only policy is in the way—and not be discouraged.

In addition to individual staff members being totally professional in their interactions with inmates and alert to any overtures that may signal an inmate trying to start an intimate relationship, supervisory staff constantly must be alert for the signs of any unusually close relationship between an inmate and a staff member. Staff who receive overtures from an inmate (verbally or in writing) should report them to supervisory personnel at once as a safeguard against later allegations of improper conduct that might be made by the inmate.

Homosexual Activity

Correctional officers should be prepared to encounter homosexual behavior among inmates in the correctional setting. Because of the abnormality of the single-sex setting, and because sex drives continue regardless of the environment, it is common for an otherwise heterosexual inmate to be involved in homosexual activities while in prison. Many of these inmates return to a heterosexual lifestyle once they are released to the community.

Some passive-partner male homosexuals play the female role in sexual activity, but do not adopt any female behavior. In their outward appearance, they may act rough and talk tough, but they can be identified by the company they keep. Others act in a directly feminine way, and if permitted to do so, many use makeup, wear feminine clothes, and generally act in a way to attract male attention.

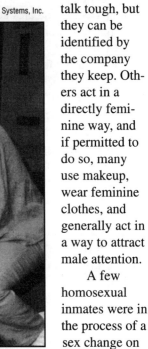

Courtesy Capitol Communication Systems, Inc.

Correctional offiers, especially females, should never give an inmate the idea that she is interested in developing a relationship with him outside of prison. However, proper communication is to be encouraged.

A few homosexual inmates were in the process of a sex change on the street when they were arrested, convicted, and sent to prison. They still retain their male sex organs, but they were taking estrogen and have had breast implants.

Aggressive males involved in homosexual activity often act as "wolves," or "jockers," sexual aggressors who take the traditional masculine role in oral or anal intercourse during a homosexual encounter, and prey on weaker, younger, or newer inmates to get sexual partners. These individuals should be watched carefully because of the trouble they can cause through their predatory sexual activity.

In male prisons, homosexuality can cause a great many problems. Sexual activity in a male institution not only reflects the sex drive, but also represents issues of power or dominance. Competition, rivalries, and death can result from homosexual relationships that are allowed to develop or continue. For this reason, they represent not only a threat to the participants, but also to the institution's overall security.

No staff member should initiate or allow any personal or intimate relationship with an inmate to start.

In female institutions, sexual activity can have less of the aggressive or power overtones that occur in male institutions. Some inmates do adopt "male" roles, and some dress and act the part. However, there is also a "family" context that sometimes emerges as well, which is thought to satisfy some of the different emotional needs that female inmates have.

Homosexual affairs in prisons or jails are no joke, and should not be treated as such. Overt, weak homosexuals should be supervised properly and may need protection from "wolves." Some prisons and jails require that known homosexuals be kept under strict surveillance; some place them in isolation. On the other hand, homosexuals should not be ridiculed or unnecessarily singled out for special treatment. They are entitled to the same fair, professional treatment that any other inmate receives.

To decrease homosexual activity, correctional officers must supervise inmates closely. This includes making sure inmates are in their assigned areas. The correctional officer must supervise shower and bathing areas, and encourage inmate participation in recreational activities as an outlet for their energy. The correctional officer must not allow the view into cells to be blocked by blankets, towels, sheets, or other objects.

When an inmate indicates a sexual assault has taken place, staff should act immediately. Supervisory personnel should be notified, and a decision made whether to place the victim in locked status or protective custody. The victim should be interviewed to identify the person or persons who committed the assault. In some cases, criminal prosecution may be indicated for the attackers, in addition to internal inmate disciplinary procedures. The victim should be referred for a medical examination and any appropriate medical care. A referral to mental health staff also may be indicated, as the trauma following such an event may lead to serious psychological problems.

Finally, there is the less common possibility of an inmate making a homosexual overture to a staff member. Just as in the case of sexual activity between opposite sexes, this is forbidden and should be reported to supervisory staff at once.

Inmates in a Texas prison's locked unit.

Disciplinary Procedures

Every correctional institution has rules to ensure good work performance, high sanitation and safety levels, and most important, institutional security. These rules, if properly enforced, result in an orderly and acceptable way of life in the prison; they are especially necessary when large numbers of people live and work together.

If rules are disobeyed in prison, some form of punishment must be imposed. This punishment can range from a verbal reprimand to disciplinary status in a segregated unit, from loss of good time to prosecution for a new offense committed in the institution.

Understandably, discipline and punishment are as unpopular within a correctional facility as they are in any other type of community. But discipline is most effectively imposed when inmates believe the process is fair. Well-defined rules of conduct, along with firm, fairly administered but not overly severe penalties, are critical to any disciplinary program.

American Correctional Association standards require each institution to provide inmates with a rule book that contains all chargeable offenses, ranges of penalties, and a description of disciplinary procedures. The rule book should be available in the languages spoken by significant numbers of inmates. When a literacy, language, or physical disability problem (vision and/or hearing impairment) prevents an inmate from understanding the rule book, a staff member or interpreter can help the inmate understand the rules.

Clear, specific regulations also should help staff members understand and implement the inmate discipline policy consistently. Institutional personnel who work with inmates usually receive periodic inservice training on the rules of inmate conduct, the rationale for the rules, and the sanctions available.

Although there is no legal penalty for not following an ACA standard, the United States criminal justice system has accepted ACA standards as the benchmark for measuring the quality of correctional programs and services. Those institutions that do follow ACA standards, or have adopted their own state standards, are managed more efficiently and safely and with humane concern for the victims of crime, for staff, and for offenders, whether accused or adjudicated.

Reporting Incidents

When very minor infractions or incidents occur, the officer has the option of resolving them informally. This should be done only in the case of very minor violations, to keep discipline consistent across the entire institution. Having too many informal resolutions can begin to erode overall control. Many institutions require a documenting memorandum for informal resolutions, so that supervisory staff can see patterns developing.

If a more serious incident occurs, most institutions require that an incident or disciplinary report of some kind be filed. If in doubt, report. The report describes the event itself (from start to finish) in factual terms, including any unusual inmate behavior, witnesses (staff or inmate), physical evidence (weapons or property), and force used (what kind and by what staff or inmate), during the incident. After reviewing and signing the document, the officer forwards it to the designated correctional supervisor for possible investigation and further processing.

This report becomes the basis for further review of the episode, and possible disciplinary action. Not every report filed will result in further action; sometimes, the supervisor or investigating officer will find a good reason to drop the charge or to resolve it informally. In many other cases, however, the report is used as the basis for a due process hearing against the inmate, and a significant punishment may be imposed. This places an important responsibility on the reporting officer to be fair and accurate in preparing the report.

When Prison Violations Are Crimes

Some internal institutional offenses also are state or federal crimes. Obviously, murder, assault, theft, and many other offenses committed by inmates are illegal, and they may be subject to established criminal penalties in addition to internal punishment. For that reason, when an inmate allegedly commits a criminal act, the case often is referred to the proper law enforcement officials, who decide whether to prosecute the individual.

There are also restrictions on how an inmate who may be charged criminally can be interviewed or interrogated, in order to preserve certain rights against self-incrimination in the criminal case. Agency policy spells out these restrictions, and they should be observed carefully.

Segregating Inmates

Serious violations—such as arguments or fights, possession of escape paraphernalia, and many other incidents—may require removing inmates from their units or jobs to segregated or locked units. Administrative and disciplinary segregation or detention is necessary to maintain the institution's orderly operation. This type of housing status significantly restricts inmates in their movement and other personal freedoms, including possession of personal property and access to normal institutional programs. These units are used for the short- or long-term isolation of the most dangerous, troublesome, and escape-prone inmates—individuals believed to be a danger to staff or other inmates, or to the institution's security and orderly operation. More security inspections are required in these units. Staff here should be the first to be issued personal body alarms, and stab-resistant body armor to increase their personal safety.

Separate housing areas ordinarily are designated for these functions. These may include units with vestibule

A correctional officer escorts an inmate in restraints.

or sally port entrances and special physical construction features. In an emergency, any housing unit can be designated to be used for administrative or disciplinary status and staffed and managed accordingly.

An officer may not simply take an inmate to a segregated unit; a supervisor should be involved in the decision to remove an inmate from the population. Of course, in an emergency, individual staff members may do so to prevent a problem from growing, or to control a violent inmate. In this process, the officer immediately must search the inmate involved for contraband. In many institutions, the inmate also is placed in handcuffs to be moved to the locked unit.

In any case, where an inmate is placed in locked status, a memorandum or incident report should be prepared, detailing the reason for the action. This report usually is given to the shift or watch supervisor, with copies to members of the inmate's unit or classification team, the administration, the supervisor of the segregated unit, and to the inmate, so long as that is not a risk to institutional security.

American Correctional Association standards establish clear requirements for the operation of a segregated unit. Among them are providing basic hygiene items, as well as eyeglasses and writing materials. Inmates also should wear the same type of clothing as the general population, unless security clearly requires a distinct type of clothing, or unless it is for their protection, such as removing a belt to prevent a suicide attempt.

Segregation

Note: "Segregation" is the generic term that encompasses administrative segregation, protective custody, and disciplinary detention.

Removing an inmate from the general prison population for a short time is an accepted correctional practice that requires no due process hearing. An inmate may be placed in administrative segregated status by the warden, disciplinary committee, shift supervisor, or members of an inmate's unit team, depending on the institution's specific policy. Ordinarily, an inmate in administrative segregated status is permitted to retain most personal property items, but is locked in a cell for most of the day with limited access to recreation, television, showers, and other normal institutional activities.

Inmates generally may be placed in short-term administrative segregation for the following reasons:

- Awaiting or following a hearing on a violation of rules
- Awaiting an investigation or trial for committing a criminal act
- Awaiting transfer or as a holdover between institutions
- For the inmates' protection

A correctional officer attaches restraints to an inmate's hands.

Pending Classification

In some institutions, an inmate may be placed in administrative segregation only if charged with an offense for which disciplinary segregation could be imposed, or if he or she is found guilty of the offense. Local regulations spell out specific restrictions of this type.

In many institutions, this same general category includes inmates requesting or requiring protection from others in the general population. They are subject to many of the same restrictions of other administrative-status inmates. However, court decisions have said that institutions must allow protective-custody cases to participate in as many of the usual programs as possible, as long as this imposes no threat to them or the institution's security. Take care so that inmates do not come to see placement in protective custody as desirable. Each case should be reviewed frequently, with the goal of ending the separate housing assignment as soon as possible.

In many states, inmates are able to list enemies during classification hearings. Take care when moving inmates from institution to institution so that he or she is not forced to request protective custody because of an administrative oversight. The same care needs to be taken to ensure the inmate is not using this to manipulate his or her housing.

Disciplinary Segregation

The use of disciplinary segregation unit housing is often the subject of considerable concern and litigation. The courts generally hold long-term segregation in disciplinary status to involve an inmate's liberty interests, and, therefore, require due process protections in the form of some type of hearing. As a result, except for the most unusual circumstance, an inmate may be placed in disciplinary status only after a full due process hearing has been held, in which all constitutional rights have been provided. Disciplinary status usually is reserved for inmates found to have committed major rule infractions for serious offenses, and then only for limited periods. It also can be used for repeat violators of less serious infractions if the hearing officer is using a sentencing matrix (mandatory sentencing guidelines).

The due process hearing may be the result of a multi-level review process involving investigators, unit staff review, a disciplinary committee, or a single designated disciplinary hearing officer. No matter what the actual procedure, which is determined by agency policy, court decisions on due process [*Wolff v. McDonnell*, 418 U.S. 539, 71 Ohio Op. 2d 336 (1974)], outline the rights that must be provided in such a hearing, and they include the following:

- The right to be notified of charges before the hearing
- The right to call witnesses if they are reasonably available
- The right to present relevant evidence
- The right to receive assistance in preparing a response to the charges
- The right to be represented
- The right to appeal to an impartial third party

Inmate transport is fraught with a chance for escape attempts so correctional officers need to be particularly alert.

If the inmate is found to have committed the prohibited act after a due process hearing, the inmate may be placed in disciplinary status. Other actions, such as losing good time, also may be heard in a due process hearing.

In disciplinary status, the inmate has significantly fewer privileges than in administrative status. In most cases, everything except basic personal property is removed and stored, and access to all but basic programs and services may be reduced or stopped.

General Segregation Procedures

Segregated units contain inmates who are potentially a danger to themselves, institutional security, staff, or other inmates. For that reason, procedures for either type of unit should include the same basic principles. While each institution has its own specific rules, the following procedures are common to most segregation unit operations.

All incoming inmates must be searched; their personal property also must be searched for contraband and then inventoried, with a receipt given to the inmate. This inventory process safeguards staff against allegations of pilferage and theft, and also is a prime opportunity to remove items not permitted in the unit.

Records

When any individual is moved to a segregated unit, the following information must be recorded in the general unit log and other individual inmate records: name, number, originating housing unit, date admitted, type of infraction or reason for admission, tentative release date (if known), and any special medical or psychiatric problems or needs. If the inmate needs to be walked and/or showered alone, an alert to this situation must be made known to all staff in the unit. All releases, incidents, and unusual inmate behavior also should be recorded in this general log and the individual inmate record kept in the unit.

The unit staff should maintain an individual record on each inmate, noting the following for each day: the time of meals, time and amount of recreation, showers, visits by medical staff, and other treatment professionals, as well as any unusual inmate behavior or incidents, such as refusing recreation, showers, medication, or meals. When the inmate is released from segregated status, these individual records then may be sent to the inmate's central file to serve as a permanent record of the

Inmate Supervision and Discipline

 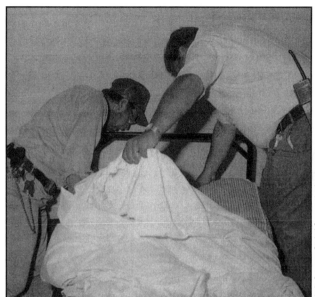

Left: A correctional officer speaks with an inmate in a security cell. Right: Two correctional officers conduct regular search procedure of an inmate's cell.

period in segregated status. They can be a valuable record in later court cases where inadequate care is alleged.

The unit also should maintain a visitor log, in which staff record the names, positions, and times of visits by all officials who inspect the units, counsel inmates, deliver medications, make medical rounds, or otherwise visit the unit for any reason. Inmate workers or witnesses for disciplinary hearings coming into the unit from the general population must be kept to the necessary minimum, and searched both going in and coming out of the unit. These inmate workers must be supervised constantly, and their selection should be approved by a supervisor.

Tools kept in the unit, and those coming in with maintenance crews, must be inventoried and carefully controlled throughout the time that they are in the unit. Only those tools required for a particular job should be permitted in the unit.

Personal Property

Personal property generally is restricted to some degree in all segregated units and may be limited severely in disciplinary status. In either case, while an inmate is housed in a segregated unit, supervisory staff may be authorized by policy to remove from an inmate's cell any item the inmate is likely to destroy or use to cause self-injury. However, in the case of personal care materials, the supervisor should permit the inmate to use the item while monitored by an officer, or find a suitably safe substitute. Plastic containers that can be purchased in the prison commissary and modified by inmates in a segregated unit to become the delivery system for urine sprayed on staff or other inmates should be replaced by a suitably safe substitute.

Most institutions require that when an inmate is deprived of any item or activity usually authorized, that decision must be made with the approval of a supervisor; in many cases, a written report is required to detail the reason why the item was taken from the inmate. Ordinarily, copies of these reports are forwarded immediately to the chief correctional supervisor/administrator.

If circumstances appear to justify the removal of all personal items in a cell, approval should be obtained in advance from the warden or designee. No item or activity should be withheld longer than necessary to insure the inmate's safety and the well being of the staff and other inmates. In no case should an inmate be deprived of an item or activity for the sole purpose of punishment without a due process hearing.

Meals

Meals ordinarily are served in cells in these units. This *Guide's* food service chapter gives additional information on this subject, but two important rules in all segregated unit operations are that inmates should not serve food to other inmates in these units, and food should not be used as a punishment or reward. Allowing inmates to serve food is a prime opportunity for extortion, food tampering, or other problems. To avoid using food as a control measure, if an inmate throws food trays or food at staff, it may be necessary to prepare nutritionally adequate sack lunches that cannot be used as readily against staff. Inmates who plug their sinks and toilets may need to have the water in their cells controlled from the outside, but at no time should food or water be withheld as a punishment. All of the control methods used must be documented properly.

Movement

Movement in restraints is a typical feature of most segregated units. Any time an inmate in segregated status is out of a cell and in contact with staff or other inmates, he or she should be in handcuffs. This process requires handcuff ports in all cell doors, shower grilles, recreation cell doors, and any other areas where inmates may be cuffed or uncuffed. Local procedures describe how that is done, and whether the handcuff should be in front or behind. In addition to handcuffs, some inmates with severe behavioral problems may require ankle shackles. This information should be maintained on the individual inmate's record maintained in the unit.

Group Activities

Careful control of recreation and other group activities is also a must in segregated units. In many high-security settings, one-at-a-time recreation is the rule. In others, carefully selected small groups may recreate together, and they should be searched carefully as they come out and go back into their cells. Use of handheld metal detectors is very effective. No matter what the arrangement, these groups should be under constant staff supervision, and the inmates should be restrained when they are in direct contact with staff. A successful control method for small group activities is through use of a television camera.

Searches

High-risk areas such as segregated units must be searched more often than other areas. These searches should be logged, so that a record of which cells and areas have been searched is available to staff on other shifts.

Recreation areas should be searched for contraband before and after each recreation period. The use of ground-sweeping metal detectors can assist staff in locating metal weapons. In addition, all security hardware and the physical features of the area should be a part of the regular security inspection system, and in this case, should be inspected not less than daily.

Searches of inmate cells should be performed on a frequent but unpredictable basis. Particular attention should be given to bars, windows, locks, lighting fixtures, and any furniture allowed in the cell. Some institutions regularly move inmates from cell to cell to disrupt any attempt to tamper with or compromise the room's security.

Searches of common areas in the housing unit should be part of the regular security inspection program, with close supervisory review of all findings. Particular attention should be paid to the bars, locking devices, door guides, and metallic items that could be used to fabricate weapons, but no portion of the unit can be overlooked. Staff should take note of fresh marks on floors or walls that would indicate a weapon is being sharpened. All cell and common area searches should be logged for reference by other staff and supervisory personnel.

Visits

Visits for inmates in segregated units often are conducted in the unit, or in a special controlled, noncontact visiting area in the regular visiting room. Because of the concern for high-security inmates in particular, special search and escort procedures may be in place for both inmates and visitors.

Services

Religious, educational, counseling, and other services typically are delivered to inmates in their unit. In many instances, this takes the form of staff members touring the unit regularly, and stopping at the cell fronts to discuss inmates' problems. In the case of library and legal reference services, those materials ordinarily are requested from a central location. In some institutions, a small law library collection is maintained in the unit, and after requesting to be put on a schedule for using the area, the inmate can be locked in the room with the legal material.

Summary

Supervision and fair, consistent discipline are the key to maintaining not only internal institutional order, but public safety. No matter how secure the perimeter, if the interior of an institution is improperly supervised, eventually the inmates will find a way to breach the security. An alert, caring, and professional staff is an absolute must.

APPLICABLE ACA STANDARDS

Records: 3-4092

Special Management Inmates: 3-4237 - 3-4261

Security and Control: 3-4180, 3-4181, 3-4183-1

Inmate Rules and Discipline: 3-4214 - 3-4236, 3-4243

BIBLIOGRAPHY

Bayse, Daniel J. 1995. *Working in Jails and Prisons: Becoming Part of the Team.* Lanham, Maryland: American Correctional Association.

Phillips, Richard L., James D. Henderson, and W. Hardy Rauch. 1997. *Guidelines for the Development of a Security Program,* Second Edition. Lanham, Maryland: American Correctional Association.

Wojda, Raymond, and Judy Rowse with photography by Grace Wojda. 1997. *Women Behind Bars.* Lanham, Maryland: American Correctional Association.

5

Security and Control

To maintain a secure institution, staff must prevent escapes, regulate contraband, and properly control inmate movement and activity. The necessary level of control is maintained through the hardware and physical security features of the institution, as well as through human action inside the perimeter. Of the two, the human factor is far more important; without it, the hardware would deteriorate and the physical plant, no matter how secure, could be defeated by the inmates.

The human factor is made up of well-trained and disciplined professional staff, using sound classification and discipline systems, and efficient communication methods. Coupled with those elements, the managers must be willing not only to listen to problems of staff and inmates, but to effectively deal with them in a timely manner. This *Guide* discusses the perimeter or external security issues first and then explains the importance of internal security measures and staff performance to the overall institution's security and control.

External Controls

External controls are the institution's physical features that make up its perimeter and support structures. In secure facilities, towers, gates, fences, lights, detection systems, and walls are a major part of the physical security.

An institution's specific security features are determined by the type of inmates it houses. American Correctional Association standards describe typical perimeter construction for maximum- or medium-security institutions as usually consisting of walls or fences, with buffer zones between buildings and the perimeter itself. Walls typically are capped by towers that overlook the interior of the compound. Fenced compounds ordinarily have free-standing towers of some sort, a mobile patrol system, or both. If double fences are used, they ordinarily are at least twelve feet high, and twenty-to-thirty feet apart, with rolled-wire reinforcements. The inner fence is embedded in a concrete curb or barrier to prevent tunneling underneath it. The area between the fences should be sanitized to suppress weed growth and to allow officers better visibility.

A limited number of sally ports or gates, ideally no more than two, should penetrate the perimeter; gates ordinarily are operated from towers or other remote locations. These fence and gate configurations are used with various combinations of electronic surveillance devices—pressure, sound, closed-circuit television, and microwave-based systems.

It is highly desirable to have a buffer zone approximately 100-to-150 feet wide between both the inner fence and the institution's buildings, and the outer fence and adjacent buildings or tree lines. The inner zone prevents inmates from using any nearby buildings to their advantage in an escape; the larger the exterior buffer zone, the easier it is to respond safely with disabling gunfire should an inmate try to escape.

Minimum-security institutions ordinarily rely on single fences, or no fences at all. A mobile patrol may be used, but if inmates are screened appropriately, the patrol staff will be concerned just as much with intruders bringing in contraband as inmates trying to escape.

In most older maximum- and medium-security institutions, towers form the backbone of perimeter security. They contain armed officers who observe a specific sector inside the perimeter. Tower officers typically are equipped with at least a rifle or shotgun, and may have a sidearm and gas in the tower as well. Some institutions may have armed posts at critical points inside the compound, including a few prisons with armed staff in gun galleries or gun walks inside the housing units. This, generally, is considered a more risky strategy than the policy adopted by most agencies, which is to never have firearms regularly stationed inside the institution.

In any case, these armed posts exist to deter and prevent escapes, or other incidents that could result in serious injury or even death to employees or inmates. Firearms should be used only when other means fail, and then only according to institutional policy. Staff should abide by specific agency policy in using deadly force. Ordinarily, the policy is to shout a warning before firing, then to fire a warning shot—if needed. If the inmate still has not stopped the dangerous activity, then shots are to be fired to stop, rather than to kill.

Post Orders

Each perimeter post should have a comprehensive set of post orders providing clear guidance to employees on the use of deadly force, hostage situations, actions regarding intruding civilians, and other situations. These post orders vary according to institutional size and security level, but they also typically indicate the location and use of surveillance devices. They show how mobile patrols fit into the perimeter security picture, provide firing distances for various points within the compound, inventory procedures for weapons and ammunition, and offer other important details.

Courtesy U.S. Bureau of Prisons

All correctional officers must be aware of their institution's policy on use of force both while on perimeter patrol and in the institution.

Correctional officers also may be assigned to mounted or other motorized patrol duty outside the prison. These methods are used for supervising work details in remote areas, and discouraging contact between inmates working on outside details and civilians passing by with whom they may come into contact.

Officers assigned to a foot patrol adjacent to the perimeter must inspect all walls and buildings where inmates might dig holes or hide tools, weapons, ropes, or homemade ladders. The fence or wall itself must be part of the regular security inspection system, as must all penetrating tunnels, manhole covers, and other security features.

Pedestrian and Vehicular Traffic

Pedestrian and vehicular traffic may enter and leave only at designated points in the perimeter—the fewer the better. Where possible, these entrances should be located close to one another; this reduces the number of ground-level officers required to check vehicles and visitors. All entrances and exits to the institution should be sally ported.

All visitors and employees must pass through a pedestrian entrance, gatehouse, or main entrance, where they are properly identified and processed into the secure portion of the institution. Larger institutions may have a secure sally port near the vehicular gate designated for work crews. Officers at each gate must thoroughly search everyone who enters, and properly identify them as they come in and out of the institution.

Usually gates separate any public-access portions of the administration building from the secure part of the prison. Officers controlling these gates or grilles (usually in the control center) must admit and release only those employees, visitors, or inmates who are clearly authorized. Most institutions that have inmate workers in the administrative area use a gate pass system of some sort to positively identify all inmates permitted through this critical traffic point.

Vehicular sally ports often are controlled by an officer in an adjacent tower. Vehicles with materials, equipment, and supplies may not pass through until drivers are cleared by the appropriate official, or the authorizing paperwork has been produced and carefully validated. Every vehicle that enters or leaves the vehicular entrance must be searched thoroughly before admittance for contraband, and before leaving the secure compound for inmates who may be hiding in the payload or under the carriage.

The drivers of all vehicles should dismount and stand clear of the cab to demonstrate that they are not under any duress. In addition, the officer on the ground who performs the search also should stand well clear of the vehicle when giving the "all clear" signal to the tower, so that it is evident that he or she is not giving the signal under duress.

Occasionally, the regular vehicular entrance is not suitable for serving large industrial operations, and a second sally port is needed for incoming materials and outgoing products, or in some institutions, to accommodate a

Security and Control

Double-wire fences and guard towers provide an extra level of security.

train track for boxcars moved by a small switch engine. Depending on physical plant constraints, the entrance also can be used for emergency vehicles such as hook and ladder trucks or ambulances.

Hostage Policy

It is extremely important that the staff assigned to gate operations be aware of the agency's hostage policy. While this policy may vary in detail from one agency to another, in general, most correctional institutions hold to the rule that no hostage has any authority, and that no inmate will be released while holding another person—visitor, employee, or another inmate—under duress.

Tunnels penetrating the perimeter, usually for utility service, are a concern. They should be secured with multiple grilles; ideally, the grilles on the outside half of the tunnel should be keyed so that they can be opened only from the outside. These are areas where technology can be used to good effect. The use of motion-detection circuits on closed-circuit television cameras, acoustic monitoring devices, and other electronic systems can alert staff to unauthorized activity in critical tunnel areas. Drain pipes and other utility piping should be designed with a sufficiently small diameter, or should go through constrictions of some type, to prevent their use in escape attempts.

In addition to the perimeter security that is obvious to the casual observer, every activity in an institution has an impact on security, and can be important in preventing escapes and disorder.

Lighting

Lighting on the perimeter and compound is vitally important. The proper amounts of lighting can aid tower and patrol staff greatly. Correct placement of lights in the interior eliminates blind spots in the shadow of buildings, makes internal patrols safer for staff, and reduces inmates' ability to move about in a nighttime escape attempt. Institutions increasingly are using high-intensity, high-mast lighting that provides lighting levels and coverage far superior to regular mercury or quartz vapor fixtures on standard light poles.

Outside-assisted Escape Attempts

Escape attempts with outside assistance typically take a relatively predictable form; a visitor brings in a weapon, a disguise, or some other contraband to assist

Correctional officers must be alert to items thrown over the fence or buried under it as well as for any obvious breaches in the hardware.

the inmate, or this individual may be waiting outside the perimeter with a vehicle. However, staff constantly must be alert for other variations on these methods.

For instance, there have been incidents where outside parties have fired on institutional towers with high-powered weapons while inmates inside have attempted to escape. There is always the possibility of an outsider throwing a weapon over a fence, and the inmate involved using the weapon against staff. These escape strategies, too, must be anticipated in yard searches and outside patrol procedures.

Helicopter-assisted escapes are a relatively new innovation for prisons, but a serious one, nonetheless. Correctional agencies do not agree on the proper policy in this area. Several schools of thought have emerged. The first involves the use of ground "clutter," such as using trees and light poles on the compound, to make it more difficult for a helicopter to land successfully. This method has been extended by stringing wires from buildings and poles throughout the compound to further complicate low-level hovering.

The use of firearms against helicopters is a particularly difficult issue. Some agencies permit firing on an inmate trying to run to a helicopter, but not the helicopter itself, because if it subsequently crashed, the possibility of an explosion could endanger perhaps hundreds of nonparticipating inmates, and even staff. If a rotor blade were hit, it also could spray the yard with shrapnel-like fragments that could kill nonparticipants. At least one location has its towers equipped with Bridger line guns, which are used in naval operations to project lines from one ship to another. In a prison application, they could be fired from a tower, over a helicopter's rotor, to tangle it and render the craft unmaneuverable. Other locations have taken the position that staff should do no more than note the identifying features of the aircraft and depend on law enforcement and military aircraft to trail the escapees. In any case, officers should be familiar with the policy of their particular agency on this important subject.

Internal Controls

After an institution's physical perimeter is secure, attention must turn to the interior. Escapes inevitably will take place, even with a secure perimeter, if inmates are not prevented from making or acquiring contraband, compromising internal security hardware, or moving at will without staff accounting for them. In truth, an institution is only as secure as its employees make it on the inside.

Inmate discipline is discussed elsewhere in this guide, but it is important to note the role that it plays in security and control. Staff must have an effective disciplinary system at their disposal for dealing with troublemakers and escape-prone inmates. If the inmate discipline system breaks down, almost inevitably the security also will break down.

Supervisory visibility is one of the central reasons why well-managed institutions run that way. The standards and expectations that top staff convey in the security and control area are absolutely vital. If top staff are active in touring the institution, talking to staff and

Left: Being prepared for any emergency is a vital aspect of the job of officers who monitor the control center. Right: A cell search should include careful inspection of any area where contraband may be hidden.

Photos courtesy U.S. Bureau of Prisons

inmates and thereby staying familiar with the institution and its climate, then security and control are far more likely to be intact.

Staff need clear, written guidelines to direct them. Each institution or correctional system should have a security manual that outlines security procedures. Topics should include security inspections, inmate counts, control of weapons and chemical agents, suppression of contraband, key and tool control, as well as cell equipment, emergency procedures, and supervision of inmate programs and activities. This manual of policies and procedures should be available to all staff, and should be used as the basis for annual refresher training. In addition, the manual should be the starting point for any internal agency review of procedural or policy compliance, through a structured audit program.

Design Issues

There are some internal physical plant items that greatly contribute to security and control. The importance of the control center cannot be overemphasized. Ideally, the control center is outside the secure perimeter, away from direct inmate activity. It is the center of all communication functions and is staffed around the clock. Staff here monitor key traffic points, take inmate counts, issue and inventory keys, and coordinate internal and perimeter security networks. They monitor various systems—fire alarm, public address, smoke and thermal detection, radios, computers, walk-way and perimeter lighting, and other mechanical and electrical systems. All of these mechanical systems must be tested on a regular basis, and the results of those tests logged. Gas and other equipment should be maintained on an inventory, checked regularly, and outdated items should be replaced with fresh supplies. An institution is only as secure as its employees make it on the inside.

The control center must be the institution's most secure location—completely invulnerable to inmate attack. In addition to ballistics-grade glazing in all windows, it should have bars over the windows, to further resist attack by rioting inmates. All walls and ceilings should be of reinforced construction, and the control center should have independent power and ventilation systems that enable it to continue operations in the event of a widespread institution takeover. The entrance should have an interlocked, double-door sally port that ensures that only authorized personnel enter. Often, counts are taken in the control center, and keys are issued from this point.

Housing Units

The construction of housing units has a great deal to do with the degree of supervision that can be exerted in

Top: A correctional officer opens the control panel in a secure unit. Bottom: An officer equipped with a communication device and key ring stands at cutoff grille in the corridor of the Bay County, Florida, Jail.

an institution. Facilities with dormitories generally are far more difficult to control than those with single cells, at least from the standpoint of the officer in the housing area. On the other hand, even a dormitory may be better than a single-cell housing unit that is so poorly designed that there are blind corners and hiding places where inmates can be totally out of an officer's sight. In short, there can be difficulties in either type of housing area. Staff need to learn the weaknesses of the particular design in their institution and find ways to compensate, either through specific procedures, additional staff, or additional technology.

Internal Movement

Physical design also can affect internal movement control by preventing inmate access to unauthorized areas. Control can be facilitated by such means as cutoff fences in the yard and at the ends of blind courtyards between buildings. It also can be maintained through manned checkpoints with fixed metal-detection equipment, where staff stop inmates, search them, and check passes. It also can be obtained through closed-circuit camera coverage of key locations where staff cannot be posted. Each of these strategies and many others prevent inmates from moving to areas where they can pursue unauthorized activities.

Correctional Officer Resource Guide

Entrances

The entrances to buildings and program and recreation areas are other posts that can be used effectively to monitor and control inmate traffic. In addition, the construction and location of windows, doors, mirrors, closed-circuit television, stairwells, elevators, and other physical features of buildings greatly can affect internal building supervision. The use of cutoff grilles in corridors and crash doors in units can be effective traffic control devices, particularly in an emergency, when staff need to gain additional time to contain a situation.

Inmate Accountability

Inmate accountability is far more than simply counting inmates. It involves movement control, pass systems, census checks, and record systems, also. Every correctional institution must have at least one official count each shift, and most institutions count inmates formally at least five times daily. The most common times are before and after typical working hours, after any mass movement, and at bedtime, coupled with two or more counts during the night, when the inmates are locked in their cells or dormitories. During those counts, inmates must be in place and not move from one point to another. As much as possible, all inmates should be in their assigned housing unit, in their cells, or at their bunks, during the count.

When officers count a unit, they must be sure that they actually see each inmate. Inmates who sleep under the covers may have to be disturbed just enough to be sure they are, in fact, there, and that a dummy is not in the bed. In dormitory units, two officers must be present, one to count and one to provide back up and be sure no inmate "bed-hopping" occurs to cover for a missing inmate.

Outcounts

Inmates whose jobs require them to be out of the housing unit during counts are on what is called "outcount" to that job area. The staff member in the work area must submit the names and numbers of those inmates in writing to a supervisor for approval, usually at least one hour before the time of the count. Those inmates then are approved, and the officer taking the count is given the signed, approved outcount approval form for the count records.

Counts made as outcounts on the job site are done differently than in a housing unit, where inmates are required to be in their immediate living areas or cells. On-the-job counts require that all inmates assemble in one area to be counted by staff. The numbers are called in, just like those from a unit, and recount procedures are also the same. Inmates may move about in the work area after the count has been cleared by telephone, but they may not leave the area until the entire institutional count has been cleared.

Courtesy Richard Phillips

An officer in the control center in a Colorado prison surveys a wide area.

The count numbers for each unit are called in to the control center. If the count is correct, inmates in the unit may move about, but they may not be released from the unit until the entire institutional count has been cleared. The officers counting must submit a signed count slip, attesting to the count they called in by telephone. In the event an officer calls in an incorrect number, a recount of that unit must be conducted, and local policy may require multiple recounts to verify the actual number.

The count ordinarily is taken in the control center or designated count room. The officer maintaining the master count record is provided up-to-the-minute information throughout the day on all inmate housing moves, work assignment changes, admissions to the hospital, and so forth. All inmates in legal custody are included in the master count, and there is a written record of all temporary absences from the facility. In effect, the count officer continually must know where every inmate is, and how many inmates are in each unit. This ongoing process is necessary for another reason; if an escape occurs, the count records in the control center are used as the basis for an emergency count. In addition, count records should be retained in enough detail to reconstruct any count held in the last thirty days, should there be any question about a particular count.

On the job or in the cellhouse, accountability is somewhat different, because official counts ordinarily are not held during working hours. Instead, crews are checked at the beginning and end of work periods against the assigned detail roster or by using some other system such as a crew kit card. Job supervisors as well as unit officers also take informal counts, or census checks, which are frequent but irregular checks made to verify that all inmates are present. Unless otherwise required, reports of these counts are made only when an inmate is missing.

Inmate Movement

Correctional officers often are required to transport inmates between institutions and to and from other locations outside the institution. The officer in charge ordinarily verifies the identity of all inmates as they board the vehicle and verifies the count onboard each time the vehicle stops and starts. Policies and procedures are designed to guard against escape. Restraints ordinarily are used for all but minimum-security cases.

Line counts may be used to count work details and other large groups out of their housing units. To avoid being distracted by inmates, officers should conduct line counts from behind. Large details usually are easier to count when inmates are assembled in columns of two.

Restrictions on inmate movement may vary depending on the classification of the inmates and the type of institution. Written procedures ordinarily specify how officers should regulate inmates moving from area to area. They may use a combination of pass systems, telephone contacts, intercoms, or other methods.

To these add the use of well-designed record systems, such as unit identification and assignment cards, inmate crew kits for work details, control center cards and pictures, and gate passes. These internal identification structures help staff control inmate activities and movement in the institution. A related category is the need to maintain central file pictures that are kept current for use in escape flyers, in the event an inmate successfully escapes from the facility.

Searches and Contraband Control

To detect and prevent the accumulation of contraband, institutions must conduct frequent unannounced searches of inmates, their property and quarters, and other areas of the facility. A comprehensive search program can detect and prevent the introduction of contraband, recover missing or stolen property, and help prevent escapes and other disturbances.

Although contraband is defined differently in each correctional system, in general, it is any item not authorized to be received by an inmate, sold in the institution, or received from the outside, as well as any otherwise approved item that has been modified in an unapproved manner. Contraband can be sold or traded (as in the case of drugs), or it can be used for aiding in an escape attempt, destroying property, or endangering human life. Carrying or possessing contraband is a violation of institutional rules. The local definition of contraband should be included in the admission and orientation program and in any inmate handbook used in that program.

American Correctional Association standards stress the need for a written policy regarding searches of facilities and inmates to control illegal articles. Frequent searches of inmates and their living areas are not conducted to harass or agitate inmates. They are a basic responsibility of institution staff, and are necessary to discover and eliminate contraband. However, abusing the power to reasonably search inmates may result in courts restricting the use of specific search procedures. As a result, staff should be well trained in policies regarding searches, and the search policies should be reviewed at least annually and updated, if necessary.

Generally, search procedures will not be questioned if the officers conducting them are professional and considerate of inmates and their possessions. However, problems can occur when officers use abusive, ill-timed methods; those tactics can cause inmate grievances,

A correctional officer watches the grounds from a guard tower.

Courtesy South Carolina Department of Corrections

disturbances, or litigation. Repeated confiscation of articles properly belonging to inmates, even though later returned, are certain to cause resentment. At the same time, an officer should not neglect to examine an article simply because it is not considered contraband. Some innocent-appearing objects can be converted into dangerous weapons or hiding places for drugs.

Preventive measures to keep contraband out of an institution begin at the institution's perimeter—the walls or fences. These must be adequately guarded and patrolled. However, most search activity is conducted inside the institution.

Careful inspection of vehicles entering and leaving the institution is a vital security function of the correctional officer.

Individual Inmate Searches

The technique used in searching inmates is important; officers must avoid using unnecessary force, or otherwise embarrassing or humiliating inmates. Good search techniques are learned best by doing searches; however, during routine "patdowns," officers generally do the following:

- Require inmates to remove hats, unbutton coats or jackets, and empty all personal articles from pockets

- Working from behind, run hands under the inmate's shirt collar and down the upper part of each arm to the wrists

- Bring hands back along the undersides of arms to the armpits

- Sweep hands down from the shirt front to the belt

- Run thumbs around the inside of the belt from front to back

- Run hands down the front of legs to shoe tops and up the backside of legs

- Sweep hands down the back from the shirt collar to the waist

- Examine subject's hat and other personal articles, including the inside of the hatband, cigarette cases, glass cases, or anything that appears unusual

Body Searches

Unless it is an emergency, body or "strip" searches should take place in a private area, such as in a booth or behind a curtain. Officers should stand behind the person being searched, unless the inmate is in restraints.

The technique generally involves the following: The staff member directs the inmate to remove all clothing, dentures, and prostheses (false limbs), and to move away from the clothing, which should be searched for any concealed contraband. The officer then should visually inspect the inmate's entire body, looking for contraband; the inmate should be required to open his or her mouth and allow the officer to look inside for concealed items.

This procedure should include directing the inmate to lift his or her arms to expose the armpits, lift each foot to expose the soles of the feet and to allow inspection between the toes, and bend over and spread the buttocks to ensure nothing obvious has been concealed in the crotch or in the rectum.

An inspection of an inmate's body cavities only takes place if there is reasonable belief that the inmate is carrying contraband. Inspection of body cavities, such as the nasal cavities, rectum, or vagina, whether manually or by instrument, only should be conducted with good cause, and when authorized by the warden or designee. It must be conducted in private, by health care personnel or other staff who have been specifically trained in these procedures.

When officers search a large group of inmates, such as a work detail, they should order the inmates to line up and present themselves one at a time for the search. The first person searched then forms the start of a new line far enough from the unsearched people to prevent the passing of contraband. After the searches are complete, the officer should scan the area where the inmates stood to locate any contraband that may have been dropped or discarded.

Housing Unit Searches

Searches of housing units, cells, or rooms should be performed without warning and irregularly. Cells always should be searched before being occupied by new inmates.

Ideally, two officers should conduct room searches, taking care to leave a room in the same condition in which it was found. Inmate property must be respected and not willfully discarded, broken, or misplaced. Officers doubting whether or not an item is contraband should consult the institutional rule book or a supervising officer.

Although it is impossible to list every hiding place for contraband, the following are the most obvious places in which officers should look:

- Holes or cracks in the wall, floor, and ceiling
- Lighting and wall fixtures; any items mounted on the wall, such as outlets, conduits, and so forth
- Washbowl, toilet, and plumbing stacks
- Shelves, drawers, and medicine cabinets as well as their contents
- Bedclothes, pillows, mattresses, and blankets
- Books, magazines, and newspapers
- False bottoms on large tobacco cans, ashtrays, or drawers
- Hollow legs of beds and other metal furniture
- Window bars, window frames, and overhead ventilators
- Sliding doors and grooves

Some critical areas, like segregated units and their recreation areas, must be searched more often than other sections of the institution.

In conducting searches in rooms, but in any other area as well, staff should be alert for bombs and booby traps. A suspected bomb should not be touched. Supervisory staff should be called at once. Another hazard of searching is the possibility of being stuck by hidden needles used by inmates for drug injection. Since these needles can carry the AIDS virus, take great caution if you discover any needles or syringes during a search.

Contraband Disposal

In most cases, officers are required to submit a disciplinary report on any inmates possessing contraband on their person or in their personal living area. All items confiscated during searches should be secured properly, in line with local procedures that normally require a report documenting the circumstances under which the contraband was found. This report ordinarily is submitted to the appropriate supervisor who also disposes of the contraband.

In most institutions, there is some type of secure contraband locker, where items are held for evidence pending a disciplinary hearing, or for possible criminal action. These items are disposed of outside the institution at regular intervals when they are no longer needed.

Local procedures describe how items with evidentiary value for a criminal case must be handled in order to preserve the "chain of custody" that proves that a certain item at trial is actually the item taken from the inmate.

Vehicle Searches

All vehicles and machinery must be searched thoroughly when entering or leaving the institution. Because people and contraband can be concealed in a very small space, an effective vehicle search process includes careful inspection of passenger and freight compartments, motor compartments, and the undersides or suspension gear. Mirrors, "creepers," and even inspection pits can help ensure the undercarriage is inspected thoroughly. Inspections also may include removing hubcaps, examining spare tires, and inspecting dashboards, seats, and head and door linings.

Commercial vehicles must be searched, and the driver's records listing the contents checked against the actual payload. If the list of cargo includes any narcotics, pharmaceutical supplies, gas equipment, arms ammunition, or equally dangerous substances, the vehicle ordinarily is not allowed inside the institution. Any such items intended for the institution are unloaded outside, and then taken by staff to the designated storage area.

All shipments leaving the institution must be well searched also. Barrels or tanks of liquids and loads of loose materials, such as hay, grain, and refuse, usually are probed with a rod to detect any hidden inmates. Large boxes and crates are accompanied through the gate by the officer who supervised their packing, or are locked in storage until after the institutional count and before being loaded onto trucks or freight cars. Another option is to lock the entire vehicle in the sally port through one or more counts.

Searches in Connection with Visiting

Visitors must be searched before being allowed to enter the institution. This search ordinarily is limited to passing through a metal detection device, and depositing all packages, bags, purses, and other property in a locker or other designated storage area. A sign indicating the institution's policy on contraband and other restrictions should be displayed prominently and read by all visitors, who may be required to sign an acknowledgment form regarding the notice before entering.

Visitors ordinarily are not required to submit to a body search unless they volunteer for it. If staff strongly suspect that visitors possess contraband, the officer processing them should consult with a supervisor, who may deny the visit or even call for local law enforcement officers to investigate. Each agency has different regulations on detaining visitors in such cases, and staff processing visitors should be familiar with those rules to avoid unlawfully detaining a visitor. Inmates should be searched before and after visits, to prevent them from bringing contraband into the visiting room or taking anything obtained from a visitor back to the compound. In most institutions, there is a sally port-type vestibule area between the visiting room and the general-population area where inmates are given a visual body search before and after each visit. Most institutions also limit the amount of property permitted in the visiting room, and some require the inmates to wear a special jumpsuit and shoes to reduce the likelihood of concealing contraband in standard institutional clothing during a visit.

Immediately before and after visiting hours, officers must conduct a thorough search of the visiting room for contraband, and inmates must not be permitted in the area during this search. During the visit, officers should watch for outside visitors passing illegal items to inmates, cross-visiting between inmates, and any attempt to exchange clothing or engage in sexual activity. Local regulations describe the kind of items that legally may pass between an inmate and a visitor, such as legal materials during an attorney's visit. After the visit, all trash left in the visiting area should be removed by staff and disposed of outside the institution, to prevent inmate workers from retrieving concealed contraband. The rest room should be searched thoroughly before and after visiting hours. Sinks, towel dispensers, and toilets should be given careful attention, because they could be used to hide contraband that could be picked up later by inmate janitors.

Tool Control

Every item in a prison must be considered a potential weapon, including work tools, kitchen utensils, and maintenance supplies. This is particularly true of tools, and as a result, staff must supervise and control all tools very carefully. The procedures for handling, storing, and monitoring all equipment, as well as securing certain

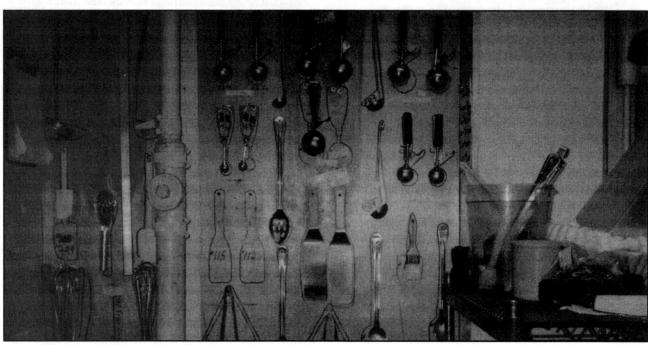

A shadow board allows officers to tell at a glance if any tools are missing.

"hot items," usually are outlined in the local tool control policy, and are specific to each institution. However, as in many other areas, most institutions use some common procedures.

First, there must be a central authority, usually in the form of a tool control officer, who coordinates the purchase and control of all tools. Employees in most institutions are not permitted to purchase tools independently, or to bring their own tools into the institution.

Tools must be accounted for at all times. This is done by maintaining a written inventory of each set of tools and prominently posting the inventory where the tools are stored. This inventory must be checked daily by the responsible employee and verified at least monthly with a member of the correctional force.

Tools generally are classified into two or three categories:

Class A Tools (Extremely Hazardous). This includes hacksaws and blades, cutting torches, torch-cutting tips, large pipe wrenches, knives, bolt cutters, axes, and hypodermic needles. Portable welding equipment ordinarily is removed from the institution each day; if removing it is impossible, the equipment should be kept in the institution's most secure area, with the tips and mixing chambers removed. Class A tools are issued only to employees; these items must be used under direct staff supervision at all times.

Class B Tools (Hazardous). These tools include items such as shovels, picks, and hammers that could be used to effect an escape but are less hazardous than Class A tools. Class B tools may be used by inmates under intermittent supervision.

Class C Tools (Nonhazardous). These tools are not considered hazardous and include small hand tools that cannot be used as weapons and are not considered contraband. (Some institutions combine Classes B and C into a single Class B category.)

Tool Storage

Tools should be stored on shadow boards, with each space on the board either covered with a tool or a receipt for a tool; only one tool should be stored per shadow. Shadow boards containing any Class A tools must be locked in a secure room or tool crib. Items not adaptable to shadow boards should be kept in locked drawers or cabinets in a secure area.

Bolt cutters should be stored in the control center or armory and issued only when needed. Because of AIDS, hypodermic needles must be carefully handled, and used needle disposal must be handled according to procedures established jointly with the appropriate health officials.

All tools should be marked with numbers or symbols etched on them, so that a missing tool can be identified easily. Any missing tools should be reported immediately to the proper superior officer and an effort made to locate the equipment before inmates leave the area. Broken or otherwise unserviceable tools should not be discarded

Proper numerical marking of keys and their color coding allow officers to immediately tell which key is for what area.

directly; they should be exchanged for a replacement item, and the old tool disposed of outside the institution.

Food Service Items

When not in use, Class A items, such as butcher knives, vegetable knives, meat and bone saws, skewers, cleavers, and ice picks, must be locked in a shadow-board storage cabinet, which should be in a locked room. These items are issued by the kitchen steward or officer, who records the name of the inmate to whom the knife or other tool is issued. Before the kitchen closes or a shift changes, the items should be checked.

Foods such as yeast, nutmeg, sugar, and mace are kept under lock and key, and used only under employee supervision. Extracts with an alcoholic base should not be used, but if their use is unavoidable, they too must be secured.

Hospital Items

Surgical instruments (such as scalpels) are considered Class A tools, and doctors and dentists must be aware of the dangers of these items falling into inmate hands. A regular inventory procedure should be in place for these items, as for any other Class A tool.

Bulk supplies of medications such as psychotropics (usually medication for mental health cases), morphine, codeine, barbiturates, and tranquilizers, if kept in the institution, must be locked in a safe or vault, with the combination given only to certain officials. If daily use quantities must be kept available for emergencies, they should be in a relatively secure container, with shift-to-shift accountability maintained. When these items are used, they can be replenished from the separate bulk supply area or vault, which must be jointly inventoried by medical and correctional staff members at least once a month.

Any hazardous or toxic fluids, or those that may be sniffed, also must be inventoried and secured. These include flammables, carbon tetrachloride, degreasing compounds, some duplicating fluids, and all aerosol cans.

Key control is a vital security operation. When a key is removed, a chit must be left in its place.

Lock and Key Control

Along with inmate accountability and tool control, absolute control of all keys is a must for any institution. Very elaborate systems are necessary to ensure that keys do not fall into inmate hands.

Key Records

Key records are maintained to cross-index all keys alphabetically, numerically, and against key ring numbers. Cross-indexing of this type provides a structured method of controlling and inventorying all key blanks and pattern keys in the institution. Records must be maintained that will show which keys are on each ring, which lock each key fits, and where each lock in the institution is in use. Keys opening multiple locks must be identifiable so that if one is missing, it will be immediately evident which locks must be changed.

Key rings, once assembled, should be marked with a tag that identifies the ring itself by a distinctive alphabetical and numerical code, as well as a tag that indicates the number of keys on the ring. All keys in use in the institution—both those in regular circulation and emergency keys—should have the split rings soldered or spot-welded closed to prevent tampering or removal. This measure helps ensure accurate key counts, and also eliminates the temptation for staff to remove a key from a ring to lend to another individual for a short time.

Once during each working day, preferably during the morning watch, all key rings should be reconciled as to count, to ensure that no keys have been lost or stolen. Employees who have keys on their person at that time should call their key count into the control center, and the control center officer should count all the keys on the key board to obtain a key total.

Emergency Keys

The emergency key system enables staff rapid access to every part of the institution to respond to a riot, fire, or any other crisis. The system must be clearly separate from all other keys on the central key board. Each set of emergency keys should take staff from the perimeter, or whatever starting point is designated for that set, through every necessary door in that part of the institution. Various systems are in use, using color codes, metal tags, etching on the shank of the key, and other variations, which enable staff to quickly determine which key opens a given lock. Whatever system is adopted, all staff must be trained in it, so that in a crisis, anyone issued any set of keys can use them quickly and easily.

Regular-issue keys should be rotated into and out of the emergency key rings to ensure that wear on the locks and keys is even. In addition, all emergency keys need to be tested periodically, not only by the locksmith but by other staff, to ensure that personnel unfamiliar with the peculiarities of the locks involved can operate them effectively. Also, supervisory personnel need to be trained to use the emergency keys. Ideally, a backup set of emergency key rings should be located either in the armory or in one of the towers for safekeeping.

Restricted Keys

In addition to the emergency key system, a number of areas should be accessed only by restricted keys. These include the laundry and clothing issue area, the business office, the personnel office, the commissary,

Security and Control

An officer tests the locking mechanism as a part of his regular security duties.

warehouses, and many of the administrator's offices, as well as the armory and the control center, themselves. These keys should be issued only on the authorization of the watch commander or some other senior staff member, and the issuance of the keys should be logged by the control center officer. No restricted or emergency keys should leave the institution, and local procedures and staff supervision should enforce that requirement.

Key Handling

The following general rules apply to key handling:

- Keys never should be thrown or left in a lock; staff should carry key rings on a secure belt keeper or chain to prevent loss.

- Entrance keys never should come inside the facility; to do so constitutes a serious security violation.

- Keys to the armory never should come in direct contact with inmates.

- Grand master keys never should be in open circulation inside the institution. The loss of just one of these keys could require a total overhaul of the key system, or at a minimum, rekeying of major portions of the facility.

- Only in rare instances should employees be issued keys for their personal key rings, and even then, a security key should not be taken home. The number of keys maintained on personal key rings should be reduced to an absolute minimum.

- Inmates ordinarily are not permitted to have keys other than those for personal lockers, living quarters, or

work assignments, when appropriate. They never should carry security keys or be permitted to closely see the security key profiles.

Security Inspections

It does not take long for inmates to become aware of security breaches and to find ways to take advantage of them. A functional security inspection procedure in an institution will prevent this from happening.

A typical security inspection system includes thorough searches of all physical security features at pre-identified zones by a specific staff member. General, nondefinitive inspections cannot substitute for specific checks, for which certain staff are responsible and accountable. Checks must be made for compromised bars, windows, locks, manhole covers, and other modified, inoperative, or tamper-security features. Bars should be tapped regularly, locks tested, and other security devices checked. Security inspections must be paralleled by a scheduled maintenance procedure that ensure that all locks, windows, doors, and other devices are fully operational.

Each inspection must be followed by a signed, documented report of the inspection, which is maintained on record for not less than thirty days. Supervisory personnel should have a list of the employees responsible for each inspection zone, and follow up immediately if an inspection form is not returned.

A two-way radio allows officers to communicate with other staff. However, such a device must not be used if there is a bomb threat because radio vibrations could trigger the bomb.

Communications

From a technological point of view, effective communication systems make it possible for officers to be in constant touch with each other. These systems include radios, tower intercoms, personal body alarms, and closed-circuit television. The way that each institution uses these technologies may differ in detail, but their use is fairly consistent in most institutions.

Good communications in the nontechnical sense also help managers to make critical day-to-day operational decisions. As discussed in Chapter 4, they also ensure staff and inmates know policies and procedures, and that staff learn about changing policies before the inmates do. Clear information, circulated widely to staff and inmates, reduces the chance of day-to-day problems and larger disturbances. Good post orders and other internal information systems allow for a well-informed, effective staff.

Handling High-security Inmates

Special precautions may be in order when unusually high-security cases are known to be in an institution. In many instances, the high-security inmate will be held in a special housing unit. Procedures there may include issuing an order for two or three staff, so that extra staff are available when the inmate is out of the cell.

In other instances, the inmate may be in the general population, and other precautions will be necessary. A special information file, with pictures, may be set up in an area inaccessible to inmates. This file allows employees to review the backgrounds of these individuals, as well as others who present special management concerns. Housing assignments should be restricted to the most secure units. Work assignments should be selected with great care; if possible, tower officers supervising the immediate work area should know the identity of all high-security risk cases in that area. In general, inmates in this category should receive extra supervision by all staff.

Special Supervision Units

Certain units in some institutions operate totally on a high-security basis. Segregation units for administrative and disciplinary cases are one example. But there are several other categories that should be mentioned.

Special management units or control units are used to confine inmates who have demonstrated that they are so dangerous, predatory, or violent that they cannot be held successfully or safely in the general population of any regular institution. These inmates are held in some systems in a separate segregated unit that resembles administrative segregated status, except that they are confined there for very long periods. In most cases, a due process hearing is required to place an inmate in this type of unit, and special classification and review procedures must be in place to determine when an inmate is ready for release.

Protective custody units are operated in a segregated unit setting. Even so, inmates in this category are to be provided approximately the same privileges and access to programs as nonprotective custody cases, to the degree that institutional security and the inmates' personal safety needs permit.

Witness security units are a special type of protective custody unit. While inmates in regular protective custody status may have provided information in a variety of ways, true witness-security programs are for inmates who actually have provided testimony in exchange for a formal agreement that the government will protect them during confinement. The level of programs and services in these units is ordinarily above those found in typical segregated or protective custody units.

Inmates sentenced to death may be held in a separate section of a regular administrative locked unit, or they can be in a separate segregated unit. Some systems even permit selected inmates under a death sentence to be in a nonlocked unit. In a segregated unit environment, however, these inmates should be handled as extremely high-risk cases, and staff constantly should be aware of the possibility of a serious incident when dealing with an inmate who presumably has nothing to lose in an escape attempt or hostage takeover of a unit.

Summary

Security and control are prime responsibilities of institutions and their staff. In addition to the perimeter security that is obvious to the casual observer, every activity in an institution has an impact on security and can be important in preventing escapes and disorder. If adequate procedures are not in place and carefully followed inside the institution, then public safety and that of the staff and the inmates can be threatened.

APPLICABLE ACA STANDARDS

Administration, Organization and Management: 3-4004, 3-4011 - 3-4017
Inmate Rights: 3-4269
Institutional Services: 3-4272
Safety and Emergency Procedures: 3-4164, 3-4212
Security and Control: 3-4167 - 3-4198

BIBLIOGRAPHY

American Correctional Association. 1983. *Design Guide for Secure Adult Facilities.* Lanham, Maryland: American Correctional Association.

Freeman, Robert. 1996. *Strategic Planning for Correctional Emergencies.* Lanham, Maryland: American Correctional Association.

Phillips, Richard L., James D. Henderson, and W. Hardy Rauch. 1997. *Guidelines for the Development of a Security Program,* Second Edition. Lanham, Maryland: American Correctional Association.

6
Firearms, Gas, and Use of Force

Using deadly force or armed intervention in a crisis is a serious step requiring clearly established policy, well-trained staff, and sound judgment. Even the use of unarmed force can present serious problems if not done properly. All correctional officers should be well versed in the policies and procedures of their particular agency in these areas, so that if and when the use of force becomes necessary, it will be done in an effective but a restrained manner.

Procedures and Authority for Use

Weapons and other security equipment (such as shields, batons, helmets, gloves, and body protectors) used in a correctional institution are chosen by administrators based on the physical plant and the number and type of inmates in the facility. Because of the inherent risk in their use, carefully developed policies and procedures specify who may be issued weapons, as well as how this equipment should be used. Agency and institution policy clearly should spell out all armory, weapon, and use-of-force practices.

The institution's armory should be in a totally secure location, ideally outside the facility's perimeter. It should have a double-door entry, and a pass-through or "Dutch door" arrangement for issuing equipment in an emergency. The armory should be climate-controlled, have sufficient storage space for all weapons and ammunition, and have a telephone and a battery-powered emergency lighting system.

The authority for using weapons and force ordinarily is found in state or federal law and in specific agency policy. Detailed procedures for storing, handling, and accounting for weapons in continuous use in towers and patrol posts should be spelled out in the post orders for these posts. Similarly, there should be clear procedures for inspecting weapons and counting ammunition when first assuming a post. With the tremendous variation in types of armed posts, it is impractical to describe these procedures in any detail. However, this chapter describes a number of the more common issues and practices encountered in typical prison settings.

Weapon Storage and Upkeep

In most correctional systems, weapons and gas equipment are stored in secure areas that are inaccessible to inmates but easily accessible to personnel in emergencies. Small amounts of tear gas, a few batons, and shields may be stored in the control center for emergencies, but for the most part, these items should be kept in the armory or in a secure location outside the perimeter, such as a tower.

In a few institutions, weapons are maintained on armed posts inside the perimeter; storage and handling procedures at those locations are quite different. Because of the relatively few locations that do this, these procedures will not be described in this *Guide*; local policies should be followed carefully at those institutions.

All ammunition and gas munitions should be stored in suitable metal cabinets within the armory or other designated secure-storage area. The area itself should be climate-controlled, with the temperature and humidity within ranges that will maximize shelf life for all chemical agents and prevent the rusting of weapons.

All security equipment in storage, including ammunition and expendable supplies such as grenades, must be identified, and inventories maintained for each category of equipment and supplies. These inventories must be reviewed at least monthly to assess the condition of the equipment and expiration dates of any expendable items such as gas grenades and cartridges. Ammunition, tear gas, and other items that can leak or lose effectiveness because of aging must be replaced, as needed; the outdated items may be used for training.

Records must be maintained, noting to whom each item of security equipment is issued, or in the case of weapons maintained in towers, on which post the weapon is located. These records are necessary to establish responsibility and accountability for the use of this equipment.

Except as otherwise provided by state law, personal weapons should not be used for official purposes, nor should employees use nonagency ammunition. In certain instances, where employees live in agency housing near the institution, personal staff weapons and ammunition may be stored in the armory, but they should be in a separate area of the armory, under lock and key. This will prevent inadvertent issue during a crisis.

In many locations, a separate armory officer is identified for the purpose of maintaining the weapons' program; in some, the armorer and locksmith functions are combined in one position. In any event, all weapons should be subject to a regular maintenance program that ensures that they are cleaned, fired regularly, and repaired, as necessary.

Loading and Unloading Areas

Safe firearms handling is a constant concern in a correctional institution. Since loading and unloading a weapon is an inherently risky activity, most institutions have a specific area designated for these functions. This area is commonly a large barrel or other container full of sand, into which the barrel of the weapon is pointed when it is being loaded and unloaded. These areas ordinarily are located near entrances where weapons are unloaded before being secured, and are intended for use by both institutional personnel and visiting law-enforcement officers.

Armed Supervision

To reduce the risk of firearms falling into inmate hands, correctional officers who are in contact with inmates must not carry any weapons. Employees who use firearms while transporting or supervising inmates must be trained in the handling and use of these weapons, and safe techniques for inmate supervision.

A well-arranged armory allows for efficient and fast deployment of needed weapons.

Courtesy U.S. Department of Justice

Inmates ordinarily are assigned to jobs in the prison, especially if they would require armed supervision if they went beyond the institutional perimeter. However, if such inmates must work outside, great care must be taken to place them away from any armed officers. In supervising work crews, armed staff should arrive before the inmates and remain until after they leave. Officers carrying firearms while transporting inmates outside the facility must be separated from them either by being located in a separate, secure compartment, or by riding in vehicles preceding or following the inmate vehicle.

Documentation of Use

Whenever firearms are discharged or chemical agents used, officers must document exactly what happened. The report describing the incident must list the staff and inmates involved, the actions that caused the weapon use, and the person who authorized the action if advance approval was obtained.

When to Use Deadly Force

Staff should abide by specific agency policy in using deadly force, but in general, firearms should be used only when other means fail, and then only if less

Firearms, Gas, and Use of Force

extreme measures will not serve the same purpose. In most jurisdictions, an officer may fire under the following circumstances:

- At an inmate or other person carrying a weapon or attempting to obtain a weapon in order to harm others

- At an inmate or other person whom the officer has seen kill or seriously injure any person (whether or not a weapon is used) and who refuses to halt when ordered

- At an escaping inmate who cannot be stopped by nonlethal measures

- To protect equipment or vital property

Mass weapon firing should be used only as a last resort during escapes or serious assaults. Staff should shout a clear warning before shooting, if time permits. Warning shots may be required by some agencies, and should be fired only if there is no reasonable likelihood of serious injury or death to innocent people. If circumstances require a staff member to shoot an inmate, the fire should be aimed to stop, rather than to kill.

Nondeadly ammunition can be used to control some violent situations. These include wooden or rubber bullets for shotguns, "beanbag" rounds for handguns, and other specialty cartridges. However, staff using them should be aware that even these rounds may be deadly at close range.

Firearms should be used inside the perimeter only as a last resort. Within the enclosed institution, there may be staff or uninvolved inmates who could be exposed to direct gunfire or dangerous ricochets. Therefore, officers must exercise extreme caution when firing at targets within the security area.

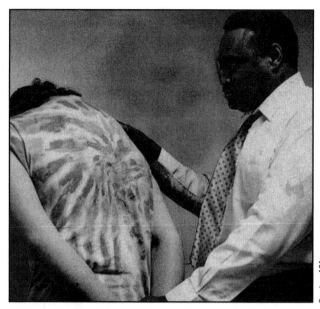
Correctional officer conducts a patdown of inmate in handcuffs.

Just as important is the concern for public safety when fire is directed at an escaping inmate outside the perimeter. Many institutions are located in urban areas or have staff housing or other occupied buildings nearby. Tower or patrol staff particularly must be careful that their fire does not needlessly endanger innocent third parties.

Use of Sharpshooters

The use of sharpshooters is a special case for deadly force situations. Only those staff who are properly trained and qualified on the specific weapon involved should be permitted to draw and use any sharpshooting weapons. Most institutions have a system set up for ensuring that only qualified staff draw and use these weapons.

These individuals not only must be thoroughly trained in the use of this equipment and experienced on the specific weapon they will use, but carefully briefed on the "rules of engagement" under which they may fire. In many cases, precise fire only is authorized upon the specific orders of a supervisor. In others, the shooter may be preauthorized to fire if specific acts take place, such as a threatening act taken against a hostage. These conditions should be spelled out in advance, to the extent possible, and then additional briefing information provided at the time of a specific incident.

Rifle training is one aspect of the education of a correctional officer.

Training in the proper level of the use of force is an important part of the education of the correctional officer. The SWAT or special emergency team requires additional training.

Firearms Training

All personnel authorized to use firearms must receive appropriate training that covers the use, safety, care, and limits on the use of firearms. They must demonstrate proficiency in the use of institutional firearms on at least an annual basis, and the records of these qualification tests should be retained by the institution. Furthermore, each facility should have a system for assigning only these properly qualified staff to armed posts. As with so many other areas of practical corrections, safe firearms handling and use is best taught in a hands-on environment. However, a number of basic principles can be reviewed here.

The first rule of handling weapons should be that all weapons should be treated as if they were loaded. Many lives have been lost because a loaded gun was believed to have been empty.

In addition to the presumption that all weapons are loaded, all firearms should be kept pointed in a safe direction, that is, away from other people. Weapons never should be pointed deliberately at anything other than the intended target. This rule is particularly true when loading and unloading a weapon, a time when, with some weapons, the action must be cycled. Weapons on post should be loaded; pistols should be carried in holsters and removed only for inspection or firing. Weapons in storage always should be unloaded.

Officers should keep their fingers away from the trigger on a weapon until they are ready to fire. If a finger is on the trigger, an officer's reflex may cause a firearm to discharge accidentally, especially a firearm not equipped with a mechanical-safety device.

Firing Positions

The following information is intended as a general guide for firing certain categories of firearms. Specific training in weapons use is provided by the institution, and these firing positions may be taught somewhat differently from state to state. Actual aiming depends on the type of sight on the weapon: open, peep, laser, or telescopic.

Rifles

There are four basic firing positions used for rifle fire.

Standing. Stand at a forty-five-degree angle to the right, with feet spread one-to-two feet apart with body erect and well balanced. Place the left elbow under the rifle, grasping it in front of the balance with the left hand, and resting the rifle in the palm of the left hand. Firmly hold the butt of the rifle high on the right shoulder, with the right elbow approximately level with the shoulder. Press the right elbow approximately level with the shoulder. Press the right cheek against the stock and as far forward as comfortably possible.

Firearms, Gas, and Use of Force

Kneeling. Kneel on the right knee and support the body with the bent left leg. The right knee should point along the line of fire approximately at the target. The point of the left elbow should be over the left knee. Lean forward.

Sitting. There are several variations to the sitting position, and every officer must find the one that is most comfortable and steady. Sitting at an angle to the intended target, and with legs spread comfortably at rest, lean forward and place each elbow on a knee, taking aim from that braced position.

Prone. Lying face down approximately forty-five degrees with the line of fire, spread the legs wide apart and turn the heels inward. Flatten the stomach close to the ground, and place the point of the left elbow to the front and well to the right under the rifle. Raise the right shoulder, and with the right hand on the rifle butt, place the rifle against the right shoulder and flatten it out again. Position the right cheek snugly against the stock. Grasp the small of the stock with the right hand and keep the thumb along the stock, not across it. Extend the elbow and, drawing the body back, position the chest and body as close to the ground as possible. The left elbow should be directly under the gun. Extend the right elbow to raise the muzzle and bring the elbow in to lower it. In this position, the body will absorb the recoil.

Shotguns

The intimidation value of a shotgun is often enough to deter even the most hardened inmates. In many cases, just the appearance of a shotgun on the scene will be enough to disperse a group of rioters. In other cases, a warning shot will have the same effect.

Although all of the positions described for rifle fire can be applied to a shotgun, ordinarily these weapons are fired from a standing position. In actual fire, however, the shotgun is used somewhat differently than a rifle. Rather than aiming for a specific point, this weapon is capable of hitting a wider area with multiple, smaller shot pellets. A particularly valuable firing strategy is to aim the weapon at the floor or ground, which will further spread the shot pattern and have the effect of striking more rioters. This also keeps the shot pattern low, reducing the chances of serious injuries.

One of the other keys to the proper use of the shotgun is selecting the correct ammunition. In the past, OO buckshot and other large shot sizes have been issued in institutions, and when fired, have caused serious injuries and death. If the intended purpose of weapons use is to disable, then using large shot sizes is inconsistent with that goal. As a result, many institutions have shifted their shotgun ammunition use toward small bird shot sizes that can disable inmates, but are less likely to kill them or harm bystanders hit by large ricocheting shot pellets.

Handguns and Pistols

Handguns are the third major category of weapons used by correctional staff. They are less accurate at a distance than rifles, less powerful than shotguns, but have the clear advantage of easy portability and concealability for escort work. Their use in tower or patrol operations is generally as a backup weapon.

The following general information is provided to give a picture of how pistols should be handled and used:

Grip. Grasp the butt of the gun so that the crotch of the thumb and forefinger are well up toward the hammer. Curl the second, third, and fourth fingers firmly (but not too tightly) around the butt of the gun. Lay the thumb up along the frame, parallel to the barrel. Lay the forefinger along and outside the trigger guard so it is ready to pull the trigger instantly.

Stance. The recommended position is comfortable and relaxed, and usually means you face the target at a forty-five-degree angle. Spread the feet twelve to twenty inches apart, the body should be erect with weight resting evenly on hips and feet; keep the back straight and the shoulders square, with the head held erect. Raise the right arm so that it is level with the shoulder, and slightly bend the elbow. Turn the head, still held erect, to the right.

Trigger Squeeze. Usually, considerable slack is taken up in pulling a trigger before the gun actually fires. While aiming, exert a steady backward pressure on the trigger to take up slack, and continue a steady pressure until the gun fires. Trigger snapping, or a quick hard jerk on the trigger, accounts for more poor shots than any other factor.

Gas

In a riot situation, other less forceful methods may not restore order. In those cases, the warden or designated senior officer, after reviewing the situation, may authorize staff to use tear gas or smoke compounds.

Gas may be used, within agency policy, under the following general conditions:

- To prevent serious injury or loss of life
- To prevent or suppress escalating riots or disturbances
- To prevent extensive, willful destruction of property

Tear gas creates tears and causes difficulty in breathing, stinging sensations, and other physical effects that disorient or disable individuals. Once secured or subdued, individuals exposed to tear gas should be permitted to wash and then be examined by a health care employee as soon as practical after exposure. They also should be monitored until no effects remain.

Periodic inspection of tear gas grenades and other chemical weapons is the duty of the security staff.

Gas may be deployed in several ways. The most common are the grenade and the 1.5" (37mm) gas gun. Both can be used to spread gas in a relatively controlled manner in specific areas. Different types of grenades and gas gun cartridges are available, from blast dispersion types for a near-range problem, to long-range projectiles that can be fired over, or even through, barricades at a distance. Many of these munitions have burning components and should be used with caution where a fire hazard may exist.

There are several additional methods of dispersing gas. These methods include aerosol dispensers, ranging in size from a handheld unit for use in a cell to fire extinguisher-size containers for larger areas. There are devices that use the exhaust of a small gasoline engine to heat and propel the gas into large areas. There also are fixed-placement gas systems that sometimes are used in dining areas and other locations where large numbers of inmates may gather.

Smoke compounds also are among the more common types of munitions, which can be used to confuse rioters, or to supplement and simulate gas. Smoke munitions should be as carefully controlled as gas, and their use should be authorized by the same level of official as that for gas use.

Staff should receive specific training in the use of gas guns, grenades, and other devices before being permitted to use them. Used in the wrong way or in the wrong circumstances, these munitions can be just as deadly as a standard firearm.

Officers using riot control gases should be taught, at a minimum, the following subjects and skills:

- Agency policy on the employment of riot and control gases
- Characteristics of specific gases
- Squad organization and the use of gas
- Tactical deployment of gas
- Individual protection and first aid procedures for all people who have contact with gas
- The use and upkeep of gas munitions and equipment

Special safety precautions must be observed when using gas and smoke munitions and projectile devices:

- All weapons and munitions must be handled with caution to prevent accidental firing and resulting harm to personnel or damage to property; they never should be aimed at a person.
- Safety pins must never be removed from grenades until officers are ready to throw them; employees must know the delay period for each specific type of grenade.
- Grenades must be thrown immediately after the safety grip is released.
- Safety rings never must be used for carrying grenades, or for hanging grenades from pegs or hooks.

Use of Restraints and Force

Force may be used to control inmates, but it must be in proportion to the threat posed by the inmate or inmates involved, and also follow any statutory procedures that apply. Justifiable circumstances often include self-defense, protection of others or property, or to prevent escapes. In no case is physical force justifiable as punishment. When force is used, the incident must be thoroughly documented, and a full report sent to supervisors for review. American Correctional Association standards limit the use of physical force to instances of justifiable self-defense, protection of others, protection of property, and prevention of escapes, as a last resort, and in any other situation approved by law.

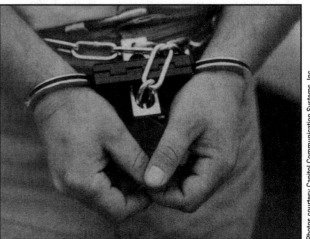

Inmates in black box restraint need additional help with eating and other daily functions.

Photos courtesy Capitol Communication Systems, Inc.

Firearms, Gas, and Use of Force

Restraint equipment is a protective and precautionary measure to prevent assaults, prevent escapes during inmate transfers, serve medical purposes at the direction of a medical-staff member, prevent inmate self-injury or suicide, or prevent damage to property. Restraints never should be applied longer than is absolutely necessary.

Types of restraining devices may include:

- Swivel nonlocking handcuffs
- Belly chains
- "Black boxes"
- Ankle shackles
- Restraining belts
- Plastic flex-tie handcuffs
- Thumb cuffs
- Strait jackets
- Restraining sheets
- Restraining straps

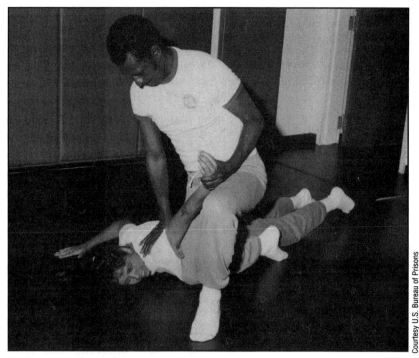

Training in self-defense enables correctional officers to carry themselves with confidence and project a no-nonsense image.

Restraint use involves the following general principles:

- Handcuffing inmates does not render them harmless. Inmates still can assault an officer or attempt to escape.
- Maximum-security, segregated, or detained inmates must be restrained before moving them out of their cells.
- For high-risk cases, handcuffs may be applied from behind; extra restraints like "belly chains" and "black boxes" may be applied when indicated by agency or institutional policy.
- Restraints should be checked periodically by officers transporting inmates.
- Inmates ordinarily should not be secured to any motionless object, including an automobile; they never should be secured to a moving vehicle.
- Officers must be alert in applying or removing restraints; that is when they are most vulnerable.

Unarmed Self-defense

Unarmed self-defense techniques for staff can be useful in the correctional setting; they involve using self-protection moves that require no special equipment. Officers may employ basic defense holds if threatened or assaulted by an inmate, but in no case may physical force be used as punishment. The following techniques are listed to show the variety of self-defense maneuvers that are available to trained staff:

- Come-alongs
- Breaks for choke holds
- Defensive moves against weapons, such as knives and clubs
- Defensive moves against swings to the head and body
- Defensive moves against the pinning of the arms

As in using firearms, constant practice and supervision in unarmed defense are necessary to maintain proficiency in the techniques. In addition to the many manuals and visual aids available, employees also need to watch qualified instructors demonstrate the holds, and then practice the movements under supervision.

Deadly Force

In *Tennessee v. Garner* (1985), the United States Supreme Court ruled that a police officer only could use deadly force to prevent the escape of a fleeing felon if the officer had probable cause to believe that the suspect posed a threat of serious bodily harm to the officer or to others. With respect to corrections, the question that arises is "Do the correctional officers responsible for perimeter security around the correctional institutions have to make that same decision?" A clear answer has yet to emerge from the courts. *Kinney v. Indiana Youth Center* (IYC) (1991) provides an example of a suit by an inmate subjected to deadly force during an escape. In June 1988, Kinney and another inmate attempted to escape from the IYC, a double-fenced, secure youthful offender institution with guard towers manned by armed officers. As Kinney and his companion approached the inner fence, the tower officer yelled at them, asking "What are you doing?" The two inmates did not respond and continued toward the fence and climbed over it. As the inmates began climbing the second fence, the officer, who had selected a .22 rifle instead of a shotgun, yelled at them "Halt, or I'll shoot!" As the two inmates reached the top of the second fence, ready to jump over, the officer fired two shots attempting only to wound them. They both fell to the ground and neither made any further move. Only Kinney was hit, and he suffered a severe injury to his mouth.

The court found that the officer's conduct in shooting Kinney while escaping did not amount to cruel and unusual punishment because he gave notice to Kinney that he would be shot if he ventured over the fence. The court indicated that any prisoner who is escaping may pose a serious enough threat to justify using deadly force.

California's recent addition of electrified fences to a maximum-security prison (Caliptra) (and its planned construction of twenty more at maximum- and medium-security institutions in the next few years) adds another dimension to the use of deadly force in escapes. The thirteen-foot-high fence is located between two twelve-foot-high fences topped with razor wire, and carries 4,000 volts and 650 milliamperes—only 70 milliamperes are required to kill someone. Signs warning inmates that this fence is dangerous "show a man hit by a bolt of electricity falling backward [and say] 'Danger, Peligro, Keep Out. Alto Voltage, No Entre.'" California estimates saving $2 million by reassigning ten of the prison's twelve tower correctional officers to other duties.

The question arises as to whether the courts will find the use of deadly force without human decision making constitutional or if the fact that prisons hold dangerous people would be sufficient to apply current case precedents to escape.

Emergency Response Teams

Almost all institutions provide basic emergency response training to all staff, including training in squad formations and tactics. However, many institutions have a special emergency response team, which is trained specifically to respond to institutional crises such as fights, riots, forced cell moves, or hostage situations.

These employees almost always are selected according to written criteria and receive additional training in squad tactics, use of special weapons, and other emergency reaction strategies. These staff may be on call throughout the day by radio, and even may carry paging equipment when off duty so that they can be recalled quickly to the institution during nonduty hours.

Other locations take the approach that since all correctional workers are trained in emergency response tactics, a special team is not needed. The advantage to this approach is that it is less expensive, and also that at any given time, a response team can be assembled. The disadvantage is that the specific group assembled for a given crisis may never have worked together before, and may not be as efficient.

There is no single best solution to this problem, and local administrators choose the most practical response team strategy for their institution based on available staff and other factors. For instance, in a camp setting, there is a low probability of ever needing a response team at all, so there would be little need to provide training and ongoing support to a special response team; regular staff training is sufficient. However, in a high-security institution where there are a relatively large number of forced cell moves and other confrontational incidents, a trained, well-disciplined team that works together regularly can be a tremendous asset.

ACA Firearms Standards

ACA standards regarding firearms include the following provisions:

- Weapons are subject to stringent safety regulations and inspections
- Except in emergency situations, officers carrying firearms are assigned only to watchtowers, gun walks, mobile patrols, or other positions inaccessible to inmates
- Officers supervising inmates outside the institution perimeter follow procedures that ensure the security of weapons
- Officers are instructed to use deadly force only after other actions have been tried, and were ineffective, unless the officer believes that a person's life or institutional security immediately is threatened
- Officers on duty use only firearms issued by the institution, and use them only when directed by the warden/superintendent or officer in charge

Firearms, Gas, and Use of Force

Forced Cell Moves

Unarmed techniques also may be used to remove inmates who refuse to come out of their cells and forcibly must be restrained and taken to a locked unit. All forced moves of this type should be directed by a supervisory staff member, and a full report filed on each such incident.

The staff assigned to a forced cell move should be equipped properly for their personal safety. Jumpsuits, helmets, defensive shields, and even bulletproof or penetration-resistant vests should be provided.

Many institutions now use a coordinated move strategy that greatly simplifies the process of subduing, restraining, and removing a rebellious inmate from a small cell. This involves each staff member being assigned a specific limb to subdue or function to perform (such as applying leg irons or handcuffs or pinning the inmate with a shield). In the confusion of a fight with an inmate, this strategy can prevent several people grabbing for one of the inmate's arms and no one restraining the other arm, or no one grabbing the inmate's legs, allowing the inmate to kick and injure staff unnecessarily. With each staff member on the team assigned a specific role, the move can proceed quickly and efficiently, with a minimum of injury to staff or the inmate.

If possible, the forced move itself should be videotaped, to use as evidence against the inmate if a criminal prosecution results. In many institutions that use the videotaping strategy, the mere presence of a camera deters the inmate from any violent action. The presence of a camera also is a reminder to staff to be totally professional in their actions.

Sometimes just the sight of a fully armed riot squad will quell a disturbance.

Summary

Correctional officers must know the correct procedures for using firearms, gas, and physical force, and clearly understand who may authorize it. Written reports are needed for discharge of a weapon, use of chemical agents, or use of force to control inmates remaining in restraints at the end of the shift.

This chapter should be regarded only as a general introduction to this topic. Individuals must develop the necessary firearms, gas, and self-defense skills through training and practice.

APPLICABLE ACA STANDARDS

Security and Control: 3-4166, 3-4191 - 3-4197, 3-4198

Training and Staff Development: 3-4086 - 3-4089

Use of Chemical Agents: 3-4089

Use of Firearms: 3-4088

Use of Force: 3-4087

Use of Restraints: 3-4194, 3-4183-1, 3-4362

7

Emergency Plans and Procedures

Day-to-day application of such sound correctional practices as inmate accountability, security inspections, and tool and key control contributes greatly to an institution's security. However, crowding, inmate idleness, understaffing, severe budget constraints, and even natural disasters can create situations that lead to disruptions of institutional routines. In those moments, the existence of a well-developed set of institutional emergency plans will pay tremendous dividends. The correctional officer must be aware of these plans and know what to do in case of an emergency. If the training is not provided by preservice or early-on inservice, the correctional officer must seek it out. Knowing what is expected during an emergency can save your life and the lives of those around you.

American Correctional Association standards require that institutions have written plans to be followed in situations that threaten institutional security. These plans—including but not limited to riots, mass food strikes, disturbances, and hostage taking—should be available to all institutional personnel, and reviewed and updated at least annually. Emergency plans must include a command structure to handle the emergency, notification of law enforcement agencies about the emergency, temporary measures pending the arrival of top officials, actual riot control, instructions for separating and temporarily housing ringleaders, and steps for resuming normal operations, or continuing normal operations and handling the incident at the same time.

The plans developed for each institution will be unique to that facility. The physical plant, staffing patterns, and even statutory requirements in which it operates determine the specific way a plan is developed. However, there are a number of general principles common to all emergency plans.

Emergency Plan Structure

Each institution should have a complete set of emergency plans that include strategies for dealing with at least the following situations:

- Riots
- Escapes
- Fires
- Bombs
- Hostage situations
- Civil disturbances
- Inmate work/food strikes
- Fog/reduced visibility
- Employee job actions
- Natural disasters including tornadoes, hurricanes, floods, snow, and ice storms
- Emergency staff recalls
- Hazardous material spills

Each problem situation should be the subject of a separate plan. Each plan should include a set of general guidelines for detecting the signs of impending problems and preventing the problems, and then provide an overall structure for developing a specific response to each individual crisis. The plan at least generally should identify the major issues that will have to be dealt with and describe possible response options, and vital telephone numbers and locations. Plans must be developed and refined specifically for each institution; a single plan for all facilities in an agency is not practical.

In addition to the specific content of each plan, a formal cover sheet should be included in each, with the

After an incident occurs, debriefing is necessary both to understand what has happened and to devise a plan so that it does not reoccur.

warden's signature, indicating approval of the plan. Regular high-level review of all plans is a necessity; an administrative review should be conducted not less than once a year as an integral part of the emergency plan system. It is necessary to update the plan as policies, staffing, and institutional construction change.

These plans ordinarily are maintained in looseleaf binders so that changes and updates can be made easily. With the increasing use of computers, the plans can be revised and reissued easily each year at the time of the annual review.

Often, there are some major problems in the way correctional administrators currently approach emergency plan testing.* The contents of the emergency plans would be covered in initial and refresher training, and staff should be required to review all plans at least annually so that they are familiar with their provisions. This often is done through a checkout system. The emergency plan review system also should require staff to sign off on a review documentation sheet after they review each plan.

This training and review process is important because there is no way of predicting who will be on duty in a critical post in a time of crisis. A senior officer may be acting in a supervisor's position, a department head may be acting as an associate warden—each of these individuals and staff at every other level need to know the overall plan for response.

Common Emergency Plan Information

Although each agency's emergency plan differs, most contain at least the following basic information:

- A definition of the emergency situation for each plan
- Key indicators of potential problems in that area
- Preventive steps to take, if possible; this may be the most important element in many plans, especially those for riots and escapes
- A notification system for reporting the problem
- Immediate operational steps to take to secure the institution, which could be in a checklist form. All departments should have checklists for each type of emergency.
- The chain of command during nonduty hours (most problems seem to crop up after normal duty hours)
- The telephone, beeper numbers, and identity of key officials to be notified
- The sequence of notification (with space for date, time, and caller's initials)
- People authorized to call in additional staff
- A command structure with clear lines of authority to handle the emergency initially, and expand as top officials arrive and assume command
- People authorized to notify outside authorities
- The location of a command center for emergency operational control
- The person authorized to notify the media and release information

  NOTE: In most instances, the correctional officer is not authorized to talk with the media, and talking may jeopardize a particularly sensitive situation.

- Current telephone numbers for all staff and key outside parties, such as the state police
- A statement containing the agency's hostage policy
- Memorandum of agreement between the institution and outside agencies, such as the local hospital emergency room and ambulance service. These should be reviewed and updated, at least annually.
- Secondary operational steps to take to resolve the situation

For situations such as riots, escapes, and other preventable incidents, each emergency plan should emphasize signs of tension and unusual circumstances in the institution, and other contributing factors that staff can be aware of, which often telegraph a major impending problem. In addition, the plans should emphasize preventive measures that can be taken when these signs are in evidence.

For any emergencies, joint training with other agencies on emergency-plan implementation can be a tremendous benefit. To effectively deal with a riot or fire, for instance, it is important to have employee

---

*See Freeman, R. *Strategic Planning for Correctional Emergencies.* Lanham, MD: American Correctional Association.

Emergency Plans and Procedures

emergency plan training in cooperation with local firefighters or state police. (Encourage the fire company responsible for your area to visit and tour your agency. During an emergency is not the time to learn their way around a prison).

This joint training should include drills during which the agencies involved participate in simulated responses to institutional emergencies. This is a valuable training strategy, and also develops closer cooperation and understanding among the various agencies involved in emergency responses to institutional crises.

The established command structure used to address the emergency should be practiced on a regular basis by the various shifts of operation. Setting up the command and exercising the lines of authority and the roles of those in this command help assure an appropriate and timely response to the emergency. Mock drills are very effective in exercising the command structure and providing a general understanding of emergency responses.

All emergency plans should include information on media access and notification because any major disturbance in a correctional institution attracts news media attention. In fact, such news media involvement often is the first thing demanded by inmates during a crisis. All relevant plans would include specific information about media contacts by staff, establishment of a briefing area, and other important details. An official spokesperson should be identified. (During times of emergency, all inmate telephones should be cut off). Media representatives should not be involved in any emergency activities.

Fire drills and fire-prevention training is necessary to insure the safety of officers and inmates.

Preparedness Checklists

In addition to regular training, some agencies have adopted a regular emergency preparedness checklist strategy. Checklists might include, but not necessarily be limited to, regular reviews of the following areas or items:

- Firearms and ammunition; weapons must be operable and ammunition fresh
- Gas munitions and equipment; gas supplies should be current, but old gas may be used for training purposes
- Emergency lighting equipment and facilities, including those available from outside agencies
- Fire fighting equipment and personnel; air-pacs should be available for immediate response to smoke-filled areas
- Shut-off valves for water, electricity, gas, heat, and ventilation
- Emergency evacuation routes for uninvolved staff
- Emergency entrances to all buildings
- Emergency key systems and their use
- A general alarm system
- Availability of emergency personnel, including current telephone lists and call-up systems
- Amplifiers, public address systems, and other communication equipment
- Location and secure storage of critical supplies and equipment, especially those that can be burned or used as weapons, such as gasoline, poisons, ladders, and torches
- Portable welding equipment, bolt cutters, and other specialized response equipment
- Current floor plans of all parts of the institution
- Alternative housing for inmates

Security Inspections

Some physical features of the institution have a bearing on emergency responses to fires, escapes, riots, and other crisis situations. A regular security inspection program, as described elsewhere in this guide, should ensure that the following items are operating as intended. It is particularly critical to ensure the full operating status of:

- Emergency doors
- Locking devices
- Sally ports in key areas

Correctional Officer Resource Guide

Riot squads should be used when other methods of quelling disturbances have failed.

Courtesy U.S. Department of Justice

- Emergency power systems
- Fire fighting equipment
- Communication systems and alarms
- Specific plans

Riots

Institutional disturbances may range from a minor outburst involving several inmates to a major riot involving the entire population, from a passive "sit-down" demonstration to large-scale, random destruction of life and property. Disturbances can start with inmates' spontaneous reactions to a stabbing, or they can be organized, calculated movements of mass resistance supported and assisted by outside groups or led by inmates using revolutionary tactics. They also may start as a result of a disturbance in another institution somewhere in the state's prison system or the country. Each type of disturbance requires different response tactics. Therefore, it is essential that the riot plan be sufficiently flexible to cover all possibilities, but contain specific tactical and administrative information that will help shape the proper response.

A well-written riot control plan provides administrators with sufficient response flexibility, and is clearly and concisely written so that it is easily understood by all. It ensures deployment of all personnel and equipment to the problem areas as quickly and efficiently as possible.

A well-developed plan will have basic content of the following elements:

- *Reporting.* The emergency plan should emphasize the need to report a disturbance immediately to a central location, usually the control center.

- *Security.* Secure the perimeter of your institution. Isolate and bring the problem under control before it escalates and involves a greater area or more inmates.

- *Notification and call-up procedures.* Upon being notified of a disturbance, the control center officer should contact the shift supervisor. The plan then should specify prompt notification of staff on perimeter posts, front and rear entrances, the powerhouse, all areas where there are likely to be groups of inmates, and then administrative staff—the warden, the associate warden, the chief correctional supervisor, and others. If the shift supervisor cannot be contacted, the control center officer ordinarily is authorized to initiate these emergency notification procedures independently.

- *Intelligence gathering.* The plan should address the need to quickly gather information about the nature and scope of the disturbance, number of staff hostages (if any), and other key facts. If the situation continues, then an ongoing intelligence-gathering and analysis process must be in place.

- *Selection and assignment of officers for emergency squads.* The plan clearly should identify the categories of staff to be mustered for response action, how they are to be organized, where they will be staged, methods of timekeeping, and other administrative details.

- *Developing options for action.* The riot plan should include general information on the tactical options available for retaking the institution, from securing a single, small area to the entire compound. While each crisis will differ, similar principles can be employed in many riot situations. The plan should contain information on squad use, deployment of gas, utility controls, and other crowd and riot suppression activities. It also should include an awareness of the importance of not overreacting to the crisis and creating even greater problems.

Emergency Plans and Procedures

- *Notification of outside parties.* Specific authority to notify local law enforcement authorities should be contained in the plan; local utility companies also may have to be notified to assist staff in maintaining or cutting off utility service in the institution. The power company should be aware of your possible needs as part of your emergency plan training.

- *Use of outside organizations.* The plan should describe staff deployment methods, and provide that only trained correctional officers are assigned inside an institution during a disturbance, unless the situation is so serious as to require the police or National Guard to assist in providing additional coverage in retaking the facility. Outside law enforcement personnel and institutional staff who are untrained in riot control may be used to secure the perimeter, to control gates, or to supervise areas where they are unlikely to encounter inmates.

- *Curtailment of normal programs.* The plan must provide for a measured, nonpunitive response to small-scale incidents, so as not to alienate the majority of inmates, who may not be active participants, as is often the case.

- *Selection and use of equipment, including firearms and gas.* The plan should provide for rapid issue of emergency equipment to staff, including items such as riot helmets, batons, communication equipment, shotguns, gas and gas equipment, shields, emergency keys, cutting torches, wrenches, wrecking bars, ropes, ladders, and portable lights. This often is done by maintaining ready boxes of enough personal equipment to outfit one squad, and preprepared weapon kits that have a firearm, ammunition, and other necessary gear ready for issue from the armory.

- *Weapon, key, and equipment accountability.* All equipment issued must be accounted for through a preprepared, positive identification system of some type. The confusion of a riot is no time to try to set up an accountability system.

- *Follow-up.* The riot plan must address not only the actual emergency and the retaking of the institution from a tactical point of view. It at least must consider the following pre- and postriot considerations:

  - Taking an official count of all inmates
  - Accounting for all staff
  - Ensuring due process for participants who may be prosecuted
  - Securing evidence for subsequent prosecutions
  - Evacuating unserviceable sections of the institution, as well as temporarily evacuating areas where gas has been used and decontamination is necessary
  - Maintaining or resuming physical plant operations
  - Revising dining schedules to serve meals in cells, or to serve smaller groups in the central dining area
  - Assigning additional personnel to living quarters and dining rooms until the atmosphere in the institution returns to normal
  - Conducting an extensive, thorough investigation beginning with interviewing staff, ringleaders, and other participants
  - Assisting staff or law enforcement personnel in preserving and/or photographing physical evidence or damaged areas, which later may be used as legal evidence
  - Arranging for physical examinations, treatment, and psychological care for staff, particularly former hostages
  - Arranging for physical examinations and medical care for injured inmates
  - Preparing a full report for the appropriate agency or

A critical incident stress debriefing team may include line staff, a clinical director, and a mental health worker.

Courtesy Bowden Institution

A regular procedure for inspection and testing of emergency equipment is part of the emergency preparedness program.

authority, summarizing the origins of the riot, the actual events, staff response, and the events in the aftermath

Escapes

No matter how secure the institution, inmates will try to escape. During an escape attempt, officers must act quickly to stop the attempt and recapture the inmate(s). That is why a functional escape plan is vitally important for every institution. While the methods used by inmates in escape attempts vary, escape plans should contain the fundamental search and surveillance techniques that cover most situations.

A functional plan includes the following elements:

- *Defining an escape.* A clear definition is needed of what specifically constitutes an escape and the use of deadly force to stop escapees, in the particular jurisdiction involved, as opposed to an inmate being "off-limits," "out of bounds," or some other lesser infraction.

- *Reporting an escape.* Staff in the institution must know whom they should notify in the event they believe an inmate is missing. In most cases, this is the control center.

- *Alerting the perimeter and gateposts.* As soon as an inmate is believed to be missing, the perimeter and gatepost staff and any outlying patrol staff should be notified.

- *Securing the area.* The entire institution should be secured; inmates must return to their quarters/cells.

- *Providing a count.* The inmates in the institution should be counted immediately, to determine the identity of the missing inmates; in most cases, a picture card (identification) count will be needed to verify the identity of those missing.

- *Notifying top staff.* The plan should specify the order in which top staff should be notified, usually starting with the warden.

- *Stating hostage information.* The plan clearly should state that no inmate with a hostage is to be released, and that no hostage has any authority.

- *Identifying key posts to continue to staff.* Some areas can be secured and their staff assigned to the escape hunt; others, such as the powerhouse and food service, must continue to operate; these positions should be identified in advance so no confusion results from removing staff from a critical post.

- *Establishing a command center.* This area includes not only internal communications and command functions, but also communication with local and state law enforcement personnel assisting in the escape hunt.

- *Recalling staff.* Using a current list of all employees and preestablished call-up procedures, off-duty employees should be told to report.

- *Notifying local law enforcement.* This section of the plan should specify who is authorized to notify local law enforcement personnel of the escape, and by what means; it also may involve distribution of escape flyers.

- *Using internal searches to apprehend hideouts.* The plan should specify internal search procedures to apprehend inmates who may be hiding inside the facility, awaiting darkness, fog, or some other time when it may be more favorable to try to escape the secure compound.

- *Planning external searches.* Plans/procedures need to be in place that include the use of force regarding "fresh pursuit," and coordination with allied agencies.

- *Establishing outside escape posts.* The plan should establish fixed and roving escape posts, identify the equipment that should go on each post, and describe the other procedures necessary to staff these posts, including issuance of equipment.

- *Providing staff support on escape posts.* The plan should provide for the regular relief, feeding, and checking of staff on remote posts.

- *Offering strategies for apprehending and restraining escapees.* The plan should provide staff with clear guidance on actions they should and should not take when apprehending an escapee. At least two officers should be present to search any escapees after they are captured; if only one officer captures an inmate, the inmate should stay "spreadeagled" on the ground until backup assistance arrives.

- *Notifying of capture.* When inmates have been captured, the procedures must specify who will notify all law enforcement agencies, communities, and the media.
- *Interviewing escapees.* The plan must ensure that any interviews with escapees are done in a way that does not hamper the criminal prosecution of an escapee by compromising any constitutional rights.

Fires

Fires in institutions can threaten hundreds of lives, endanger the facility and surrounding communities, and result in tremendous financial losses. Moreover, because of the confined quarters and crowded conditions of many institutions, fires can present an even greater danger than in an ordinary setting. American Correctional Association standards provide a clear view of an effective fire prevention program, which includes, but is not limited to, the following elements:

- Adequate fire protection service from a combination of inside and outside sources
- Regular fire inspections and quarterly testing of equipment
- Annual inspection by local or state fire officials or other qualified people
- Fire protection equipment located appropriately throughout the institution, as required by the National Fire Protection Association's Life Safety Code
- An up-to-date copy of the Life Safety Code on the site
- A full-time crew of inmate firefighters who meet custody standards and training levels necessary to cope with any type of fire in and around the institution
- Availability of fire fighting equipment that includes, at a minimum, a modern fire truck complete with pressure pumps, tanks, and modern, portable extinguishers
- An automatic fire alarm and smoke detection system certified by an independent, qualified inspector; if the institution relies on a local fire department, the system may be connected directly
- In cell/room/dorm equipment to notify the hearing/vision impaired of a fire emergency
- Quarterly tests of all systems and annual certification by a state fire official
- A written evacuation plan for fires and other emergencies, certified by an outside inspector trained in the application of national fire safety codes

A well-developed fire plan incorporates the basic concepts of the American Correctional Association standards and has the following elements:

- *Prevention.* The first line of defense in any fire plan is an aggressive fire prevention and safety program.
- *Staff training.* Initial and refresher training should cover basic fire prevention and suppression topics, as well as the use of basic fire fighting equipment; this should include institutional familiarization tours by local fire fighting personnel and joint training exercises.
- *Inmate information activities.* Inmates should be advised in orientation (multilingual, if necessary), unit meetings, and through other programs (inmate handbooks), of the hazards of carelessly handling cigarettes, flammable materials, and welding equipment.
- *Control of flammable materials.* The proper control of hazardous substances is very important to preventing accidental and purposely set fires.
- *Notification.* The same sequence of notification as used for the riot plan may be employed in the fire plan; procedures for notifying local fire authorities should be specified.
- *Inmate fire crews.* The use of trained inmate firefighters under officers' supervision can be an important factor in fighting an institutional fire; the procedures for their use should be spelled out clearly in the plan and these inmates should be housed together for quick response to a fire alarm.

Here, an emergency response team is at full alertness.

The Maryland TAC team practices their maneuvers.

- *Evacuation plans and routes.* Evacuation charts with clearly identified escape routes should be prominently posted; officers must be familiar with release and backup systems for inmates.

- *Escort procedures for outside firefighters.* The plan should specify gate processing procedures for community fire fighting crews and equipment, including search and escort procedures whenever trucks and other equipment are brought inside the institution.

- *Fire drills.* Quarterly drills should include evacuation of all inmates, except when there is clear and convincing evidence that institutional security would be jeopardized; in those instances, staff should walk through their roles in quarterly drills.

- *Postfire care of inmates.* The plan should provide direction for moving and housing inmates, and for providing injured staff or inmates medical care and transportation to hospitals.

- *Postfire investigation.* In the case of major fires, the institutional staff should preserve the fire scene to the degree possible, to enable trained investigators to properly determine the fire's origins.

Bombs

Although some institutions, like a metropolitan jail, may have bomb threats relating to their perimeter, bombs inside the institution are more commonly a concern. However, sophisticated bombs smuggled in by a visitor or other third party are not the primary problem inside a prison; inmates easily can fabricate bombs from match heads and other simple materials, and bombs of that type are far more common. For that reason, staff need to be prepared to deal with these dangerous explosive devices.

The plan should emphasize proper reaction to bomb threats and actual bomb handling, and include the following elements:

- *Telephone threats.* The plan should instruct switchboard and control center staff in particular, but all staff in general, on the procedures to follow and information to try to obtain if a bomb threat should be telephoned into the institution.

- *Notification.* If a suspected bomb is discovered, the staff member should immediately secure the area and notify a supervisor.

- *Movement of bombs.* Suspected bombs never should be moved.

- *Evacuation.* The plan needs to emphasize "evacuating people not bombs." This point cannot be driven home too strongly, and it should be included in bold type and underlined in each copy of the bomb plan.

- *Use of radios.* Bombs that are wired to explode may pick up enough electrical energy from nearby radio transmissions to be detonated; most bomb plans call for stopping all radio traffic until the device is deactivated or removed from the institution.

- *Expert assistance.* Few institutions have staff with the expertise to safely examine and deactivate even the simplest explosive device; local law enforcement or

Emergency Plans and Procedures

military expertise should be arranged in advance, and the notification procedures should be contained in the bomb plan.

- *Booby traps.* Inmates have set booby-trap bombs in various locations, severely injuring staff; employees conducting searches must be very careful not to disturb any potential bomb or trigger a booby-trap device and to call for help immediately.

Hostages

Inmates occasionally take hostages with the intent of trying to effect an escape or to gain some concession from the administration. Hostages often are taken in the course of a riot.

Although not clearly defined, the role of the line correctional officer during a hostage situation can take many forms. The correctional officer may be a member of the Quick Response Team, or Special Emergency Response Team. Your role would be clearly defined.

The problem with a hostage incident or many emergency situations in an institution is that while the emergency/hostage situation exists, the rest of the institution still must operate even if it is in a "lock-down" posture with all inmates returned to their cells and no inmate movement within the institution. All custody staff not directly involved with the hostage/emergency situation will supervise the inmates not involved in the emergency. There is not total agreement on the issue of hostage negotiations versus retaking the hostages by force. Conventional wisdom generally holds that if the hostages quickly can be recovered by a tactical response, then that course of action should be taken. However, once some time has passed and the hostage takers have had a chance to become organized, the history of a great many prison hostage situations seem to point toward the wisdom of patient, fair negotiations to free hostages.

A typical hostage plan includes sections on the following:

- *Understanding hostage policy.* Hostage plans clearly should indicate that no one held hostage has any authority, and that no inmate will be released while holding anyone under duress. To do otherwise would encourage inmates to view every staff member as a potential avenue for escape, and no one would be safe. If all inmates understand that taking a hostage will not result in their release, the risk of this kind of incident is greatly reduced.

- *Issuing post orders.* In addition to being in the hostage plan itself, most institutions include a hostage statement in all emergency plans and in the post orders of all perimeter and gatepost positions, as well as at the control center. This is particularly necessary for the plans that relate to disturbances and escapes, although any emergency, conceivably, could be used as a diversion for a hostage-type escape; thus, all plans should contain this information.

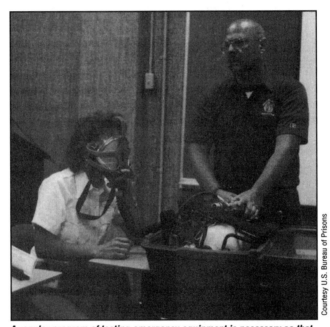

A regular program of testing emergency equipment is necessary so that officers can be prepared for any emergency.

- *Securing the area.* This section of the plan should ensure that staff take the proper precautions to secure the area in which the hostages are being held, to prevent additional inmates from joining or otherwise reinforcing the hostage takers by bringing in weapons or supplies.

- *Identifying the hostages.* As quickly as possible, the staff in charge of the incident need to know who the hostages are, if they have any special health problems, and other vital details. (It is critically important that the control center know who both custody and treatment staff is inside the secure perimeter of the institution at any time.)

- *Identifying the hostage takers.* The identity of the hostage takers often is critical to successful management of a hostage incident in a prison. Special details about their cases, background, or behavioral characteristics can be used in negotiations and in briefing the response teams that may be called on to free the hostages by force.

- *Notifying of nonprison officials, hostage families, media, and other agencies.* The plan should identify the people responsible for notifying noninstitutional parties, starting with the appropriate law enforcement agencies and members of the hostages' family.

Use of correctional officers in towers adds to the security of an institution but it does not replace the need for vigilant security within the the walls of the institution itself.

- *Establishing negotiations.* Once it is apparent that the hostages cannot be safely retrieved at the onset of an incident, then the plan should provide for the option of negotiating for their release. The area of hostage negotiations is quite complex, but basically this plan should include the assignment of trained hostage negotiators who are familiar with the institution or correctional operations, but who are not authority figures. The media and third parties should not be part of the negotiations.

- *Profiling the hostage takers.* The facility should attempt to construct a psychological profile of the hostage takers for use by the negotiators.

- *Making concessions.* In general, no substantial concessions ever are made in hostage negotiations. Minor exchanges of photographs or notes by hostages, for some equally minor favor, can be the basis for larger exchanges later, like the release of some hostages for turning on the water again. However, under no circumstances can a major concession like release of the hostage takers ever be part of the negotiations.

- *Establishing prosecution policy.* The issue of prosecution often comes up in the negotiations. Agency policy usually states that there will be full prosecution for all crimes committed during the course of a hostage incident, and prosecutors for that jurisdiction usually take that position also.

- *Caring for hostages after release.* The plan should provide for the immediate, positive identification of all released hostages, their medical examination, and any necessary follow-up psychological or psychiatric care.

- *Handling hostage family issues.* Whenever possible, the families of hostages should receive special information briefings in a private area where they can remain free from harassment by the media and other third parties throughout the crisis. A ranking official should be available periodically to brief them, and other staff, such as chaplains or psychologists, can assist them as they wait for the release of their loved ones.

Civil Disturbances

In rare occasions, institutional operations are disrupted by civil disturbances in the vicinity of the facility. This may be deliberate, in the case of a radical group trying to disrupt institutional operations, or it may be a side effect of another local problem unrelated to the prison.

The institution's plan for these occasions should include the following points:

- *Maintaining staff coverage.* If the disturbance disrupts staff access to the institution, then the plan should outline alternate coverage for key security posts and vital services such as utilities and food service.

- *Establishing outside law enforcement liaison.* The plan should include information on notification, liaison personnel, joint command centers, and jurisdictional issues.

Emergency Plans and Procedures

- *Preventing intrusion.* Clear information should be provided on blockading or barricading the institutional property; methods for preventing unauthorized access to the institutional property; deterring, repelling, or apprehending intruders; and other issues.

- *Establishing limits of staff authority.* In the event that a civil disturbance results in unauthorized entry of civilians on the institutional property or overt acts against institutional property, the plan clearly should state whether institutional employees have the power of arrest or detention.

- *Monitoring inmate reaction.* Staff should be alert to spontaneous, disruptive inmate reactions to an outside disturbance, as well as the possibility of a coordinated effort between outside agitators and inmates.

Inmate Work/Food Strike

Inmates sometimes stage food or work strikes as a form of protest against institutional conditions, or in reaction to outside agitation or events. Each institution should have a plan that ensures that essential services are maintained in the face of these disruptive events.

Typical plans for food and work strikes include these factors:

Prevention. The signs of these disruptive acts are often similar to those of an impending riot.

Identification of leaders and agitators. Identify inmates who may be trying to agitate a strike (by circulating among groups, getting signatures on petitions, and other actions). Once a strike is underway, staff should be alert to the inmates who actively advocate its continuance. Removing the leaders from the general population is a key step in strike management.

Determination of actual grievances. There should be options in the plan for gaining credible information from inmates about the reason for the strike. This may be through interviews, surveys, or unit meetings, but they should focus on the broadest possible range of sources, not just the inmate leaders.

Curtailment of normal programs. The plan must provide for a measured, nonpunitive response, so as not to alienate the majority of inmates, who may not be active supporters, but who feel pressured to go along with a few verbal, aggressive agitators.

Alternate food service operations. In the event a work stoppage involves food service workers, staff must arrange alternate coverage in the food preparation area, and have plans ready for serving meals to inmates in smaller groups, on extended schedules, or via sack meals in their cells. In some prisons, the contingency plan could provide for the use of minimum-security camp inmates in meal preparation, but care should be taken that they do not come in contact with the higher-security strikers.

Fog/Reduced Visibility

Each institution should have a reduced visibility plan that ensures inmates do not have an opportunity to use fog or other weather conditions to cover an escape. This plan should state the following:

- *Supervisory responsibility.* Identify the supervisor responsible for making the decision to implement the plan.

- *Criteria for decision making.* Give some general criteria for visibility that will be used to make that decision.

- *Special posts.* Identify any additional posts that should be staffed until visibility improves.

- *Special precautions indicated.* Describe any internal movement restrictions that will be in place, such as escorted movement, special counts, or curtailment of work assignments.

Employee Job Action

Although most agencies do not face the likelihood of an employee job action, because of laws prohibiting public employee strikes, there should be some contingency

Proper storage of handcuffs and other restraints enables easy access when they are needed.

Courtesy U.S. Department of Justice

plan for this type of crisis. While the most common such action might be a "blue flu" or mass sick call, a full work stoppage by staff is not totally beyond the realm of possibility.

A contingency plan for this kind of situation involves developing options in these areas:

- *Assessment of the nature of the action.* Administrative staff should attempt at the earliest possible moment to learn the type of job action planned, how extensive it might be, and how long it might last. This information will assist in plans to bring in workers from other government agencies, including the state police or National Guard. It also will form the basis for beginning to develop a response strategy to the leaders of the job action.

- *Notification of other agencies.* Once a job action of this type is clearly about to occur, or is underway, the plan should identify the responsible authority who will notify other government agencies, as well as the media. As the employees participating in the action already may have notified the media, a public information structure also should be put in place.

- *Assignment of alternate post coverage.* To ensure that vital institution functions are continued, the plan should identify key posts to keep active, and a priority listing of those areas that can be shut down for the duration of the job action. In addition, supervisory and management (custody and treatment) staff, and any other employees who are not members of the bargaining unit who report for work, should be ready for assignment to these critical posts. This part of the plan also should provide for timekeeping and relief of staff.

- *Curtailment of inmate services.* To the degree possible, inmate activities should not be curtailed, unless they involve security risks. In some instances, a limited "lockdown" may be necessary in the housing units to keep other areas such as food service in operation.

- *Communications with inmates.* This is very important. To prevent any undue inmate reaction to the job action, managerial staff should keep inmates advised of the steps being taken to continue near-normal operations, and to restore the institution to normal functioning as soon as possible. Staff on duty should be alert to the possibility of inmate agitators taking advantage of this situation to stir up the inmate population, as well.

- *Process for returning to normal operation.* As staff return to work, there should be a strategy for reactivating posts and programs that have been curtailed by the job action. This ordinarily would include expanding food service operations to normal, and carefully restoring work, recreation, education, and other programs as more employees are available for the proper level of supervision.

Disasters

While unlikely, the threat of disasters such as tornadoes, floods, a nearby train wreck with a hazardous material release, and other events must be anticipated in the institution's contingency planning process. These plans differ greatly according to the facility's location; it is unlikely that an institution in Oregon will experience a tornado, or that a facility in an arid part of the country would experience a flood. However, the problems presented by most disasters are similar in certain respects, and a general plan can help staff to think about how they would deal with the following issues. It is important for the line correctional officers to keep their immediate supervisors up-to-date on what is happening in the officers' area of responsibility (their assigned post). Keep all lines of communication open. Know who your first responder is in case you need immediate help. Insure that all information for the inmate population is passed on to them as you receive it.

- *Notification of impending disaster.* Most institutions can monitor local emergency radio or weather networks that would signal a coming severe storm or a nearby major accident that might affect institutional operations. In other areas, contacts with local law enforcement and civil defense/emergency management personnel can ensure that the institution will be warned as soon as possible of an impending problem. These warnings usually are received in the institution's control center.

- *Agency notification.* In most cases, only one institution in an agency would be affected by a severe storm, flood, or other disaster. The parent agency should be notified at once, so that assistance from other institutions and state agencies can be coordinated.

- *Staff notification.* As soon as the institution is notified, supervisory staff on duty and other officials should be advised, especially the institutional maintenance supervisor. It also may be advisable to notify staff on posts, and even to begin an advance staff recall, so that enough employees are available to supervise an evacuation or other unusual response to the crisis.

- *Inmate communications.* This area is vitally important. Once the impending crisis is thought to have an effect on the institution, the inmate population should be advised and told of the response, if any, that will be required of them. In most cases, no dramatic inmate movement will be involved, but there may be a curtailment of activities; inmates should be told why, how long it may last, and what they can expect to receive in the way of activities and privileges in the meantime. As in many other crisis situations, staff carefully should observe the population for signs of agitators and others who would take advantage of this situation.

- *Evacuation procedures.* The emergency plan should contain a set of options for evacuation of selected portions of the institution, as well as the entire facility, if necessary. This part of the plan entails supervision, restraints, transportation, outside assistance, and liaison with other institutions if a mass transfer is needed. Remember, if the disaster affects the local civilian population, most state police are mandated to respond to the local community first.
- *Supply issues.* If an extended emergency prevented delivery of perishable food items and other critical supply items, the plan should cover contingencies for delivery.
- *Staff housing and meals.* In the event staff are stranded in the institution, or enough staff cannot report for duty and employees must be held over, then accommodations must be available for them, including the need for personal hygiene items by the staff.
- *Utilities.* Continuation of key utilities will be a priority, if only to ensure that security, fire safety, and sanitation systems are available. Key staff should be a part of the plan.
- *Assistance from other agencies.* In addition to notification of the impact a crisis may be having on the institution, it may be necessary to call on other agencies, such as the National Guard, for support. The contact points and telephone numbers for these agencies should be in the plan.

Emergency Recall Plan

The staff recall plan can be a separate plan, or a subsection of other emergency plans. This is basically a local system for quickly notifying off-duty staff that they are needed at the institution for some emergency. Any recall plan is only as good as the employees want to make it. Correctional officers need to make a family member aware of the recall system, and the importance of notifying you immediately. If you are not available, alert a family member to the need to make the call to the employee you are responsible for notifying in case of an emergency recall.

The "pyramid" style of telephone-call notification speeds up staff call-ups in emergencies. This is a structured call-up system that specifies certain employees who are called first, and they, in turn, call several other specified employees, who themselves call several others. This method considerably speeds up telephone notifications in a crisis, and does not unduly burden any one staff member with a large number of calls.

In recent years, new technologies have become available that can be used to speed this process. One in particular allows for a computer equipped with a specific accessory board to be connected to a telephone line, and to automatically make a sequence of calls, telling those who answer the telephone that the institution is calling in all employees.

Summary

Effective emergency procedures are fundamental to all institutions. They cover the general steps to be taken before, during, and following institutional crises. The possibility of emergencies occurring means that officers continually must review the emergency response plans and practice the necessary emergency skills.

APPLICABLE ACA STANDARDS

Physical Plant: 3-4206, 3-4209, 3-4120, 3-4121, 3-4127

Safety and Emergency Procedures: 3-4121, 3-4199 - 3-4210

Security and Control: 3-4204, 3-4205, 3-4207, 3-4211 - 3-4213

BIBLIOGRAPHY

American Correctional Association. 1990. *Causes, Preventive Measures, and Methods of Controlling Riots and Disturbances in Correctional Institutions.* Lanham, Maryland: American Correctional Association.

Freeman, Robert. 1996. *Strategic Planning for Correctional Emergencies.* Lanham, Maryland: American Correctional Association.

Phillips, Richard L., James D. Henderson, and W. Hardy Rauch. 1997. *Guidelines for the Development of a Security Program,* Second Edition. Lanham, Maryland: American Correctional Association.

8
Food Service

Food service operations have the challenging mission of providing inmates with three meals a day, 365 days a year, without fail. In addition, the meals must be nutritious, tasty, attractive, and produced under sanitary conditions, at reasonable costs.

Food service operations have an enormous effect on inmate morale and health. Many work and food strikes, and even riots, started with inmate complaints about food. To the degree that institutional staff can make sure that the meals served are nutritious, appealing in appearance, and sufficiently varied, they will be ensuring that this major management variable will not create unnecessary problems.

In some locations, a contract with a private food service company is used to provide food services. Even when private parties are involved, however, the basic principles described in this chapter still apply. Some of the information contained in this chapter is not strictly related to correctional supervision. Additional detail is included because food service is such an important part of institution life, and because correctional staff often are assigned to work in the kitchen to supervise the general area.

Food Service Organization

Most correctional institutions in the United States have extensive food service facilities and equipment. The most common method used to provide meals to inmates is a modified cafeteria system. However, others plate up the meals and serve them on hot trays or through hot cart systems. Architectural designs and the arrangement of equipment vary from facility to facility, but a food line, with individuals selecting quantities of most items, is the most practical way of serving large numbers of inmates.

American Correctional Association standards provide a general picture of how a well-organized food service department should operate. In almost all institutions, a full-time staff member who is experienced in food service management supervises food service operations. This individual is given the resources, authority, and responsibility to manage the department effectively, both in terms of labor and financial resources. The administrator of the food service department ordinarily supervises all the food service staff and others such as dieticians, bakers, and butchers. Depending on the system, a number of correctional officers also may be assigned directly to the department. More commonly, however, correctional staff are posted in the preparation and dining areas, but still work for the correctional department.

Menu Preparation

Ordinarily, menus are prepared at least one week in advance. The administrator should plan all menus, including special diets, in connection with an independent review by a registered dietician. That review will ensure compliance with applicable nutritional standards, which must be documented. Many institutions actually prepare longer menu cycles. The federal prison system, for instance, uses a thirty-five-day cycle to reduce the monotony of short-cycle menus. State systems often use the twenty-five-day cycle. Menus should reflect the inmate population's cultural and ethnic preferences, as well as provide for their religious and medical needs within the limits of legal requirements.

Food Supplies and Storage

Food should be the best quality possible within the institution's budget, and of sufficient quantity to guarantee a wholesome diet. Available sources of food supplies

Food preparation provides both a job and an opportunity to learn a skill that can be used on the outside.

Food Preparation

Food usually is prepared according to a standard recipe system that is available to all food service staff and inmate workers. This standard system ensures that the quantity and quality of meals are uniform from meal to meal, and that staff variables do not enter into the preparation. For this purpose, many institutions use the standard U.S. Navy system or the Bureau of Prisons' *Food Service Manual* as their guide for food preparation.

Sanitation measures in the kitchen are absolutely critical. Each institution should have a hazardous analysis critical control point system in place to ensure that proper food handling procedures are followed from receiving, storing, preparing, holding, to serving of foods. Each institution must have a daily cleaning and inspection system that ensures that the food preparation, storage, serving, and dining areas are totally clean. This is far more than a cosmetic issue. The health of every inmate and staff member in the institution hinges on the cleanliness of the food service area.

The personal habits and cleanliness of all food service staff and inmate workers are a constant concern. Adequate facilities for washing hands should be provided in the kitchen area. Clean uniforms and aprons always should be available, and food handlers should be required to wear head coverings while cooking or serving food; serving gloves should be worn when serving and during hand preparation of food.

depend largely on the nature and location of the institution. Common sources are local wholesale food distribution outlets and contracts obtained through bidding to supply the institution for designated, quarterly periods.

In rural institutions, an institutional farm may provide such items as fresh vegetables, meat, eggs, milk, butter, and cheese. Other items, such as cakes, pies, and bread, can be prepared in an inmate bakery. All foodstuffs should meet, or exceed, government inspection levels.

The delivery and storage should ensure that food supplies are fresh and delivered in a suitable condition. All incoming food not immediately used or processed in some way should be properly stored to prevent spoilage or waste.

In most locations, a cold storage facility is available for such perishables as meat, milk, eggs, and fresh vegetables and fruits. Each refrigerated container or locker should have a thermometer on the door or exterior wall, so that staff can check the temperatures easily. Dried foods such as fruit, potatoes, and moist-dry foods may be stored in temperature-controlled storage rooms.

Less perishable items such as sugar, spices, crackers, and canned foods are handled best by a general storage facility. Shelf goods should be stored at temperatures of 45 to 80 degrees Fahrenheit; refrigerated foods should be maintained at 35 to 40 degrees Fahrenheit; and frozen foods should be kept at zero degrees Fahrenheit or below.

Attractive, tasty meals help prevent one of the major causes of riots.

Special Diets

Special medical diets are made available to inmates, but only on medical authorization. Diet orders should be specific and complete, furnished in writing to the food service administrator, and rewritten according to the requirements of the institution. Special diets should be kept as simple as possible, and should conform as closely as possible to the foods served other inmates.

A separate area in the kitchen under staff control may be used to store all diet trays, or they may be kept in a single hot cart behind the line for issue under staff direction. Many institutions use a diet card or pass system to ensure that only authorized inmates receive these meals.

Inmates also may have specific religious beliefs that require them to eat or not eat certain foods. Religious diets ordinarily are approved only by a chaplain. They should be specific and complete, and furnished in writing to the food service manager. In many systems they, too, are reviewed periodically. An example would be Islamic and Orthodox Jewish inmates who are forbidden by their religion from having contact with pork or pork products. In the event a staff member observes an inmate approved for a special diet of any type eating unapproved foods, that fact should be reported to a supervisor so that the special diet status of that inmate can be reviewed.

Meal Service

Gathering large numbers of inmates together presents a security risk under any circumstances. That fact makes the dining room a potential location for serious disturbances and incidents. As a result, it is critical that correctional staff enforce an orderly system of food lines and seating, as well as portion and utensil control.

The degree of staff supervision required and the nature of the institution's design will determine the system used for serving meals. To the extent possible, dining rooms should be designed to enhance the attractiveness of the meal-time atmosphere. Meals assume a magnified importance in inmates' daily routine, and are important to institutional personnel, also. Thus, the condition and cleanliness of the kitchen and dining areas can influence an institution's entire atmosphere.

Food should be served as soon as possible after preparation, and at an appropriate temperature. Temperatures ordinarily are maintained by keeping the food items in warmers of some type, either cabinet or pan style. Direct service is usually from a steam table or some other type of cafeteria-style warming equipment.

Food distribution should be supervised at all times. Frequently, an inmate serving food will take advantage of an officer's temporary absence to "take care of" friends, or to not give other inmates their entitled portions.

The eating utensils used in a given institution should be based on a control system dictated by the type of population confined there. Many institutions use a full array of metal items, while others, particularly those with high-security populations, have gone to highly durable, washable plastic utensils. Control of eating utensils can be maintained by requiring inmates to dispose of them in a carefully positioned and supervised receptacle when they drop off their trays.

Dining Room Routines

Inmates should be given enough time to wash before eating. Inmates working as painters or in other active occupations should be allowed to change clothing before entering the dining room.

ACA Food Service Standards

American Correctional Association standards for food service operations require the following:

- The food service manager should regularly inspect all areas and equipment related to food preparation, such as ranges, ovens, refrigerators, mixers, dishwashers, and garbage disposals, to ensure sanitary operating conditions. This equipment should be designed and located to allow efficient and thorough cleaning.

- All people involved in preparing food are to be medically examined before, and periodically after, they begin working, in accord with local requirements for restaurants. This requirement is to prevent individuals from transmitting illnesses, such as diarrhea or skin infections, to others through food or utensils.

- Food handlers, at a minimum, must be in good health and free from communicable diseases and without open or infected wounds.

American Correctional Association accreditors inspect food service.

potential for a line-cutting dispute to develop into a far larger confrontation. Close staff supervision can deter this activity and prevent it from growing into a larger problem when it does occur.

Finally, the inmate dining room is not to be used as a shortcut to other areas, nor should inmates not assigned there be permitted to remain unless authorized. The dining room should not be used for loitering or congregating.

Unit Dining Rooms

In some institutions, the prepared food portions are brought in on individual hot trays or in bulk to the housing units, and served from smaller steam or electrical heating equipment. In these units, the inmates may eat in a common area, or in their cells, depending on the security level and the type of space available.

Inmates must be fully clothed while in the dining room, and smoking should not be permitted at any time. Staff supervising the entrances should enforce the dress and smoking codes before inmates enter the area. Staff then can perform random inmate searches for weapons.

The dining room should provide normal group eating areas and permit conversation during dining hours. When possible, there should be "open" dining hours, thus reducing traditional waiting lines. Many facilities have eliminated forced seating based on housing unit, shop assignment, and other means.

Serving and dining schedules should offer a reasonable amount of time for inmates to eat. When setting schedules, institutions with this kind of meal program must consider the types of food served and the eating pattern of the inmates for that particular meal. Schedules often are set up according to housing units, but noon meals may be scheduled by work details.

Tables and chairs in the dining room should be arranged for good traffic flow and supervision; the actual arrangement will depend on the space available and the location of entrances and exits. Continuous rows of tables with adjacent aisles usually facilitate the orderly movement of inmates into the dining room, past the steam tables, and back to the eating tables.

The steam tables normally should be located next to the kitchen. This cafeteria-style arrangement usually permits enough supervisory space for officers to observe inmate activities on the line and in all parts of the dining room. It also enables extra food to be passed out by inmate waiters after the first helping has been served to all inmates, in systems where that is done.

Even with the best of traffic flows, line cutting can be a problem. In the crowded dining room, there is great

Food that is served to locked units must be kept hot.

Unit dining rooms have some advantage for high-security institutions, because they eliminate the large numbers of inmates brought together by centralized dining. There are drawbacks, however, to these decentralized operations. Among them are the problems of food transportation and cleanup of multiple dining and food service areas. In addition, it is far easier for inmates to retain foodstuffs in their cells in this situation.

Special Housing

Food service in special housing or locked units usually is provided to inmates in their cells. In some units, selected inmates are permitted to eat in common areas in small groups. In these units, portable steam tables, microwave reheating, or thermal containers can be used successfully, and there are good reasons for using each in particular settings.

Food service operations in these areas differ from institution to institution. However, there are several common principles that apply in almost all cases:

- All food carts should be thoroughly searched by staff for contraband being sent into the unit from cooperating inmates in the main kitchen area.

- No inmates ever should be used to serve food to other inmates in segregation status; this is a prime opportunity for pressure activity, as well as tampering with unpopular inmates' food.

- Inmates must be required to give back all utensils and other items on the food tray; this not only is for the safety of staff, but also because keeping food in cells is likely to attract vermin and insects.

- Staff should ensure that all inmates' meals arrive at their cells at the proper temperature.

- Food service supervisory personnel should regularly tour the segregated units during mealtime to ensure that inmates are properly served, with meals at the proper temperature.

Commissary Operations

Home-cooked foods are not allowed in an institution. However, the commissary or inmate store is available in most locations for inmates to purchase a wider variety of discretionary food and other items. Selecting the articles to be sold in a commissary requires careful study. Most commissaries limit the selection to snacks and light foods that are not in conflict with the regular food program. Some items are virtually required, such as milk and sugar for coffee, in order to prevent kitchen theft from developing. Watch for hording as a signal for a potential riot/disturbance.

Supervision Issues

Correctional officers are called on to provide area supervision in the food preparation and dining areas. These duties differ from institution to institution, but there are a number of common concerns.

Controlling Food Service Traffic

Traffic control in and out of the food service area is important. The unrestricted movement of inmates not only presents an accountability problem, but it also permits easier theft of food items and pilferage of other contraband from the kitchen. The more traffic there is, the harder it will be to detect these items. For that reason, the kitchen area should be out of bounds for all nonkitchen workers, and correctional staff should enforce that rule very closely.

Searching Inmates

Searching inmates moving in and out of the institution is a companion issue. In addition to searches of inmates going into the area (to prevent the movement of weapons), searches of departing inmates are important. These deter food theft and reduce the likelihood that inmates will attempt to steal a kitchen knife or other hazardous contraband for use on the compound.

Controlling Kitchen Items

Control of items coming into the kitchen through the loading dock is always a concern. The possibility of contraband coming in through regular food shipments from fixed sources of supply is quite high. Therefore, each institution should have a specific system for

Left: Food storage areas must be kept clean and orderly to prevent spoilage and theft. Right: Inmate workers and staff set up the food service line.

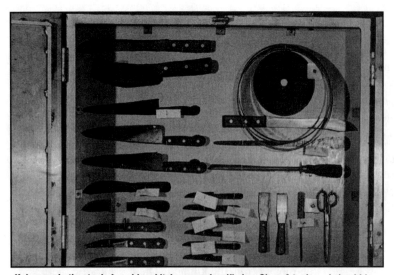

Knives and other tools found in a kitchen are classified as Class A tools and should be monitored.

searching vehicles, loads, and drivers moving supplies into the compound.

However, just because a delivery has been searched does not mean that an officer assigned to the kitchen does not have to be concerned about this issue. The contraband could have been overlooked, or placed in the supplies after they arrived and were searched. In any event, officers never should assume that any items in warehouses, storage areas, or even in the preparation areas are totally contraband-free.

Controlling Trash

Trash control is a related issue, particularly relevant to escape attempts. Every facility has a different process for collecting, securing, and removing trash from the compound. The general rule, however, is that any trash truck or dumpster load should be kept locked in a sally port-type area through one or more counts, to be sure that no inmates are hidden inside. Probing and other search techniques also may be used. The same concerns and search techniques should be used for boxes or containers of food prepared inside and sent to satellite camps or other locations; inmates can be hidden in those containers, also.

Trash compactors, too, are an avenue for escape. Inmates have successfully (and at times unsuccessfully) fabricated skeletal frameworks or "crushproof" containers to hide in to escape from a dumpster. Sally porting is the safest way to eliminate this as an avenue for escape attempts.

Controlling Kitchen Tools

Tool control in the kitchen consists primarily of knife control. However, in facilities with butcher shops, saws and other tools used in those processes can be dangerous, as well. In most facilities, kitchen tools are stored in a locked cabinet in a secure area. Inside the cabinet, the tools are hung on hooks, so it is easy to see if any are missing. When an inmate or staff member checks out the tool, a durable metal tag with that person's name or other identifier is placed on the hook, so that it is clear who has that item. A written inventory list of all items in the cabinet should be kept in it, and at each shift the responsible staff member should check the inventory and initial the list. This inventory also should be checked jointly with a correctional staff member on a regular basis, not less than monthly.

Yeast, Sugar, and Extract Control

Yeast, sugar, and extract control are other concerns in an institution. Sugar and yeast can be used to make home-brew alcoholic beverages, and many extracts have alcohol in them. These items should be kept under lock, with a strict inventory maintained. Even yeast residues (the wrappers or containers, for instance) should be disposed of by staff outside the institution, because the small amount of remaining yeast is enough to start fermentation.

In this connection, inmates with large amounts of sugar or fruits, or even small amounts of unbaked bread in their possession, should be viewed with suspicion as potential brew makers. Even if the institution does not have a possession limit on these food items, an officer encountering them in large amounts should refer the matter to a supervisor for advice.

Inmates have a tremendous amount of ingenuity when it comes to finding places to brew alcoholic drinks. While it is impossible to list all the likely places,

Sugar and fruit are two of the ingredients needed for home brew, and correctional officers finding large amounts of either or any yeast should alert authorities.

Photos courtesy Capitol Communication Systems, Inc.

staff should know that tubes, pipes, and elaborate equipment are not necessary—brew has been made in every possible simple container, from toilets to garbage bags. Locations include cells, job sites, behind ovens, in pipe chases, and anywhere that temperatures are likely to stay warm and staff are not likely to suspect. In short, ingenuity is the only limit to where brew can be made.

Accommodating Inmate Work Assignments

Using food as payment for work, or as a special privilege, is unjustified and never should be permitted. When inmates work in outlying jobs, or on odd shifts, it often is necessary to provide lunches or extra food to cover the shift portion of the day. Some institutions take into account the fact that some work assignments are more physically demanding than others, and provide extra rations from leftovers. Often, larger lunches are needed for farm workers who work extra hours during harvesting and for night workers in a dairy or piggery. In cases like this, supervisory staff, not line employees, should decide who gets what, and how much.

Summary

Nutritious and tasteful meals, served in a pleasant and safe environment, have great significance in an institution. This is true not only because food takes on magnified importance in the institutional setting, but also because the dining area can be a breeding ground for serious disturbances.

Although food service responsibilities typically are assigned to a food service manager, the correctional officer must ensure that proper security and supervision practices are observed in the food preparation area, that distribution of food is fair, and that order is maintained in the dining area. Teamwork is essential between food service staff and correctional officers to ensure smooth day-to-day food service operations.

If you have an interest in this area, join the society of correctional food service professionals who are interested in the advancement of food service in corrections: the American Correctional Food Service Association. Call (612) 928-4685, fax (612) 928-1318 or write ACFSA, 4248 Park Glen Road, Minneapolis, Minnesota, 55416.

APPLICABLE ACA STANDARDS

Food Services: 3-4294 - 3-4309

BIBLIOGRAPHY

American Correctional Association. *Certification Standards for Food Service Programs*. 1989. Lanham, Maryland: American Correctional Association.

———. 1996. *Correctional Food Service Correspondence Course*. Lanham, Maryland: American Correctional Association.

9

Sanitation and Hygiene

Crowding in correctional institutions is of increasing concern today. Outdated or poorly designed facilities are the realities of many correctional institutions. Many of these institutions are hard to maintain and keep in a high state of sanitation. Yet, the demands of congregate living mean that it is even more important now than ever before to emphasize sanitation in institutions and the important hygienic steps needed to ensure inmate health.

An effective sanitation program raises inmate and staff morale; no one likes to live or work in a dirty, smelly, poorly maintained institution. Ironically, some of the least expensive and most effective improvements in the atmosphere of an institution can be made with soap and water, disinfectant, and inmate labor. The only essentials are the necessary administrative support and supervisory initiatives.

The Role of Supervisors

Sanitation is an area where supervisory standards are critical. If the warden and other top staff personally do not set high standards of hygiene and sanitation, and if they are not active in setting up programs to enact those high standards, then a clean, sanitary institution will not be achieved.

Individual correctional officers, on their own initiative, can have a tremendous positive impact in this area, but for an entire institution to be neat, clean, and orderly, the administrator must set and maintain high standards and expectations.

Once those standards are communicated to mid-level and line staff, then other systems must be in place to support those efforts. Those systems include regular purchase of the proper equipment and supplies, systematic inspections of the institution, and prompt corrective action when deficiencies are found. Maintenance staff involvement is an important part of this effort.

The Inspection System

The institution must be inspected at least annually by appropriate officials to ensure the health of personnel and inmates. In addition, all institutional areas should be inspected at least weekly by a designated staff member (often the safety or sanitation officer), who should submit a written report to the appropriate department for corrective action.

The sanitation and safety system also should include regular inspections by unit and area staff. Moreover, supervisory correctional staff should inspect the institution as a part of their daily routine. This is not only necessary for sanitation itself, but for the supervisors to have the opportunity to keep in touch with the actual job performance of the line employees.

Individual room or dormitory inspections are a regular part of most institutional routines, and inmates whose living areas are not acceptably clean should be recalled from wherever they are and required to complete the job. In extreme cases, disciplinary action may be needed to bring a specific inmate's room into compliance.

Unit inspections also should include noncell areas, including showers, toilets, and sinks, as well as ventilators, fan outlets, light fixtures, and other parts of the unit that often are not cleaned in the day-to-day course of business. These sanitation inspections should not be confused with security inspections, which are intended to detect deficiencies in the security hardware and construction of the institution.

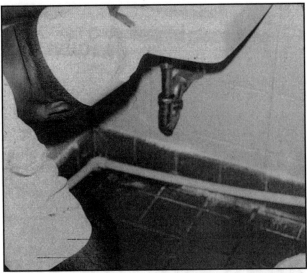
Inspection of sinks and toilets is crucial since contraband can be stored in pipes.

standard of cleanliness is maintained, there is less need for dramatic cleanup activity. Preidentified areas ordinarily are assigned to specific inmate orderlies, and unit officers should include specified tasks such as mopping and waxing floors, when appropriate. Standards for waxing floors and maintaining unit common areas such as day rooms and showers should be a clear part of the institution's overall sanitation plan. A supply system should be in place that permits staff access to necessary cleaning materials. Correctional officers should supervise inmate use of toxic cleaning materials.

Personal Property Policy

The personal property policy should state the quantities of food purchased in the institution store or commissary that are permitted in cells. Foods that attract vermin should not be allowed in cells, except as otherwise provided.

In crowded institutions, a large amount of personal property can make an already small housing area seem smaller. For that reason, controlling personal property is an important part of maintaining not only a sanitary institution, but one that is neat and uncluttered. Clear limits on the amount and type of personal property in cells or dormitories will prevent them from becoming cluttered fire hazards. Radios, televisions, and tape players, if allowed, should be engraved with the inmates' commitment number, and a numbered property receipt issued. Insisting on only reasonable amounts of personal property also aids security, because it is far simpler for officers to search more modest amounts of property.

Living Quarters

Each institution, and every housing unit in it, should have a clearly defined program for daily cleaning. This program should include the use of inmate orderlies for cleaning common areas, as well as individual inmates' responsibility for their own living areas.

Standards for Unit and Cell Upkeep

The standards for unit and cell upkeep should specify that dirt and trash are not allowed to accumulate in any part of a living area; when a consistent, high

Inmates should not be permitted to hang sheets, blankets, or any other items on bars and windows, which might obscure visibility into a living area. These visual barriers prevent staff from properly supervising the interior of cells and dormitories, allowing inmates to engage in improper behavior. Hanging items also constitute a fire hazard. For many of the same reasons, many institutions limit the number of pictures or other materials that can be placed on cell walls.

Wires, antennas, cables, and hanging plants also should be regulated in housing areas. Not only do they constitute a general safety hazard, but they may be unsightly, and they may contribute to the unit's overall cluttered, crowded appearance.

Photos courtesy Capitol Communication Systems, Inc.

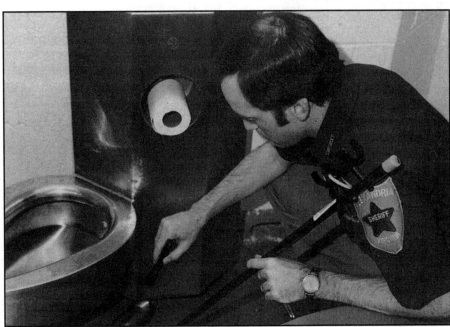
A correctional officer must take nothing for granted and be sure to inspect every nook and cranny.

Toilet Facilities

Toilet facilities must be maintained at a high level of cleanliness. These are areas where the disease-transmission potential is quite high, and staff must take necessary steps to be sure that all toilets and urinals are cleaned and disinfected regularly.

Likewise, sinks in cells and congregate areas must be maintained at a very high level of cleanliness. Not only is it personally offensive to anyone to have to wash in a dirty sink, perhaps caked with the soap scum residue and hairs of a dozen others, but it clearly creates a high risk for disease transmission. Officers in housing areas must place a major emphasis on this area.

Bathing Facilities

There should be sufficient bathing facilities in housing areas to permit general-population inmates to shower at least three times a week. In institutions where there is cellblock bathing, bathing facilities must be maintained in a sanitary condition at all times, with regular scrubbing of all surfaces to avoid soap film and moldy buildups. In many institutions, a regular schedule of bathing is used, and in those locations, inmates should proceed directly to the shower at the designated time and, after bathing is completed, return to their cells.

For institutions with a central bathing/clothing issue system, at the conclusion of the bathing count, check the laundry slips, and sign and place them inside the laundry bags with the soiled clothing. A duplicate record should be kept in the cellblock office to ensure proper counts and amounts of clothing are being returned. Upon return, clean clothing should be checked carefully and stored in the clothing room for distribution.

Upkeep of Nonunit Areas

The nonunit areas of the institution should be subject to a structured cleaning system, as well. Some areas require cleaning only once a week; others once a day or shift; still others need constant cleaning, like corridor areas near doorways in inclement weather. It is up to local staff to set up a schedule that meets the institution's needs, realizing that inmate labor is plentiful. Supervise cleaning activities at all times to ensure that work performed is proper and thorough. Pay particular attention to keeping the facility's floors clean, dry, and free of hazardous substances.

Shop and Work Areas

Shop sanitation is important for several reasons. First, a cluttered and disorganized shop is unsafe. Second, unclean working conditions in a kitchen or warehouse can breed disease or vermin just as easily as in a housing unit. Finally, the housekeeping conditions in a

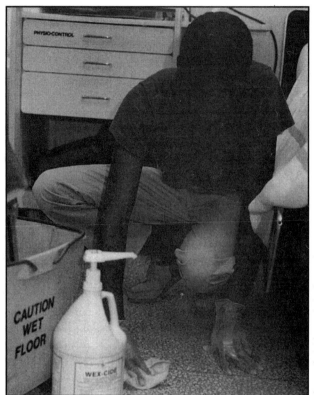

Keeping floors clean is a vital part of safety and sanitation.

work area telegraph something about the general security and supervision provided in that area. Supervisors who permit dirty, cluttered work areas also are likely to permit lax tool or key control, and probably are not as concerned about inmate supervision.

Yards and Other Outdoor Areas

The institution's overall housekeeping plan also should provide for regular cleaning of all outdoor areas, including the yard, interior courtyards, and interior building facades. This should include a well-defined system of inmate orderlies or grounds keepers, with specific areas of responsibility. In general, these inmates should be supervised by staff on the grounds, but some additional coverage can be provided by tower officers in secure locations. In particular, tower officers should be concerned about watching for unusual activity on the part of these yard workers, which might indicate they were assisting in or participating in any escape or contraband-related activity.

Cleaning Sensitive Areas

Higher-security areas, or those with clear security implications, never should be cleaned by inmates. This category ordinarily includes the control center, armory, key storage area, lock shop, and towers. Staff should have a regular system for cleaning these important areas.

Correctional Officer Resource Guide

Operation of commercial laundry equipment requires attention to temperature controls.

Preventive Maintenance Program

An institution without a well-structured preventive maintenance program is a facility that inevitably is going to deteriorate. First, the maintenance department should have a schedule for reviewing the institution's equipment and repair needs. Repetitive maintenance tasks, such as painting and filter changing, can be scheduled.

However, it also is vital that officers who observe conditions requiring maintenance and repair have a clearly defined system for the timely reporting of those conditions to the proper department. Once that is done, a properly designed system will include a method for supervisory follow-up to ensure that the required work is completed.

The trusty supervisor is explaining the work detail to inmates.

Waste Disposal and Pest Control

Waste disposal and pest control programs are essential to maintaining a sanitary institution. These programs include regular inspections for pest and rodent infestation and proper documentation. Most institutions also have contracts with licensed pest control professionals, who are available to provide pest control services.

Liquid and solid wastes must be collected, stored, and disposed of in a manner that protects the health and safety of inmates, staff, and visitors. To do this effectively, most institutions have a regular trash pickup and disposal system. Staff will determine the best methods for the particular institution for pickup, and short-term storage inside and outside movement of refuse. Any hazardous wastes generated in shops, industrial operations, or health care operations should be controlled in accordance with local policy and disposed of in accordance with state and federal regulations.

Since regular trash movement out of the institution is a prime escape route, each institution should have a particular routine for ensuring that inmates do not hide in the trash truck, dumpster, or other receptacle for garbage, industrial waste, and other refuse. Most of these policies and procedures include keeping the container or vehicle locked in a sally port or other area through one or more good counts before allowing it to go outside the perimeter.

Laundry Programs

All inmates should have clothing that fits properly, suits the climate, and meets their needs. All government clothing and bedding supplies issued to an inmate are that inmate's responsibility, and the inmate is held responsible for their use and care.

It is critical to have facilities for thoroughly cleaning, disinfecting, and storing government-issued inmate clothing. Make strong efforts to maintain a high standard of inmate laundry services.

In some locations, inmates are permitted to have their own clothing, and in others, none is allowed. For that reason, the issue of storage, cleaning, and accountability systems will be different in each institution.

In general, though, if the institution permits personal clothing, then a system must be available that provides reasonable assurances against theft in the laundry process. The inmate's personal clothes must be returned with a minimum of delay, each inmate receiving his or her own clothes from the laundry. In many locations, however, this personal clothing system takes the form of laundry equipment in the housing units, with the inmates washing their own clothes. Where the institution does provide clothing, a central laundry often is used, with a centralized clothing exchange based on inmate register number, bin numbers, or some other system.

All inmates must be supplied with adequate bedding and linens. In most institutions, this takes the form of standard issue items, but in a few facilities, personal linens are permitted, using the unit laundry system to keep them clean. Where linens are issued, a regular exchange program is used, and sheets and pillowcases typically are changed and laundered at least weekly; blankets should be laundered monthly and sterilized before reissue. Mattresses should be aired at regular intervals.

Protective and special clothing ordinarily is issued to inmates assigned to the institution's food service, hospital, farm, garage, plant maintenance shops, and other special work details. Special laundry procedures ordinarily are established for these items.

Hair Care Services

Facilities are provided in most institutions where inmates can obtain needed hair care services. A central barbershop, a single room in the cellhouse, or any multi-purpose room may be used. In any event, hair should be cut under sanitary conditions and in an area that permits observation by officers.

Equipment and supplies should be stored securely when not in use. Scissors, razors, and any other hazardous items should be controlled like any other Class A (highly dangerous) tool—engraved, shadowed, checked out, and inventoried at least daily.

Female institutions with more elaborate hair care facilities should review carefully the chemicals used in various hair treatments. Some contain highly caustic or poisonous materials, and should be used under controlled circumstances, if at all. Portable hair dryers or other items that have significant security implications should be controlled as Class A items.

Cleaning of Possible Contaminated Areas

As a result of fights or assaults in the institution, blood and/or body fluid must be cleaned up and the area decontaminated. Clothing and cleaning equipment must

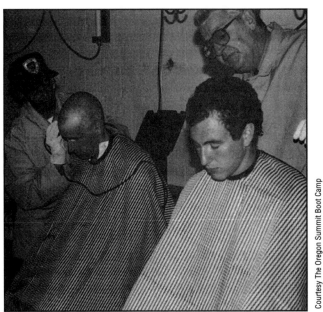

Barber tools are considered in the category of Class A tools—those that are very dangerous.

be disposed of properly. A select group of inmates should be trained in proper body-fluid cleaning techniques, and special protective clothing provided. All equipment that is necessary to neutralize a body-fluid spill should be contained in locked and inventoried cabinets, clearly marked as such, and located throughout the institution. Lists of trained inmates should be available to all shifts.

Summary

One of the major responsibilities of any institution is to maintain the health of inmates. Proper sanitation and hygiene are major ingredients in this process, and they also improve the morale of those who live or work in an institution. A decline in personal hygiene may signal a personal problem on the part of an inmate, and a drop in overall sanitation or hygiene in an institution similarly can indicate major supervisory problems at one or more levels.

While the actual housekeeping and maintenance chores may not be a direct responsibility of the correctional officer, the supervision of these activities is. In addition to being aware of proper procedures to follow for sanitation, the officer immediately should report any condition that may affect the health or safety of an inmate or staff member.

APPLICABLE ACA STANDARDS

Sanitation and Hygiene: 3-4134, 3-4310 - 3-4325

Food Service Inspections: 3-4304 - 3-4306

10

Health Care

When the state confines individuals, it deprives them of the opportunity to choose their own personal health care. In doing that, the state then must assume responsibility for providing at least basic health care for these individuals. It is the institution's responsibility to maintain physical and mental health care services, and to take necessary steps to prevent serious illnesses and accidents in the inmate population. For the purposes of this chapter, medical and dental care are covered together under the general term "medical."

Failure to meet the duty to provide adequate health care can be cruel and unusual punishment, a constitutional violation. However, negligence (sometimes called medical malpractice) or a simple disagreement between an inmate and doctor over treatment do not constitute cruel and unusual punishment (Of course, negligence and malpractice are unacceptable and may become the basis for successful legal action.).

American Correctional Association standards and standards of the National Commission on Correctional Health Care provide a picture of how a good institutional health care system should be set up. They require institutions to have a designated health authority who is responsible in a well-defined way for health care services. The health authority may be a physician, health administrator, private health contractor, or government health agency. Even when this authority is not a staff physician, final medical judgments still must be made by a designated physician from some other source.

Remember, whether a particular inmate needs medical care is a matter to be decided by trained medical personnel. The officer on duty in the cellhouse, the shop supervisor, or other nonmedical employees should not unnecessarily restrict or control inmate access to medical personnel who can decide when medical care is needed.

The institution also must make available to inmates the services of an adequately equipped medical facility that meets the legal requirements for a licensed general hospital with respect to the services it offers. If the institution does not have its own licensed hospital inside (and many do not), it ordinarily will have an infirmary for basic care inside the institution, and provide hospital care through a contract with an outside hospital.

In every facility, space should be provided where inmates can be examined and treated in private. In an institution's health services area, the type of space available and equipment in the examination or treatment room depend on whether it is an infirmary or a full-scale hospital, as well as on the qualifications of the medical staff, but security personnel should be satisfied that it is properly secured.

The information contained in inmate medical and psychological files is confidential. Correctional staff must trust the medical staff to inform them if something beyond "universal precautions" is necessary in dealing with a specific inmate.

The accountability of medical equipment from shift to shift is the responsibility of the medical staff/contractor. This includes responsibility for sharps—needles and syringes. However, security should audit the accountability procedure on a regular basis to insure compliance with the institution's policies or standards.

Initial Medical Contacts

In addition to any initial medical intake screening, all inmates should receive a full medical screening upon their arrival at the facility, as part of the admission procedures. These screenings, using a combination of specific questions about the inmates' medical history, tests, and observation, are designed to prevent newly arrived inmates who pose a health or safety threat to themselves or others from being admitted to the facility's general population.

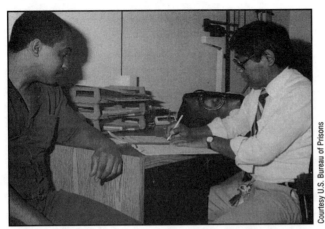

Above: The doctor must be sure to schedule follow-up visits when these are required. Right: For cases of tuberculosis, correctional officers should watch the inmates take their medication to ensure that they actually follow the prescribed regimen. This is known as directly observed treatment.

Test results, particularly for communicable diseases, should be received and evaluated before an inmate is assigned a job. Initial screenings ordinarily are performed by health care personnel. In some institutions, they are done by a health-care trained correctional officer at the time of admission.

Sick Call

Since it is not practical for an institution to allow inmates to leave their jobs or housing units whenever they want to go to the infirmary or hospital, some form of routine sick call is used in almost all correctional institutions, except for emergencies. This ordinarily consists of an appointment sign-up procedure; it also can be a specific time when inmates can go to the hospital for screening and, if necessary, a full examination by a nurse, physician's assistant, or a physician.

No member of the correctional staff should approve or disapprove inmate requests for attendance at sick call. Sick call ordinarily is initiated by the inmate, but officers should consider unusual conditions (such as a severe cough, complaints of pain in the chest, obvious indications of a severe cold, elevation of temperature, severe stomach complaints, abdominal cramps, nausea, or vomiting) as causes to send individuals to sick call. Outstanding cooperation between custody and medical staff is very important. Bring any conflict between custody and medical staff to a custody supervisor's attention immediately.

After screening or examination at sick call by a doctor or other health care provider, further treatment may be needed. In many locations, this involves issuing a series of passes that allow the inmate to visit clinics. In some cases, it may involve transportation to an outside hospital or clinic.

When sick calls reach large proportions, they can become disruptive to other institutional programs and routines. Some institutions hold sick call when most people are out on recreation, or actually have a medical staff person hold a sick call screening at the larger job sites, like the industries building. These strategies deter malingerers or other inmates who otherwise would use the sick call procedures for nonmedical purposes. Inmate co-payment for treatment also is being used in some institutions to defray costs and cut down on malingerers.

Medication Issues

Inmates who are approved for medication cannot just walk down to the hospital when they feel like it to receive their medication. Instead, regular, prescribed medication is given out in most institutions in a "pill line" or in some other organized form. Medications are administered by a medical staff member, who makes sure the inmates take the medicine then. Some medications are given to the inmate in blister packs, and the inmate is instructed on how and when to take the medication. Custody should inform the medical unit if they find inmates hording medication in any form.

In segregated units, the medical staff ordinarily may dispense medication at the same time they hold sick call rounds. Inmates in these units should be watched carefully to be sure they actually have swallowed their medication, particularly any inmates who may be thought to be potentially suicidal, or those who may be pressured into selling or giving away their medication.

Drug Storage

Drug storage is a different issue. Any large institution, even one that has only an infirmary, will have a great many controlled medications in stock for its population. No inmates should ever be permitted in a drug storage area or be given access to any bulk supplies of drugs.

Drugs for daily use should be kept in separate, carefully inventoried containers that can be accounted for from shift to shift. When not dispensing medication from these containers (usually storage cabinets of some type), staff must secure them at all times and keep them in a secure area.

Some institutions have an emergency bag or rolling "crash" cart that staff can move to the scene of a medical crisis. These containers, or any other emergency drug supply, should be kept in a locked area as well, with an inventory posted in it, which also is checked from shift to shift. All shift-to-shift inventories should have the signatures of the off-going and oncoming medical staff jointly completing the inventory.

Keep bulk storage of medications in a vault or large safe, and closely restrict its combination. Each agency has a different process for entering this vault, replenishing daily or weekly supplies, and inventorying its contents. However, at least once a month, substances in the vault should be inventoried jointly by a responsible medical supervisor and supervisory correctional staff.

Newly purchased medications should not be delivered to the inside warehouse or storeroom, where they might be pilfered by inmates. Instead, a responsible medical staff person should pick them up outside the secure compound, and move them to the bulk storage area, ideally when there are no inmates on the compound. Of course, they should be added to the inventory as soon as they are brought to the vault.

Medical Trips

In some cases, inmates must be transported outside the institution for medical or dental treatment. Each agency has different procedures for the use of restraints, number of escorts, and types of weapons to be used. There are, however, some common concerns in all such trips.

Escorting staff should strip search the inmate and thoroughly search the clothing to be worn on the trip when they take custody. Assuming someone else has searched the inmates, or searched them as thoroughly as necessary, has been a problem in many instances where inmates later produced handcuff keys or weapons.

Weapons never should be allowed to come in contact with an inmate under escort. While there is considerable variation on this theme in different agencies, the risks of armed escort staff coming in contact with visitors and the public, and the issue of when to remove restraints on patients undergoing treatment are both concerns that should be addressed in agency policy.

Supervision Issues in the Hospital or Infirmary

Supervising inmate traffic in and out of the hospital is an important task for correctional staff assigned to the medical area. There ordinarily is a pass or door check system of some type in place that will be used to account for all inmates coming to the medical area. Officers should be aware of the need for close supervision of each inmate who comes into the area.

One of the reasons for this is the fact that in addition to drugs, needles and syringes are kept in the hospital. Unless proper controls are maintained over these hazardous items/sharps, they may fall into inmate hands

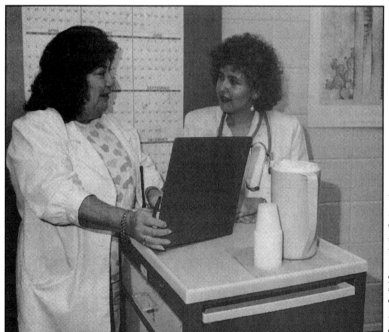

Security staff must develop a strong working relationship with the medical staff so that serious inmate medical concerns do not get overlooked. Inmates should give sick call request slips directly to medical staff rather than having a security staffer give them to the medical staff. This allows medical staff to make medical decisions and avoids issues of liability.

A large percentage of suicides occur during the first twenty-four hours of confinement. Correctional officers should know the warning signs for suicide.

and be used to inject drugs. There is also the risk of AIDS being transmitted through used needles.

Most institutions have a needle and syringe accountability program and a storage program similar to that for controlled medications. To that should be added the need to maintain secure and safe custody of used needles and syringes, and to properly and safely dispose of them in line with applicable state and local health regulations. At most locations, they are stored in a locked container until crushed and burned as contaminated medical waste outside the compound.

Common Emergencies

The use of emergency passes to the infirmary or hospital ordinarily is kept to a minimum. When an inmate's problem is clearly not an emergency, the inmate should be urged to wait for the next regular sick call. However, if the inmate becomes upset, refuses to work, or insists on seeing a doctor, it is wiser to agree. In addition, each institution has specific procedures to follow if the problem is clearly an emergency requiring immediate care.

During the early 1980s, there was a large increase in the suicide rate in crowded prisons (Camp and Camp 1989). However, between 1983 and 1993, the annual number of suicides dropped from 131 to 100. With the increased number of inmates in the prisons, this translates into a significantly lower rate of suicide.

Suicide has been the leading nonnatural cause of death within jails. 1991: 131 suicides; 1992: 124 suicides; 1993: 234 suicides (Beck, Bonczar, and Dilliard 1993). An analysis of those who committed suicide showed that:

- 72 percent of victims were white
- 94 percent of victims were male
- 75 percent of victims were detained on nonviolent charges, with 27 percent detained on alcohol/drug related charges
- 60 percent of victims were intoxicated at the time of incarceration
- 94 percent of the suicides were by hanging; 48 percent used their bedding
- two out of three victims were in isolation
- 51 percent of suicides occurred within the first twenty-four hours of incarceration; 29 percent occurred within the first three hours

Suicide Signs

Jail and prison staff can be taught to recognize and successfully intervene in situations involving potentially suicidal inmates. They may exhibit warning signs and symptoms that include the physical signs of depression:

- sadness and crying
- withdrawal or silence
- sudden loss or gain in appetite
- insomnia
- mood variations
- lethargy
- talking about or threatening suicide
- history of mental illness
- giving away possessions; packing belongings
- severe aggressiveness
- paranoid delusions or hallucinations (Hayes and Rowan 1988)

First Aid

First aid kits often are available in designated areas of the facility. The medical staff should approve the contents, number, location, and procedures for monthly inspection of the kits. Contents of first aid kits typically include roller gauze, sponges, triangle bandages, adhesive tape, and adhesive bandages. They do not include emergency drugs. The contents should be inventoried regularly and replenished after each use.

Most institutions provide some type of emergency first aid training to staff. The officer must clearly evaluate each emergency on its own, but after calling for assistance, some situations may require the officer to provide emergency care. First aid training should include familiarity with the following reaction to inmate emergencies: serious bleeding, unconsciousness, heart attack, shock, convulsions, choking, heat exhaustion, nosebleed, eye irritations, poisoning, burns, and broken bones. Although officers should be prepared to react to these emergencies, medical personnel should be notified at once in any medical situation.

Cardiopulmonary Resuscitation (CPR)

In a heart attack, the victim's heart and blood flow to it stop functioning normally, and other parts of the body stop functioning. If this stoppage continues for more than a minute or two, brain damage will occur.

Physicians' assistants and doctors often function as a team in correctional settings.

Cardiopulmonary resuscitation (CPR) has proved effective many times in keeping oxygen flowing to the brain of heart attack victims long enough for the heart to either spontaneously recover part of its function or for other assistance to arrive.

Cardiopulmonary resuscitation is a technique for assisting a failing heart to pump blood to the brain through direct chest pressure, and to get oxygen into the blood by helping to restart the victim's breathing. Many institutions teach cardiopulmonary resuscitation to all staff in the regular training program. It is not possible to teach cardiopulmonary resuscitation in a publication—it must be learned by actual practice of the techniques involved.

Medical Service in Segregated Units

Inmates in segregated or special housing units cannot go to sick call or to the pill line. Medical services must be brought to them. Typically, medical staff such as physicians' assistants travel to the unit once each shift and make the rounds of the cells, screening any inmates who have complaints. If necessary, inmates can be moved (under security escort and in restraints, when appropriate) to the medical area for further examination or treatment. Likewise, medications are administered to inmates in their cells, ordinarily by medical staff when they make their rounds.

Occupational Risk of Infection with Viral Hepatitis

Viral hepatitis is caused by at least five distinct viruses, referred to as hepatitis A, B, C, D, and E viruses. Hepatitis B virus (HBV) and hepatitis C virus (HCV) are transmitted primarily by percutaneous (needle stick) exposures to blood and by sexual contact; hepatitis D virus (HDV) also is transmitted through these routes, but only to persons who are infected with HBV. HBV, HCV, and HDV all can cause chronic infection. Hepatitis A virus and hepatitis E virus are transmitted through the fecal-oral route; neither virus results in chronic infection.

Health care workers long have been recognized to be at risk for HBV infection through occupational exposure to blood and blood-contaminated objects. Because HCV was discovered in the last few years, only recently has data been accumulated that addresses the risk of HCV infection among health care workers.

When a person is exposed to HBV, the virus enters the bloodstream and reaches the liver, which is the site of infection and viral replication. The incubation period (the time between exposure to the virus and onset of illness) ranges from two to six months and averages four months.

The most efficient route of transmission is by percutaneous (needle stick) exposure to blood. Other body

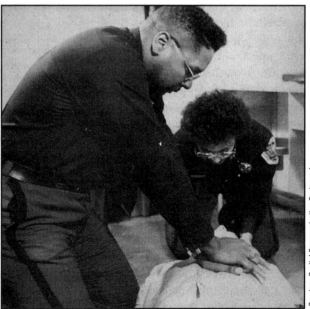

Correctional staff should learn techniques for both first aid and CPR.

fluids in which the virus is present, although in much lower concentrations, are semen, saliva, vaginal fluid, and serous exudates (sweats).

The risk to health care workers of acquiring occupationally related HBV infection has been shown to be related to several factors: the degree of exposure to blood, body fluids, or blood-contaminated sharps such as needles and other medical instruments and the duration of employment in an occupational category with frequent blood/needle exposure.

HCV is a major cause of chronic liver disease. No true confirmatory test exists for anti-HCV (antibody to HCV), but supplemental tests are available to evaluate screening assay results and should be used in the determination of anti-HCV positivity. Studies have shown an anti-HCV prevalence of 60 to 90 percent among injection-drug users. As with HBV infection, expected risk factors for HCV infection among health care workers include the degree of contact with blood or sharp instruments and the prevalence of anti-HCV among patients/inmates. The average incubation period for hepatitis C following a blood transfusion or needle stick is approximately seven weeks.

Prevention of Hepatitis B and C Viral Infection among Health Care Workers

The most important approach for the prevention of occupational HBV infection is use of hepatitis B vaccine among health care workers at risk. Hepatitis B vaccine has been available since 1981. Currently, two recombinant hepatitis B vaccines are available in the United States. These vaccines are very safe and highly effective in preventing HBV infection. In 1991, the Occupational Safety and Health Administration (OSHA) issued the bloodborne standard that requires employers to offer hepatitis B vaccine to all employees who reasonably anticipate contact with blood or other potentially infected materials, at no cost to the employee.

Effective HCV vaccines are not going to be available until quite some time from now. Consequently, preventive measures including barrier precautions and measures to protect against needle sticks are currently the mainstays for protection of health care workers against HCV infection.

The risk of HBV infection among health care workers is well documented. With widespread use of hepatitis B vaccine, the risk of infection largely can be eliminated. The risk of HCV infection among health care workers is not well defined. Although based on available data, this risk appears to be low. The risk of chronic liver disease with HCV infection is high, and effective measures that prevent transmission and infection are needed (Shapiro 1995).

Although data is not available (no study to date on the occupational risk to correctional officers of infection with hepatitis B and hepatitis C virus), the wisest course of action is to practice universal precautions and assume that the bodily fluids of every inmate are contaminated with the HBV and HCV virus.

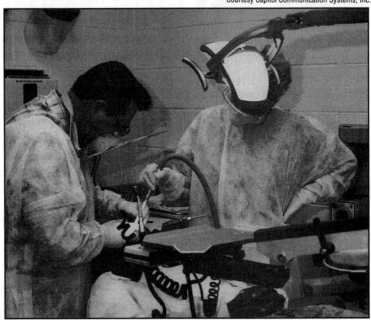

Because health practitioners may not know who has AIDS or other infectious diseases, they always should practice universal precautions and assume that the body fluids of all inmates are contaminated.

Acquired Immune Deficiency Syndrome (AIDS)

AIDS is an as-yet incurable, fatal disease caused by a virus known as the Human Immunodeficiency Virus (HIV). When HIV enters a person's bloodstream, it attacks certain types of white blood cells (the cells that fight all kinds of diseases), weakening and eventually destroying the body's immune system (the ability to fight disease). As a result of the extensively damaged immune system that develops over time, the individual becomes unable to fight off other infections or cancers and dies.

Since the discovery of the virus that causes AIDS and the development of blood tests to detect HIV infection, there has been confusion about the term "AIDS." When a person first becomes infected with the HIV virus, there are usually no significant symptoms. In fact, symptoms may not develop until the individual's immune system has become badly damaged.

As the body's immune system becomes increasingly weakened by the HIV infection, the individual develops certain symptoms or signs. This stage is commonly referred to as AIDS Related Complex (ARC). There is no clearly defined medical diagnosis of ARC the way there is for AIDS. This ARC condition confirms that the person is infected with the HIV virus, but the infection has not progressed to full-blown AIDS.

AIDS Diagnosis

The diagnosis of AIDS is not made until a secondary opportunistic infection occurs—an infection that takes advantage of the opportunity to attack the person's weakened immune system. This is usually not until several years after the initial infection, but because experience with the disease has been relatively short, this may not always be the case.

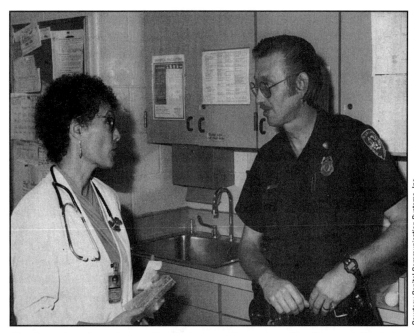

Keeping a strong level of communication between the security and health care staff leads to better management for all.

If you are exposed to body fluid for any reason, you should file a report of that contact so that your supervisor and the administration are aware of the incident. As with the hepatitis B and C virus, the wisest course of action for an individual officer is to assume that the bodily fluids of all inmates are contaminated with the HIV virus, and practice universal precautions.

While HIV can be found in other bodily fluids, it almost always is found in blood and sexual fluids. All evidence indicates the virus is transmitted primarily through two routes:

- Blood to blood contact—usually by shared needles through intravenous drug use

- Sexual fluids to blood contact—occurs in certain sexual practices, particularly by male homosexuals engaging in anal intercourse; transmission through vaginal intercourse also has been documented

Transmission of HIV occurs much less frequently by heterosexual contact than between homosexuals. Transmission of the virus during pregnancy, from a mother to her fetus, may occur frequently. In addition, the virus may be transmitted through the transfusion of blood during surgery or other medical procedures, for instance, during transfusion of blood products in the treatment of hemophilia or other diseases. However, blood and blood products now are screened for the HIV virus in all blood banking procedures.

AIDS is a fatal disease, and some treatment exists for those infected with the HIV virus. However, depending on the cause and type of the opportunistic or secondary infection, many patients may be treated successfully on an illness-by-illness basis. In addition, there are medications and treatments under study that may prove at least partially successful in treating the basic HIV infection. The development of an AIDS vaccine also is being researched, but is possibly years away.

Institutional Handling of AIDS Cases

Testing procedures for incoming inmates may include a blood test for AIDS, but that is not true in all locations. As a result, staff members may not know if any particular inmate is HIV-positive, meaning that the inmate might be capable of transmitting AIDS. In addition, most states and the federal government have strict rules on confidentiality of medical records, which means that even if the medical staff knew an inmate was HIV-positive, they might not be able to tell other staff.

The probability that correctional officers or other staff will contract an HIV infection from inmates is so small as to be virtually nonexistent, even under extreme circumstances. However, the wisest course of action for an individual officer is to assume that the bodily fluids of every inmate are contaminated. That way, the chance of even accidentally picking up the virus through an inmate contact is reduced. This does not mean that a staff member should not provide normal services or have normal contacts with inmates. It does mean, however, that when there are incidents like stabbings or other emergencies, where blood or other body fluids may be exposed, the employee carefully should follow agency policy and practices in minimizing the risks involved.

While some correctional systems have decided to separate all HIV-positive cases in one location, most have not. In most institutions, inmates with the HIV

Correctional Officer Resource Guide

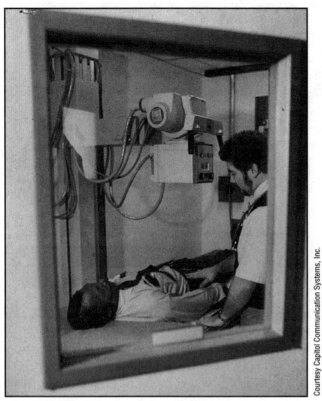

Regular screening checks for tuberculosis are important for members of the correctional staff.

virus are not isolated, segregated, or otherwise specially managed, except when their medical condition warrants it. However, inmates who are HIV-positive, and who are sexually active in prison, are predatory, or threaten staff or others, ordinarily are placed in long-term detention status to protect the staff and others.

The attitude of staff toward individuals with AIDS should, and usually is, supportive, understanding, reassuring, and as responsive as possible. These people have a fatal disease. Some systems set up special counseling programs or other individualized treatment for them, and to the extent the law allows, some are released as they near death, so they can be in a more normal setting for the final weeks or months of their life. Because it is not practical to discuss in this *Guide* the many HIV and AIDS-related situations that may occur in various correctional systems (including working with HIV-positive staff) and in different judicial districts throughout the country, correctional staff should seek guidance from their supervisors.

Regardless of these differences, staff should be aware of the specific policy for handling such cases at their institutions. To the degree that they can, they should work closely with medical personnel, other staff, and patients in proper health management and education.

Prevention/Control of Tuberculosis in Correctional Facilities

The transmission of Mycobacterium tuberculosis (M. tuberculosis) in correctional facilities presents a public health problem for correctional-facility employees and for inmates and the communities into which they are released. The Advisory Council for the Elimination of Tuberculosis (ACET) recognizes the urgent need to improve TB prevention and control practices in many correctional facilities. All correctional facilities, even those in which few TB cases are expected to occur, should designate a person or group of persons who will be responsible for the facility's TB infection-control program and the following three essential TB control activities:

(1) Screening—identifying persons who are infected with M. tuberculosis or who have active TB disease;

(2) Containment—preventing transmission of M. tuberculosis and adequately treating persons who have latent TB infection or active TB disease;

(3) Assessment—monitoring and evaluating the screening and containment activities.

Correctional-facility officials should form close working relationships with their state and local health departments, which can assist correctional facilities in formulating, implementing, and evaluating these activities.

Factors Contributing to the Prevalence of TB in Correctional Facilities

A primary reason for the high risk for M. tuberculosis infection and active TB disease in correctional facilities is the disproportionate number of inmates who have risk factors for exposure to the organism or, if infected, for development of the active disease. These risk factors include infection with human immunodeficiency virus (HIV), substance abuse, and being a member of a lower socioeconomic population that has poor access to health care. The strongest known risk factor for the development of active TB disease among adults who have latent TB infection is coinfection with HIV. Persons who are coinfected with HIV and M. tuberculosis have an estimated 8 to 10 percent risk each year for developing active TB disease, whereas persons who are infected with only M. tuberculosis have a 10 percent risk for developing active TB disease during their lifetimes.

The prevalence of HIV infection and acquired immunodeficiency syndrome (AIDS) among inmates has increased substantially during the past decade. The annual incidence of AIDS among prisoners is markedly higher than the incidence among the total United States population.

HIV infection in inmates has been associated with injection of illegal drugs, a risk factor more prevalent among inmates than among the total population. Persons who inject illegal drugs may be at increased risk for TB even if these persons are not infected with HIV, although the reasons for this increased risk are unclear. The use of crack cocaine also has been associated with transmission of both HIV and M. tuberculosis.

Residents of correctional facilities also are at increased risk for TB because many of these facilities have crowded environments conducive to the transmission of M. tuberculosis. Poor ventilation, which is a problem in many correctional facilities, also can promote transmission of M. tuberculosis to inmates, correctional-facility employees, and visitors.

TB Prevention and Control in Correctional Facilities

Although the high risk for transmission of M. tuberculosis demonstrates the need for effective TB control in correctional facilities, a 1992-93 survey of eighty-two correctional systems in the United States indicated that policies for TB prevention and control in some correctional facilities did not meet Centers for Disease Control and Prevention (CDC) recommended standards. The need for improved health care in correctional facilities has been advocated by the American College of Physicians, the National Commission on Correctional Health Care, and the American Correctional Health Services Association.

Several of the nation's courts have determined that inadequate TB control efforts constitute deliberate indifference to the medical needs of inmates and that inmates have a constitutional right to adequate TB control in correctional facilities.

The Advisory Council for the Elimination of Tuberculosis (ACET) recognizes the urgent need to improve TB prevention and control practices in all correctional facilities and recommends the implementation of screening and containment practices even though such implementation may require that stronger legislation and regulations be enacted and adequate financial resources be allocated.

Screening

Persons who have a positive skin-test result and no symptoms suggestive of TB should be screened with a chest radiograph within seventy-two hours after the skin test is interpreted. Persons who have symptoms suggestive of TB disease should be evaluated immediately. All new inmates in long-term correctional facilities should be screened as soon as possible.

A medical history should be obtained from and recorded for all new employees at the time of hiring, and they should receive a physical examination. In addition, tuberculin skin-test screening should be mandatory for all employees who do not have a documented history of a positive skin-test result.

Containment

Because crowded living conditions and poor ventilation are conducive to the transmission of M. tuberculosis, improvements in housing conditions can help prevent outbreaks. Standard engineering controls are based primarily on the use of ventilation systems, which might not prevent transmission of M. tuberculosis. These ventilation systems

Essential Facts About TB

- TB is spread through the air. One highly infectious person can infect others who share the same air space.

- Immediate isolation of infectious patients can interrupt transmission of M. tuberculosis.

- Prompt initiation of an adequate regimen of directly observed therapy (DOT) helps ensure adherence to treatment because either a medical worker, a specially trained correctional officer, or a health department employee observes the patient swallowing each dose of medication. This method of treatment can diminish infectiousness, reduce the risk for relapse, and help prevent the development of drug-resistant stains of M. tuberculosis.

- Inmates who are coinfected with HIV and M. tuberculosis are at high risk for developing active TB disease in comparison with inmates who only are infected with M. tuberculosis.

- A completed regimen of preventive therapy can prevent the development of active TB disease in persons who are infected with M. tuberculosis.

- Correctional-facility officials have an opportunity to treat inmates who have active TB disease or latent TB infection before such inmates are released into the community.

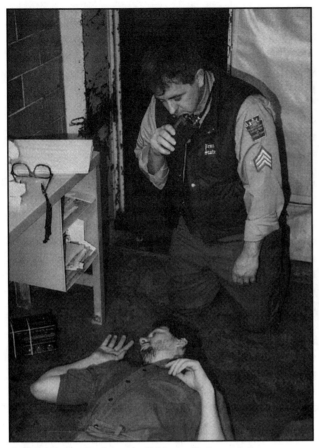
Getting help in a timely way is vital for medical emerencies.

may be supplemented with high-efficiency particulate air (HEPA) filtration and ultraviolet germicidal irradiation (UVGI) in high-risk areas (such as temporary holding areas and communal areas).

If inmates who are suspected of having infectious TB must be transported outside their TB isolation rooms for medically essential procedures that cannot be performed in the isolation rooms, they should be required to wear a surgical mask that covers their mouth and nose during transport. A respiratory protection program, including education and fit testing (for proper fit of respiratory equipment), should be included in the correctional facility's infection-control program. Medical or security staff who transport infectious TB patients in a closed vehicle or who must enter TB isolation rooms should wear a personal respirator.

Role of the Correctional Facility

The correctional facility should be responsible for in-facility TB screening, containment, and assessment unless otherwise mandated by legal statute. In all correctional facilities, officials should work closely with the state and local health departments in their jurisdictions. Correctional facilities, including local jails, should establish formal written working agreements with health departments in their areas. These written agreements should delineate responsibilities and specify procedures for the following activities:

- Screening and treatment of inmates
- Follow-up of symptomatic inmates
- Follow-up of inmates who have abnormal chest radiographs
- Contact investigations for reported TB cases
- Follow-up of inmates who are released before completing treatment for TB disease
- Follow-up of inmates who are released before completing preventive therapy

Correctional facilities also should collaborate with health department staff to provide TB education and counseling to inmates and employees (Centers for Disease Control 1996).

Epilepsy

The human brain operates with very mild electrical activity. Epilepsy results (for various reasons) from disturbances in these electrical patterns or rhythms in the brain. Many epileptic seizures can be provoked by periods of emotional excitement. Thus, if epileptics get upset, they may have a "spell."

Epilepsy may result in any one or all of these symptoms: seizures, which are often called "fits" or "spells" (convulsions); impairment of motor control (falling); loss of consciousness; and psychological difficulties. There are three main seizure types: "grand mal," "petit mal," and "psychomotor episodes."

During "grand mal" seizures, people lose consciousness and have violent convulsions. They black out at first, become stiff, and barely breathe; this is followed by severe muscle twitching and shaking of the body. Breathing can be so restricted that the person turns blue. There also can be frothing at the mouth. Sometimes, the person empties his or her bowels or bladder during the course of an attack. Many epileptics experience a warning feeling (called an aura). This allows some people to protect themselves before the attack by lying down. However, most do not have any warning and suddenly are taken by a seizure. Some epileptics involuntarily emit a cry before their attack begins. Such spells usually are followed by a period of confusion and lethargy.

In the "petit mal" epileptic seizure, the person is not aware of what is going on around him or her. Even though there is no actual convulsion, these epileptics might be hurt by their inability to respond to emergencies or even routine tasks, and may be injured by moving machinery. These episodes rarely last more than thirty seconds, after which the individual returns to normal.

During the "psychomotor" epileptic seizure, individuals do not experience a convulsion, but do experience reduced consciousness and loss of memory. They retain the ability to act, but usually in a purposeless fashion, often talking nonsense, making chewing movements with their mouth, or displaying other bizarre behavior.

Response to a Seizure

The emergency treatment of an epileptic convulsion first involves the understanding that it must run its course; there is nothing one can do to stop it. During a major attack, the person very likely will thrash about violently. A pillow or substitute, such as a coat, may be placed under the person's head to prevent damage to the skull. Nearby objects, on which the inmate could be injured, should be removed. If the person seems to be choking, he or she involuntarily might have forced his or her tongue into the back of the mouth, closing off the air intake. Roll the person over on the side, so that the tongue can be coughed out. Do not insert anything into the mouth of a person having a seizure. Loosen tight clothing, such as a belt or closely fitted collar. After the uncontrolled thrashing phase is over, let the person rest or sleep and recover. The other types of seizures ordinarily will not require this type of active assistance.

Treatment

The long-term medical treatment of epilepsy involves a physician prescribing specific medications. It is important to remember that when such drugs are prescribed, it is critical for the inmate to take them. Some epilepsy-controlling medications may represent a temptation to other inmates in the population. Also, some epileptics resist taking their medication because of the possible side effects, such as drowsiness. For these reasons, their dispensation should be closely supervised, ideally by a trained medical staff member. Also, when possible, use liquid forms of medicine.

Asthma and Other Chronic Illnesses

Inmates with known chronic illnesses frequently present a management dilemma to medical staff as well as to correctional officers and other personnel. In addition to providing for the real medical needs of these individuals, staff often must deal with inmates who may exaggerate their difficulties or fake new symptoms for other nonmedical reasons—special privileges, unwarranted individual attention, excuses from work or other assignments, just to get out of their cell for a while, or even to set the stage for a major security breach. Sometimes, the motivation may be only to break the monotony of institutional life, or to cause a disruption. On the other hand, inmates with legitimate chronic illnesses also are likely to experience significant symptoms, which may result from complications of the basic illness or even the development of new diseases.

The problem of telling the difference between real and faked or exaggerated complaints can be quite difficult even for the physician, and especially for the correctional officer. While some judgment must be exercised, the correctional officer always should make a medical referral if there is any reasonable doubt about the need for an inmate to receive medical care. Even a known malingerer may develop a real disease. Correctional officers must avoid premature judgments influenced by an inmate's previous deceptive behavior.

Asthma Cases

While these concerns should apply to any chronic illness, patients with asthma deserve special mention. These individuals are subject to sudden periodic episodes when the small air passages (bronchial tubes) inside their lungs become closed, causing a failure to inhale enough oxygen. Many such incidents may be mild and may respond well to prescribed medication, which may be in the patient's possession or available in the living unit. However, in many documented prison experiences, the margin between an apparently "mild" episode and a significant life-threatening experience can be small and deceptive. Correctional officers should be particularly alert to asthma situations and make early medical referrals.

Diabetes

The human body requires certain chemicals, which it produces, to use foods that we eat. One of these chemicals is insulin, which helps the body to use sugars properly.

A diabetic is a person whose body produces either too little, or an inactive supply of, insulin. Unless there is a proper balance of sugar and insulin, the body is unable to operate efficiently, and the person becomes ill. The treatment or control of this condition is based on either controlling the amount of sugar the body has to deal with, adding insulin from an outside source, or stimulating the body's natural insulin production in some way.

Diet is a diabetic's fundamental key to controlling the condition. Almost half the known diabetics have enough natural insulin to maintain satisfactory control by diet alone. Others are able to take pills that stimulate their insulin production. But many diabetics cannot survive without daily injections of insulin. However, with proper attention, the otherwise healthy diabetic can live and work in the same way as the nondiabetic.

Diabetes-related Problems

A diabetic coma usually occurs as a result of insulin withdrawal, or infection, and is sometimes aggravated by

Distinguishing Insulin Reactions and Diabetic Comas

Correctional officers should be aware of the ways to tell the difference between an insulin reaction and a diabetic coma:

	Insulin Reaction	Diabetic Coma
How it Starts	Suddenly	Gradually
Skin	Pale (may be moist)	Flushed, dry
Behavior	Disoriented (confused)	Drowsy
Breath	Normal	Fruity odor
Breathing	Normal to rapid	Deep, labored
Vomiting	Absent	Present
Tongue	Moist	Dry
Hunger	Present	Absent
Thirst	Absent	Present
Sugar in urine	Absent or slight	Large amounts

improper diet. An insulin reaction ("insulin shock") appears rapidly, and is much more common than a diabetic coma and is due to a dose of insulin that is in excess of the body's needs under the circumstances at the time. If a diabetic coma is suspected, immediate medical attention is mandatory; without treatment, a diabetic coma results in death.

Fortunately, most diabetics are familiar with their condition and are concerned about managing their lives in a way that will not aggravate the condition. In addition, most diabetes-related reactions are mild. Every diabetic who takes insulin should have some form of sugar available at all times to take in the event of an insulin reaction.

As a part of the diabetic's regular medical treatment program, food intake should be kept approximately constant from day to day. Some diabetics may receive a "fifth feeding" in the form of a sack meal to eat in their cell at bedtime to keep their food intake more constant throughout the day.

When an adverse insulin reaction is too rapid for the diabetic to be capable of self-help, sugar in some form should be given immediately. A lump of table sugar, a glass of fruit juice, a piece of candy, or a soft drink can serve the purpose. If the condition is not corrected, the diabetic may lose consciousness entirely. If a diabetic becomes unconscious for any reason, call for medical assistance immediately. A coma can become a serious or fatal threat to the life of a diabetic inmate if medical attention is not given immediately. A doctor is best qualified to establish the level of insulin intake.

Drug Abuse and Addiction

Drug addiction refers to the uncontrollable, usually harmful use of drugs. Alcohol, which is a drug, is described in the next section. A drug addict is someone who has a psychological or physical dependence on a chemical substance—a person who needs to experience the "lift" from a drug. There are many substances that can be abused, and each has a different effect on the people who use them; many are highly addictive.

The physical reason for drug addiction is thought to be the body adjusting its pattern of natural chemical use to the presence of the drug, so that it needs the drug to stay in balance; this results in a physical craving for the drug. The psychological reason for addiction is more complicated in many cases, but certainly involves an exaggerated feeling of well being that taking the drug produces.

In such a condition, people feel free from daily anxieties and problems that everyone has. The psychological need for this escape may cause the "cured" addict to return to drugs even after the physical need has been long gone. Addicts can be treated successfully. Unfortunately, most of them get treatment only when forced to by circumstances such as prison. In such cases, treatment may be less likely to work.

There are many drugs that can be abused; the most common categories include the following: narcotics, depressants (frequently barbiturates), stimulants (such as amphetamines and cocaine), and hallucinogens (such as LSD and PCP). Marijuana and hashish are also abused drugs, but the degree of psychological and physical dependence they present is not well established. Drug abusers or addicts often use these drugs in combination with alcohol. The abuse of any of these substances presents a serious problem in the institution.

Symptoms of Drug Use

Whatever the particular substance may be, there are certain signs that may indicate an inmate is using drugs: he or she may act silly; appear drowsy and move slowly; breathe very shallowly or rapidly and deeply; have very small or large pupils; speak slowly or slur speech; stagger or lack coordination; appear excited or overly active; be unable to sleep or concentrate; have little desire for food; and sweat greatly in cool temperatures.

In addition to these physical symptoms, drug addicts using needles frequently can be identified by the presence of punctures and scars on various parts of their body, usually their arms. Many addicts inject drugs directly in the large vein in the arm ("main line") and leave "main line scars" in the crook of their elbow. However, large dark tattoos could conceal needle scars.

If drug abuse by an inmate is suspected, the officer immediately should report this to a supervisor and, if practical, detain the inmate. Officers should be aware that extremes of behavior may occur when individuals are under the influence of drugs, and should use extreme care and caution when approaching such inmates. Institution policy should be followed if there is a need to subdue an inmate under the influence of drugs.

If drug abuse by an inmate is suspected, the officer immediately should report this to a supervisor and, if practical, detain the inmate.

Known addicts bear close watching because they may go to any length to procure or introduce drugs. The admission physical examination should be particularly thorough, for any body opening might be used to hide a "fix." Incoming mail and all other outside contacts should be scrutinized carefully. Addicts have been known to receive contraband drugs through very unusual methods, such as hidden under the stamps of their mail.

The Nature of Abused Drugs

Most narcotics are derived from opium. Addiction to them causes an intense physical craving; if addicts do not get their narcotics, they develop physical symptoms. Of the opium derivatives, heroin most easily causes addiction, and morphine is a close second. Demerol is another drug with considerable addictive potential. Codeine addiction also may occur but is less severe. Synthetic or "designer drugs" are available for the right price, and are extremely dangerous.

Correctional officers finding what they suspect to be controlled dangerous substances (CDS) immediately should report the find to supervision, but never taste (as

A large proportion of inmates have substance abuse problems and need help in overcoming them.

the television narcotic agents do), nor handle the substances without using protective gloves.

Unlike narcotics (such as morphine, heroin, demerol, and codeine), depressants (such as barbiturates used as sleeping pills) can affect the addicted person's brain and muscle control. Withdrawal symptoms may include anxiety, insomnia, tremors, delirium, convulsions, and possibly death.

In addition to drugs that produce a calming effect (sedatives) such as the opium derivatives and barbiturates, some people become addicted to stimulating drugs (amphetamines) like Benzedrine (called "goof balls"), preludin, cocaine, and others. On the street, the overstimulated, irritable, excited, restless, even psychotic conditions these drugs can cause, as well as the need for money to pay for them, may result in criminal offenses. In the institution, these drugs cause equally serious problem behavior. Withdrawal signs may include apathy, long periods of sleep, irritability, depression, and disorientation.

Hallucinogens (such as LSD and PCP) are drugs that may cause illusions, hallucinations, and poor perception of time and distance. Many PCP users have reacted to its use with acute psychotic episodes or unusually violent behavior that requires large numbers of staff to control, as well as the use of hard or soft restraints. Withdrawal signs have not been reported in the use of hallucinogens, but flashbacks can occur, where the person has signs of drug use possibly for years after having used a drug.

It is important to remember that an overdose of narcotics, depressants, stimulants, or hallucinogens can result in death. Medical assistance must be called immediately after finding an unconscious inmate who may have overdosed, so that properly trained individuals can attempt to revive the inmate.

Alcoholism

Many crimes are committed while under the influence of alcohol. Prolonged, excessive use of alcohol may cause not only criminal behavior, but also physical damage to the brain and other body organs. Some alcoholics experience relatively brief psychotic episodes, with panic and hallucinations (delirium tremens or "DTs"). DTs are actually physical withdrawal symptoms that appear when the alcoholic is unable to get a drink. In such cases, inmates are in serious need of medical care, because they may become dangerous to themselves or others. More severe alcoholics can develop permanent brain damage with accompanying memory difficulties and/or liver damage.

Being in prison or jail for short or even long terms is, by itself, no cure for alcoholism. Because of the severity of this difficulty, treatment of the alcoholic is a long-term procedure. The detoxification process (taking the person off the drug) must be conducted under medical care. In some institutions, qualified medical personnel prescribe medication to ease the withdrawing alcoholic's distress, or even maintain them on a drug such as Antabuse that will make them ill if they drink alcohol.

Some specific institutional issues that will be covered in local policy are the actual detoxification process for drunk inmates, the use of small, portable breathalyzer units to establish drunkenness, and the widespread security measures that are in place throughout the institution to search for and detect illegal "brew."

APPLICABLE ACA STANDARDS

Medical and Health Care Services: 3-4326 - 3-4379

BIBLIOGRAPHY

Beck, A.J., T. P. Bonczar, and D. K. Dilliard. 1993. "Jail Inmates 1992." Washington, D.C.: Bureau of Justice Statistics.

Camp, G. M. and C. G. Camp. 1989. "Management of Crowded Prisons." Washington D.C.: National Institute of Corrections.

Centers for Disease Control and Prevention. 1996. "Prevention and Control of Tuberculosis in Correctional Facilities." *Morbidity and Mortality Weekly Report*. June 7.

Hayes, L. M. and J. R. Rowan. 1988. *National Study of Jail Suicides: Seven Years Later*. Alexandria, Virginia: National Center on Institutions and Alternatives.

Lillis, J. 1994. "Prison Escapes and Violence Remain Down." *Corrections Compendium*. 29. June.

11

Inmates with Mental Illness

by John L. Gannon, Ph.D.

Correctional personnel face increasing demands to understand and appraise inmate behavior, particularly behavior that is related to physical health, mental health, and potential suicides. As the inmate population increases and gets older, and hospital beds for the mentally ill have been reduced, the number of persons with physical and mental health problems in correctional institutions has increased substantially. In addition, recent court cases in many jurisdictions have emphasized the considerable responsibilities that correctional institutions have in responding systematically and appropriately to problems in these areas. Consequently, correctional officers must continue to upgrade their skills in bringing such problems to the attention of health care professionals before inmates are harmed or institutions become legally liable.

Most inmates are able to adjust adequately to the psychological stresses of life in correctional institutions by using the normal coping strategies found among nonincarcerated populations. However, some inmates may engage in ineffective or self-destructive efforts to cope with life by overreacting to life's problems, or because of mild emotional problems, personality disorders, severe mental illnesses, or mental retardation. Correctional officers are not in a position to treat these conditions, but it is important to both the inmate and institution that officers appraise inmates' behavior well enough to respond to problems quickly, efficiently, and appropriately.

Crises Problems and Overreactions

Most inmates bring their own personal desires, expectations, and emotional investments in others with them to the institution. When these desires are frustrated, expectations are disappointed, or emotional bonds with others are broken through divorce or death, for example, inmates may respond with symptoms typical of emotional stress. Most of these symptoms, such as increased irritability, sleep disturbances, or changes in appetite will diminish or disappear within a short period. However, in some cases, the response to stress may be more intense and may require that an inmate's situation be brought to the attention of mental health professionals.

Specific responses to life-stressors cannot be predicted for all inmates. Nonetheless, routine and commonsense observations about changes in behavior can be helpful in determining when the inmate's adjustments to life changes are not within the normal response range. Routine attention always should be paid to significant changes in how inmates interact with other inmates or with correctional staff. Brief changes in energy levels, facial expressions, ability to concentrate, topics of conversation, or other daily habits, and complaints of physical problems, or anxiety and depression may be signs that an inmate is undergoing unusual stress. If these symptoms persist, they should be brought to the attention of mental health professionals.

Some inmates will have adopted longstanding, persistent, dysfunctional patterns of dealing with the anxieties associated with living life. These patterns are sometimes referred to as neuroses, and can be thought of as the mildest form of mental illness.

People who overreact to life's problems with severe anxiety often are upset easily and continually worried about the future; some may shake and sweat (have anxiety attacks) or experience unreasonable fears (phobias) about people, places, things, or events. They may become overly concerned about illnesses, making

Correctional officers must know what to do both to prevent suicide and what to do if they find an inmate who is hanging.

numerous medical complaints, and in extreme cases, by even becoming temporarily paralyzed or blind.

Everyone has disturbing thoughts from time to time. But for some people, irrational or unreasonable thoughts—particularly those related to sexual taboos or aggression toward others—may lead to severe anxiety reactions. Even though these thoughts may never be acted upon, these thoughts may become very distressing to the individual who is experiencing them.

In response to various anxieties, some individuals may feel strongly driven to act in unreasonable and unproductive ways. Although anyone can be excessively concerned about details at times, such as being especially neat or precise when it is not needed, for instance, repeated or persistent compulsions to behave in certain inappropriate ways can become serious obstacles to leading a normal life and, in some instances, can become debilitating.

Some compulsions can lead directly to criminal acts and incarceration. The uncontrollable desire to set fires (pyromania) or to steal indiscriminately (kleptomania), for instance are criminal compulsions. Others may be compelled to act out their sexual or aggressive urges in ways that they seemingly cannot control. It is believed that compulsive behaviors or misbehaviors partially ease the tension that results from unresolved internal conflicts. Although the discomfort these people feel is a product of their mental processes, the discomfort itself is real. The role of the correctional officer is to neither ignore it nor reward it.

Suicide Risk

Correctional officers should pay particular attention to indications that inmates may feel that they have exhausted their ability to cope adequately with life-stressors and are considering suicide. Suicide is more likely to occur in correctional settings than outside for a number of reasons.

First, a large percentage of the correctional population is thought to have a higher rate of suicide-prone behavior than unconfined populations. In the community, alcoholics, drug addicts, and sex offenders are known to have higher than normal rates of suicide, and there is a higher concentration of these types of people in correctional facilities. Second, the intention to commit suicide may be a reaction to the life-crisis caused by the person's criminal behavior and subsequent incarceration. Third, the correctional environment itself can be a direct contributor to suicidal behavior. The authoritarian environment, isolation from family and friends, shame of being incarcerated, and the basic dehumanizing aspects of being in prison all can lead to increases in the likelihood of suicide in the correctional setting.

Suicides occur most frequently during the early periods of incarceration. Screening for potential suicides is crucial in all correctional settings. Any person with a history of attempting suicide or making threats related to suicide or other forms of self-harm should be brought to the attention of supervisors and observed carefully. Other people, including those arrested or convicted of a capital offense, particularly extensive or repulsive sex crimes, or high-publicity cases may represent a significant suicide risk even though no suicide statements or gestures have been made.

Signs of increased suicide risk include depression, a decrease in interest in the surroundings, expressions of hopelessness and helplessness, withdrawal from others, discussions or threats of self-harm, and giving away valued objects that they believe they will no longer need.

Paradoxically, an increase in energy and improved mood in someone who has been significantly depressed can signal an increase in suicide potential. Many people who are severely depressed lack the energy or focus to follow through on thoughts of suicide. If they finally come to a decision to end their lives, that decision may relieve them of many other fears of the future, and they may become energized and cheerful in the belief that their current problems soon will be over.

Some inmates make suicide attempts to gain staff attention; others mutilate themselves or swallow unusual objects to accomplish the same thing. Unfortunately, many of these gestures unintentionally can turn into a fatal act.

Even when inmates' statements sound unconvincing, they should be responded to appropriately. No matter how attention-seeking the person may seem to be, acts, gestures, or statements reflecting suicidal intent must be taken seriously. Even when an inmate only seems to be threatening suicide, close surveillance is warranted, and an immediate referral to the appropriate supervisor or mental health professional is indicated.

Suicidal thoughts, gestures, and behavior typically are inadequate responses to life-crises and are not in themselves mental illnesses. However, people with more severe mental illnesses, such as psychoses or mood disorders, may engage in similar or even more bizarre self-destructive kinds of behavior, and correctional officers may save lives and avoid institutional problems if they recognize the essential features of major psychiatric disturbances.

Psychoses

Psychosis is a severe form of mental illness that is reflected in disturbances in the contents of a person's thoughts, in the form or quality of the person's thoughts, in perceptions of the outside world, or in combinations of these three.

Some people who are psychotic display distortions in the contents of their thoughts. That is, they have delusions—unreasonable, false beliefs that are maintained firmly even when contradicted by reality. They falsely may believe that they are the objects of a persecution or conspiracy to harm them, or that they are the subject of newspaper stories or radio broadcasts when they are not. People who think their thoughts and actions are controlled by others suffer delusions of influence, while those who falsely believe that they are unusually skillful, famous, or noteworthy are exhibiting delusions of grandeur. Their ideas can range from mistakenly thinking they are particularly good artists to believing that they can read minds, or are descendants of distinguished families, or that they are God.

Distortions in the contents of a person's thought can occur by itself, but they also may be accompanied by disturbances in the form or quality of the person's thinking processes. Their ideas may be normal, but the expressions of those ideas may become garbled and difficult to understand. They may speak rapidly, jumping from thought to thought so quickly that the listener is left far behind. They may make remarks that do not fit with the topic of conversation, or they may create entirely new words or use words in such a personal way that their meaning is unintelligible.

Hallucinations are disturbances in a person's perceptual experiences. People who are psychotic frequently hear, see, feel, taste, or smell things that are not there. Hearing "voices" is the most frequent form of hallucination, but many psychotic inmates see visions of things that are not really there, as well.

Understanding mental health issues will enable a correctional officer to work more effectively with a wide range of inmates.

The content of delusions and hallucinations can vary widely, from believing one has written best-selling songs and has millions of dollars in the bank as a result, to hearing the "voice" of God, to seeing the face of a murdered victim on the cell wall. Delusional beliefs and genuine experiences of hallucinations are often very distressing to these individuals, and their distress is often accompanied by appropriate behavioral and emotional responses. Claims to delusional beliefs or perceptual disturbances that are offered nonchalantly or with context-inappropriate emotion, such as being angry that special housing is not forthcoming instead of fearful when discussing apparently paranoid delusions, may reflect attempts to manipulate the correctional environment. However, such problems are potentially serious enough that correctional officers should consult with mental health staff before ruling such behavior as malingering.

People who are psychotic may experience emotional reactions that are exaggerated or distorted, sometimes to the degree that these individuals may stop moving or talking. On the other hand, their despair can be so great that they pace, wring their hands, or cry out in suffering or guilt. Others fail to exhibit any emotional reaction at all, even during joyous or tragic situations, or exhibit responses directly opposite of what one normally expects, such as laughing over the death of a loved one, or crying when they hear good news. They even may show mixed emotions by crying and laughing at the same time.

Correctional Officer Resource Guide

In general, indicators of psychosis fall into two broad categories: positive and negative signs. The positive signs of psychoses include speech and language disturbances, inappropriate emotions, delusions, and hallucinations. Negative signs include withdrawal from others, restricted facial expressions, slow movements, and unusually poor personal or cell hygiene. The more positive and negative signs that are present, the more likely that a person is suffering a major psychosis.

Gross distortions of speech, peculiar or bizarre behavior, and unusual deviances from ordinary institutional routines may provide clues to correctional officers about the psychological impairments of mentally ill inmates. Refusal to leave the cell or to take any meals in the dining room may reflect paranoid delusions of physical harm or poisoning, and easy distractibility or difficulty in concentration, in the context of other symptoms, may reflect auditory hallucinations. These and similar kinds of behavior should be reported to a supervisor or mental health professional to determine if additional mental health evaluation or treatment is appropriate.

Mood Disorders

Mood refers to the emotional states that color a person's whole personality and psychological life. Severe disorders of mood are considered major mental disorders. Disorders of mood are focused on those times when, though nothing particularly bad or good has happened recently, some individuals feel excessively sad and melancholy on the one hand or overly exuberant, positive, and energetic on the other.

In the first case, individuals may lose their appetite, have trouble sleeping, and suffer a general decline in interest in sex, companionship, or daily activities. While their thinking processes are usually clear, and they can respond appropriately to questions, their facial expressions often are restricted to a minimum, and they may move and talk slowly. Sometimes, they will spend significant periods of time

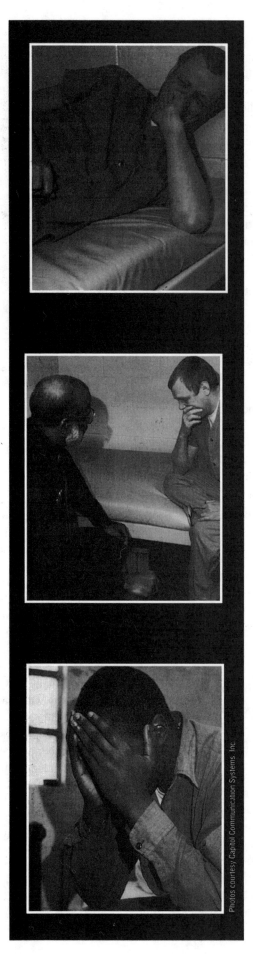

Photos courtesy Capitol Communication Systems, Inc.

lying in bed or sitting and staring at the wall. They may lose a significant amount of weight, and occasionally, they will be agitated or easily irritated.

These people are depressed, and they should be referred to a mental health professional as soon as possible. While most people who are depressed do not commit suicide, many depressed patients have recurrent thoughts of death, and a significant number of depressed patients attempt suicide or make plans to do so.

In the second case, persons may have an excess of energy. They often seem to have a strong urgency to talk, and they speak very rapidly, continuing even when they have been requested or ordered to stop. They may act out aggressively or sexually. These individuals often express grandiose delusions, such as completely unrealistic plans for the future or claims to numerous kinds of superior abilities, associations with celebrities, or personal achievements. Claims that they are affiliated with the FBI or that they have to be released to fulfill a recording contract in Hollywood are common.

These people are *manic*, and a true and severe manic episode will be identified easily by the excessive speech, high energy level, and difficulty staff have in redirecting the individual to conform to institutional rules. Low-level manic episodes are not identified as easily, but observations of unusually grandiose beliefs or other behavior consistent with the prior indicators should be reported to supervisors and mental health staff, in severe cases immediately. Manic episodes easily can escalate, and may lead to dangerous conditions for the individual, for other inmates, and for the correctional staff.

Personality Disorders

The disorders of personality are additional, diagnosable categories of psychological functioning. These disorders are not major mental illnesses, but they may be very troublesome for the individual and the institution, and they may precede major mental illnesses.

People with personality disorders tend to act out their personal distress in the social environment, and they often get into trouble as a result. Although they usually are not bothered by their own behavior and the problems it causes, they typically have difficulty adjusting to life and often resort to alcohol, drugs, or criminal behavior.

There are several types of personality disorders, but one of most interest in the correctional setting is known as the *antisocial personality*. These "rebels without a cause" often clash with society, and have lifelong histories of legal and other conflicts; they seem immune from learning the appropriate lessons from their earlier experiences. They also have difficulty postponing satisfaction of their impulses and seem to live only for the pleasure of the moment. It appears that their inability to endure tension and frustration interferes with their ability to adjust to routine tasks over a long period of time. Consequently, their work histories and institutional adjustment are likely to be erratic and unstable.

Antisocial persons live a pattern of bravado and risk taking. Since they tend toward extremes, they may commit outrageous acts that a sensible person would never consider. This inclination for risk taking makes them dangerous. Some antisocial people are pathological liars, that is, they lie for the pleasure of lying, for the pleasure of putting something over on someone, or for

Mentally retarded inmates may become the victims of more aggressive inmates, and correctional officers need to understand how to deal most effectively with inmates who are retarded.

getting attention or sympathy by a wild story. When confronted by contradictions or by clear evidence of their lies, the antisocial person is likely to casually ignore them. Although they are callous and contemptuous of others, seeing people more as objects and not as human beings, sophisticated antisocial individuals can create the appearance of reasonableness, friendliness, and charm that may be quite persuasive, and they may use their charm as subtle agitators and underminers of authority.

Among the other personality disorders, the two most noticeable in institutions are the emotionally unstable personality and the passive-aggressive personality. *Emotionally unstable people* (borderline personality disorders) characteristically lack personal control. They panic easily in emergencies. They may have problems in sexual or self-identity, and they may display explosive tempers. They cannot seem to cope with their own difficulties. Their poor judgment prevents them from forming lasting relationships with other people, and they fear abandonment. They are often genuinely sorry for their misdeeds, and feel guilty and anxious about them, but they cannot be relied upon to avoid them in the future.

Passive-aggressive personalities have difficulty expressing anger or aggression directly, relying instead on indirect ways of expressing hostility. They may engage in willful inefficiency at work, by slowing down or developing a curious "inability" to understand instruction. Typically, these people pout and shake their heads to communicate their disapproval. Firm emotional control is needed in dealing with them because they are skillful in irritating others by their indirect delaying or sabotaging tactics and ill-concealed resistance.

There are a number of other types of personality disorders that are less likely to be the direct cause of difficulties in the institution. *Cyclothymic personalities*

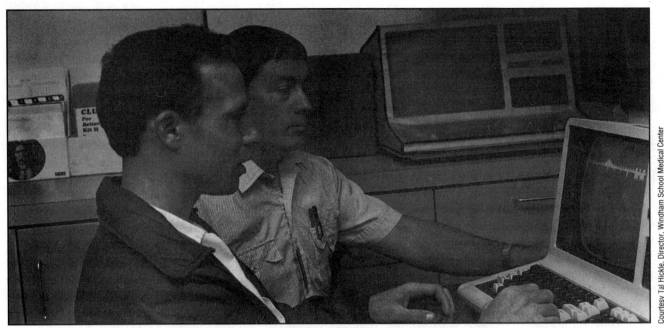
Directions to retarded inmates need to be stated slowly and simply and may need to be repeated several times.

tend to alternate between being depressed and feeling an exaggerated sense of well-being. They tend to be rather friendly, outgoing people who, because of their bubbling energy, if they are well organized, can put in a good day's work. However, they lose much of what they gain when they become depressed, and they can get into legal difficulties if their optimism overreaches them.

People with a *schizoid personality* are aloof, given to excessive daydreaming, and are unassertive. These people avoid getting emotionally involved with others. They, often but not always, are identifiable in correctional institutions by their isolation from other inmates, not so much because they are rejected, but because they prefer to be alone.

People with *paranoid personalities* are suspicious of other people and their motives. They characteristically project their own motives of envy, jealousy, and hostility onto other people, expecting the worst from others because of their own strong negative feelings. In a correctional institution, paranoid personalities can be troublemakers when they seize on petty incidents to "prove" they have been badly used or to show how things have been mismanaged. They can be vindictive and grudge-bearing. Paranoid inmates are fearful people who may retaliate against perceived threats, so they can represent a danger to correctional staff. However, given that violence among inmates is common, an inmate's fears that other inmates are out to "get" him or her may be justified, and such a complaint should not be taken automatically as a sign of mental illness.

Mentally Retarded Inmates

Mentally ill persons suffer from some form of disrupted functioning of their otherwise normal minds. The *mentally retarded*, however, are unable to adequately cope with life problems due to their below-average intellectual ability—they simply do not have the mental capacity to function normally.

Many inmates test low on intelligence tests, but this may be a cultural factor, reflecting poor test-taking skills or a lack of facts about today's society; they nevertheless may be "street smart." However, the mentally retarded person lacks a certain basic mental capacity, and therefore cannot deal with the world in a normal way. To complicate matters, there are different degrees of retardation, and mentally retarded people also can become mentally ill.

Some mentally retarded inmates are incapable of learning to deal effectively with the world in an independent fashion. They are suggestible, and may be led easily into crimes. They are easy "marks" for the shrewd operator, and need to be protected. They may be victimized in the correctional setting in any number of ways, such as by sexual assault or pressure or by holding or running drugs.

Ideally, mentally retarded individuals should not be housed in prisons; unfortunately, some are. When identified, every effort should be made to place these individuals in an appropriate noncorrectional setting. In the meantime, officers should deal patiently and firmly with mentally retarded inmates, recognizing their limitations. Communications with them must be clear, stated one step at a time. Some are capable of learning to work in routine, supervised tasks. They should not be placed in work situations that demand more of them than their basic ability permits. It may be necessary to place them in a separate housing area or even in a locked unit.

Whatever their intellectual limitations may be, the mentally retarded inmate is entitled to the same respect that any other person would get. These inmates should be protected from the contempt of staff or the ribbing of other inmates.

Dealing with Mentally Ill and Retarded Inmates

Although a mentally disturbed person's retreat from the real world may not be obvious at first, his or her ineffectiveness in dealing with life often is. The strange behavior that they may not be able to control is sometimes seen and described as faking or malingering. This can create a dilemma for correctional staff. In general, the best strategy is to take the statements and behavior at face value, at least until the actual condition is confirmed by responsible medical or mental health staff.

Remember, if officers incorrectly manage mentally retarded or emotionally disturbed inmates and treat them as malingerers, the inmates' misperceptions about the world and their ability to get help for themselves actually may worsen their condition and create liability for the officer and the institution. Facts about an inmate's behavior, appearance, and verbal expressions, not just opinions, should be noted by officers to contribute to an evaluation. How individuals act when they believe they are unobserved is particularly important.

Medication and Treatment

The treatment of each of these conditions is far too complicated to spell out in this publication. Mental health and medical staff are responsible for deciding the best course of action in each individual case. They also are responsible for seeing that correctional staff are aware of the specific problem cases in the institution population and the best day-to-day strategies for managing them.

Group and individual counseling is used with some inmates. However, in many instances, it is beyond the institution's resources to provide the intense therapy thought to be necessary to treat many of these difficult cases. The most severe cases should be referred for confinement in a mental health treatment facility.

For some conditions, medications are available to help the inmate control the problem behavior or to function more normally. Staff need to be aware that general population inmates may tease or annoy inmates who are taking medication to control their condition. As a result, the inmate may stop taking the medication. Inmates on medication should be observed closely by staff, and they should be monitored to be sure they keep taking their medicine.

One point of clarification in the area of mental health staff may be useful—the difference between a psychologist and a psychiatrist. A *psychologist* is a trained professional mental health worker who may have earned a master's degree or doctorate degree in clinical psychology and specializes in treating people with some type of emotional or mental disturbance. A *psychiatrist* is a medical doctor who has received additional training specific to the treatment of people with mental health problems. A psychiatrist can prescribe medication for patients, while a psychologist may not.

Summary

Correctional officers need to be aware of the psychological functioning of inmates under their control, and they need to know basic and appropriate ways of responding to mental problems. Correctional officers are not responsible for diagnosing and treating inmates' mental illnesses or personality disorders. However, because officers work so closely with inmates, their observation can be very useful to those who are responsible for diagnosing and treating them.

APPLICABLE ACA STANDARDS

Medical and Health Care Services: 3-4326 - 3-4379

BIBLIOGRAPHY

Bayse, Daniel. 1995. *Working in Jails and Prisons: Becoming Part of the Team.* Lanham, Maryland: American Correctional Association.

12

Reception, Orientation, and Classification of Inmates

New inmates arrive at the institution after a series of what most people would consider very disturbing events. They have been arrested, detained, tried in court, convicted of a crime, and committed to prison. Well-organized reception and orientation programs lessen inmates' shock at being confined and hasten adjustment to institutional living.

Reception Activities

The importance of thorough intake processing cannot be overstated. The primary focus is to properly identify and search inmates and all incoming personal property. In some institutions, after this initial intake processing, newly admitted inmates are placed in a quarantine section for ten days to two weeks, where they undergo thorough physical examinations, including blood tests, X-rays, inoculations, and vaccinations. A complete social history may be taken at this stage, including information about the inmates, their families, and other pertinent background facts.

Officers assigned to the receiving area perform many, if not all, of the following duties:

- Determine that the individual is legally committed to the institution

- Assign a register number to the inmate

- Completely search the individual and his or her possessions, paying particular attention to all clothing items—seams or cuffs on trouser legs, waistbands, zippers, small (watch) pockets, and all other pockets

- Mark contraband (weapons, narcotics, alcohol) properly, and process it according to institutional policy

- Dispose of all medications the inmate arrives with, following established institutional procedures

- Issue an appropriate receipt for any funds in the inmate's possession, and properly store the money in a secure area

- Appropriately search all property and dispose of forbidden personal property by storing it or shipping it to someone in the community, noting any damaged property on an inventory form

- Issue clean, properly fitted clothing, as needed

- Arrange shower and hair care for the inmate, if necessary

- Photograph and fingerprint the inmate, noting on a form any marks or other unusual physical characteristics

- Arrange medical, dental, and mental health screening

- Assign the inmate to a housing area

- Record personal data and information about the inmate to be used to create mail and visiting lists and explain procedures for mail and visiting

- Help inmates notify next of kin and families of their arrival and the institution's address

- Give written orientation materials to new inmates

- Make an immediate decision on whether the inmate has any enemies or persons from whom he or she should be separated in the institution, and take appropriate steps to safeguard the inmate, if needed

Correctional Officer Resource Guide

Fingerprinting an inmate is one of the initial intake steps.

Many of these same functions also are performed when an inmate is released. At this stage, inmates are properly identified, release authorizations are verified, inmates and property are thoroughly searched, and funds are issued, if authorized.

Admission and Orientation

Admission and orientation programs usually last about two weeks for transfer cases, and up to a month for new commitments. These programs often include classes, reviews of rules and regulations, and discussions about institutional programs and procedures. New inmates may be allowed to work, read, exercise, and attend religious services. In some states, orientation programs may be conducted in the quarantine area.

During the admission and orientation process, staff should:

- Explain institutional rules and regulations, provide a written copy of those materials (translated into the inmate's language, if necessary), and have the inmate sign a form that he or she has received the inmate handbook

- Describe available programs, their goals, and how inmates are accepted into them

- Administer tests that identify special interests, talents, or problems

- Document that the inmate has completed all phases of the orientation program

Naturally, new inmates are unfamiliar with institution rules and staff expectations. During the orientation process, staff members explain to new inmates, as well as those transferred from other institutions, how the prison operates and what will be expected of them.

During orientation, new inmates may be taken on a guided tour of the institution and then interviewed by representatives from the education, industrial, custodial, recreational, program, and religious departments. During this period, inmates may be examined by the medical staff, tested by a psychiatrist, counselor, or caseworker, who may discuss the inmate's health, family, and personal problems.

This evaluation process is vital, because the inmate's adjustment to prison is largely affected by these factors. The early days of imprisonment are difficult for inmates, particularly first offenders, who are getting the "feel" of the institution. In some prisons, counselors or caseworkers are involved in orienting the individual to the program; in others, the unit officer has that responsibility. Three goals of orientation include the following: (1) to familiarize inmates with the institution's expectations; (2) to give staff an opportunity to learn more about the inmate for classification purposes; and (3) to help inmates feel that someone is interested in helping them adjust.

At the end of the admission and orientation program, the information gathered by the staff is forwarded to the institution's classification committee or a unit team for use in the classification process.

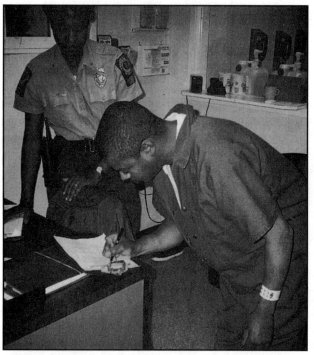

Keeping track of an inmate's property is an important task of the correctional officer.

Special Intake Cases

Some inmates require special handling immediately upon arrival in the institution. While local procedures for these cases will differ, it is important to mention the most common types:

Suicide Risks. The first hours and days of a new inmate's prison experience can be filled with fear and tension. For some, the humiliation of imprisonment is almost unbearable; for others, pressures from other inmates can be overwhelming. Correctional staff in orientation and receiving areas should be very alert to the signs of depression or presuicidal behavior mentioned in Chapter 11 of this *Guide*. Staff should be trained in the policy and procedures for handling potentially suicidal inmates and providing proper supervision and care.

Protective Custody Cases. When inmates come into the institution and declare themselves to be needing protective custody, or when reliable information is received that a new inmate may be in danger, the intake or admission and orientation staff should be prepared to take special supervision and security precautions until the degree of risk is evaluated and the inmate is removed, if necessary, to a safe, secure area.

Medical Isolation Cases (perhaps including AIDS cases). Each institution will have medical standards for screening and isolating incoming cases. These standards ordinarily require intake staff to notify medical personnel immediately if an incoming inmate displays or reports any key symptom or unusual medical history.

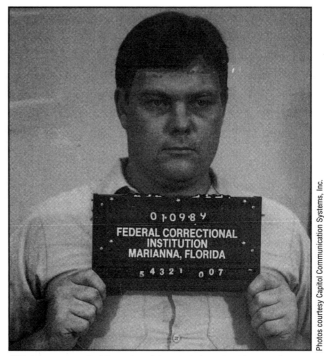
Obtaining a current picture of each inmate is important for security.

Immediate transfer to the institution hospital usually is followed by a modified orientation program conducted there, rather than in the orientation unit. In correctional systems that house AIDS patients separately, an orientation program often is conducted right in the AIDS unit.

Special Management of High-security Cases. These high-risk escape or violent inmates often are identified in advance as ultra-high-security cases. For them, the processing must involve extra staff, perhaps the use of restraints, and in most cases, a modified orientation program conducted for them while they are in a locked unit. Staff safety and institutional security must be the first concerns in handling these cases.

Parole Violators. These inmates may have returned to the institution for a violation hearing, or be there following such a hearing. If they have been in the institution before, a shortened orientation program often is used.

Classification Procedures

Classifying inmates is not, as some believe, simply separating inmates into different types and assigning them to institutions. *Classification* is a multistage process designed to fulfill three objectives: (1) to assess inmates' backgrounds and behavior to assign them to appropriately secure institutions and to appropriate levels of supervision; (2) to develop a program plan with each inmate, based on a prior assessment; and (3) to make certain that each inmate's progress is periodically evaluated and, if necessary, to modify the program and custody level.

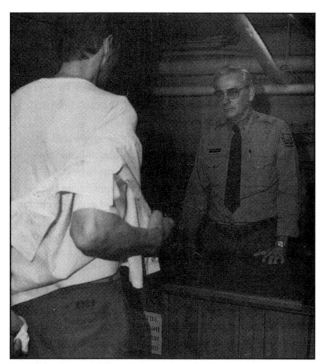
Most prisons issue clothing to inmates and the inmates are then responsible for this clothing.

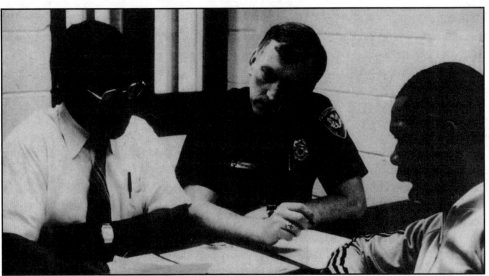
Classification involves a review of an inmate's background, security, and program needs.
Courtesy Don Bales

Proper classification ensures that inmates are confined in the least restrictive, appropriate facility without presenting an undue risk to the public, staff, or other inmates. Inmates should not receive more surveillance, or be kept in a more secure institution, than required by the level of risk they present. Keeping inmates of generally the same level of security and aggressiveness in one institution greatly reduces the likelihood of serious management problems (as opposed to a situation where weak and strong, high-escape and low-escape risk cases are all together).

Classification Approaches

Classification can be handled in several ways. In some correctional systems, all new inmates are sent to a reception and diagnostic facility where staff from various specialty areas (such as psychology, health services, social services, and education) interview, test, and evaluate each inmate. From the information they gather, staff decide where to send the inmate to serve the initial part of the sentence as well as decide on the programs the inmate needs. In other systems, cases are prescreened using probation or other court documents, and the decision on where to send the inmate is made while he or she is still in the jail or on bond. In some small systems, where only one institution serves an entire state, the inmates simply are sent to the institution's reception and diagnostic unit and, while there, evaluated for housing and custody.

In these latter two cases, the classification team (or in some cases, a unit team) begins by analyzing the problems presented by each individual. The team reviews inmates' criminal, social, and medical histories; studies individuals' psychiatric/psychological examinations; and evaluates their vocational, religious, and recreational backgrounds. In most systems, the inmates participate in this process by assessing their own needs and, to a degree, selecting programs to meet those needs.

This analysis for classification purposes can be done in one of several ways. Traditionally, classification committees have reviewed the available information, and based on their professional, subjective judgment (that is, not using any fixed or predefined rules) decided the inmate's institutional destination (if transfer is an option), custody classification, housing assignment, job, and programs.

In more sophisticated systems, however, the committee or unit team reviews a set of predetermined factors to help staff make these decisions. In some cases, agency staff gather the court information in advance and evaluate it using a security scoring form to decide where the inmate initially will be confined. When an inmate arrives at the designated institution, the additional information gathered during orientation is used to make any adjustments in assignment, as well as for other internal management decisions.

The advantage of this latter system is that it is consistent. It removes the element of personal bias from the classification process. The best systems allow staff to override a numerically determined score if, in their professional judgment, the inmate requires more or less security than the form indicates; the reasons for such overrides must be documented.

There also are classification approaches that subdivide prison populations to improve internal management, but a detailed description of them is beyond the scope of this publication. Generally, they serve the same purpose—to keep inmates with similar behavior characteristics in the same housing units, where they get along better with each other than if mixed with all other types of individuals.

Classification Policies

No matter which system is used, classification policies must include, at a minimum:

- A description of the membership of the unit, team, or institutional classification committee(s), as well as the duties and responsibilities of each member

- Detailed descriptions of procedures for classifying and reclassifying inmates, and for documenting the results of the process
- Procedures for transferring inmates from one program to another, or from one institution to another
- Provision for a transcript or some other record of the classification or team action on every case; these records can help parole authorities to evaluate whether an inmate can or should return to the community

Classification Committees

Who is on the committee? The makeup of the classification committee or unit team depends, of course, on the staff available. Members of classification teams are generally department heads and specialists concerned primarily with diagnosis, training, treatment, and custody of the inmates. They may be associate wardens in charge of treatment or custody, supervisors of classification, education, and vocational training, and/or the head social worker or sociologist. The chief medical officer, counselor, psychiatrist, psychologist, chaplain, and officers in charge of the admission and orientation unit also may sit on the committee.

Large institutions must avoid establishing large committees that occupy the time of too many staff members. Where the classification and reclassification load is heavy, it may be necessary to form a subcommittee to handle this process. Conversely, in institutions with limited staff, one committee member may assume the functions ordinarily carried out by members from more than one department. Whether there are one or more classification committees, it is important that the committee represent each service or department so that an accurate profile of the inmate is established and a well-rounded program devised.

Unit Teams

Who is on the unit team? In an institution that uses unit management, the unit team handles almost all of the functions of the classification committee. The team ordinarily consists of the unit manager, case manager, unit education representative, unit psychologist, and unit officer. This group is responsible for making almost all of the initial and reclassification decisions regarding inmates, including recommendations for parole.

Inventory processing on admission requires noting which items are to be held for inmates, which are sent to the inmate's home, which are to be destroyed, and which, if any, are to be held for evidence.

Correctional officers who maintain accurate records can make a valuable contribution to the classification process. The information contained in them is used by classification committees and unit teams to make vital decisions concerning inmates.

Summary

The way that inmates are received and classified can affect their institutional adjustment during confinement. During this initial process, staff assess inmates, assign them, and work with them to develop program plans. Proper admission, orientation, and classification procedures help correctional officers by ensuring that inmates are properly screened, are confined in appropriate facilities, know the rules, and are aware of the programs that best meet their needs.

APPLICABLE ACA STANDARDS

Classification: 3-4282 - 3-4293

Reception and Orientation: 3-4272 - 3-4281

BIBLIOGRAPHY

Henderson, James D. and Richard Phillips. 1991. *Classification: A Tool for Managing Today's Offenders.* Lanham, Maryland: American Correctional Association.

Quay, Herbert C., Ph.D. 1984. *Managing Adult Inmates: Classification for Housing and Program Assignment.* Lanham, Maryland: American Correctional Association.

13

Programming and Related Services

For most of the history of corrections in America, the idea of institutional programs meant only the activity necessary to maintain custody of inmates, and perhaps some simple work for them. As thinking about the causes of crime gradually changed, ideas about institutional programs also changed. Now, it is generally believed that in a much broader sense, programs are an important part of any institution's operation and even its security.

Correctional institutions today are geared to protecting society first, and then to providing a safe, humane place to confine inmates—a place where they can find the resources to change their lives if they want to do so. Officers are primarily responsible for the first part of this goal, providing secure and safe confinement. But even in the last area—providing opportunities for change—officers can help.

Program Models

First, some background is helpful. For many years corrections used a model for its "treatment" programs called "the medical model" (Roberts 1997). This involved assuming that professionally trained staff could identify the causes of inmates' criminal behavior and tell the inmate how to change through participation in certain programs, just as a medical doctor diagnoses a patient's illness and prescribes medicine or other treatment to cure the condition. Criminal behavior was thought to be curable in that way, and long-range "treatment" was intended to send offenders back into the community as useful, law-abiding citizens for the rest of their lives.

This opinion is less widely held now—in the era of the "balanced" model—than in the past, although there are many staff who still think this is a sound approach to prison management, and many excellent programs still operate on this basis. However, now the institution's responsibility is more commonly thought to be to provide the broadest possible range of program options for inmates, to steer them to those that appear to deal with any basic needs they have (such as educational or vocational training), and then to let the inmates decide whether to participate.

Most correctional staff understand that offering a variety of institutional programs actually helps them manage the institution more effectively.

The underlying thought here is that, "You can lead a horse to water, but you cannot make it drink." Put directly, there is no way for institutional staff to force inmates to change if they do not want to, and there are some inmates who very plainly do not want to change. For them, most correctional professionals believe that protection of society is a valid reason for confinement, and the job of correctional staff is limited to providing safe, humane conditions of confinement. This is not to say that counseling and other support services are not important, but for many corrections professionals, the time of prescribed "treatment" is largely gone.

Fortunately, the days of the custody/treatment disagreements are largely over. Most program staff realize that effective programs cannot exist in a disorderly, dangerous institution. Most correctional staff understand that offering a variety of institutional programs actually helps them manage the institution more effectively. In short, these two main segments of the institutional community need each other.

Finally, it is also important to note another trend, the movement toward ensuring equal program opportunities for female inmates. In the past, institutions have not provided the same range of programs and services to female inmates as to males. In the face of other, broader trends in society, and an increasing number of court cases on this point, correctional agencies are making equivalent programs available for female inmates.

Given these facts, what should a correctional officer do? It must be confusing to the new correctional officer to figure out just what his or her role should be. It also should be apparent that the custody officer is not alone in the effort to return the offender to society with the best possible chances of remaining a productive member of the free society. Administrators play a crucial role in deciding what programs are realistic and important to have (Lauen 1997).

In fact, there is much for institutions to do to help the offender get reintegrated into society postrelease, and programs are a valuable part of this in the prison setting. Inmates typically are educationally and vocationally unprepared for functioning in today's society. They often have poorly developed social and interpersonal skills. There are many ways that personal change can prepare inmates to function lawfully upon return to society, if they want to do so. And it is in those areas that institutions are focusing their efforts. Correctional officers can help by encouraging the "fence sitting" inmate to take advantage of academic/vocational training and to maintain a positive attitude while in any institutional program.

Social or Casework Services

Although providing for the public safety is the primary mission of correctional institutions, it would be short-sighted to think that simply locking up offenders fulfills this role. The majority of inmates will be returned to society. Therefore, it is important to provide programs which give inmates the opportunity to make personal changes and improve their chance to succeed within the mainstream of society. These programs can address basic needs such as education and vocational training or more personal issues such as reactive thinking and anger management.

To assist in providing these services, most institutions provide a case management, social service, guidance, or unit team system. Sometimes, these can be separate departments with specific responsibilities. However, the bottom line is that an individualized program should be developed for each inmate.

American Correctional Association standards describe a system that ensures inmates receive attention to their individual needs, in which each is assigned to a counselor or member of a unit management team. In this way, each inmate can be assured access to at least one employee for advice and assistance.

Employees assigned to provide case management services should have sufficient training and experience to provide guidance. Correctional officers or other untrained staff may provide informal counseling on institutional adjustment issues. However, when faced with personal problems or other noninstitutional concerns, they should refer the inmate to the appropriate staff.

Some inmates find it difficult to completely trust the badge-wearing staff member. Case management or social services staff may provide individual counseling for some issues. However, due to the personality of most inmates, group therapy is a more effective method of intervention for confronting personal change.

Reality-based cognitive therapy is seen as more successful than traditional long-term psychotherapy. In addition, social workers may be involved in release-planning services for individuals who have serious medical or mental health conditions. Providing linkage to appropriate agencies in the community will assist the inmate in receiving the care needed. With the increase in HIV/AIDS and increases in the geriatric population, more emphasis on release-planning services is needed.

Separate social services files on inmates are kept to protect confidential material. Generally, inmates will have to sign a release of information to share this information with others. However, inmates are informed that confidentiality is limited and will not be honored when the security of the institution is threatened or if a threat exists to the safety of the inmate or others. Information of a nonconfidential nature can be placed in the inmate's general institutional file.

Social services staff may be involved in crisis intervention. However, for more seriously disturbed inmates, some type of mental health unit is needed. This could involve social services, psychology, and medical staff and would involve services and specially trained staff not needed by the general population.

Education

Educational programs often assume special importance in correctional facilities. There is an inverse link between education and recidivism. Generally, the more education an inmate has, the less likely he or she is to return to crime. Often, inmates' educational backgrounds are seriously deficient: a large number of inmates lack a high school diploma, and many others have less than a sixth-grade education.

A sound institutional education program should provide a well-rounded general education. It should offer a variety of programs including the following: the Adult Basic Education (ABE) program, for inmates who have not attained an eighth-grade education; the General Education Diploma (GED) program, so that inmates can work toward their high school equivalency diploma; a postsecondary education program for those who have successfully completed high school to further their education; and continuing education courses for those who want to update their skills and knowledge. Many facilities also offer courses in life skills.

Teaching in a correctional setting requires a certain breed of professional. Inmates who have failed throughout life in various learning experiences, and particularly in the classroom setting, are a very difficult group to control and motivate. Meeting the educational needs of inmates requires a thorough knowledge of their individual learning problems.

The staff/inmate ratio is another significant factor influencing effectiveness in any teaching environment. Inmates require at least the same, and in many cases more, interaction, feedback, and personal attention than that provided to students in outside educational programs. This is, in part, because inmates vary greatly in learning ability, interest level, and motivation. Emphasis should be placed on developing programs that will deal with individual educational needs. Special attention should be paid to the needs of inmates who are unusually far behind in key areas, such as reading.

Education Staff

The education department staff usually consists of a full-time program administrator, assistant, and clerk, as well as instructors specializing in Adult Basic Education, General Education Degrees, and vocational and continuing education programs. Frequently, the full-time education staff is supplemented by contract staff or volunteers, who enrich the standard programs and offer special courses as the need arises (Bayse 1993).

Education options should be broad enough to provide for the needs, interests, and abilities of as many inmates as possible. In institutions with a significant number of non-English-speaking inmates, for example, courses in English as a second language may be necessary.

Close working relationships among educational and classification or unit team personnel are essential. Education in the correctional setting ideally is considered part of a total program, and a proper balance should be maintained between academic and vocational training and recreation.

Developing an Educational Program

The process of developing an educational program should include input from the inmate involved, and a follow-up system should be developed to regularly review program progress. Ideally, if adequate funding is available, counseling should be available to provide inmates assistance, encouragement, and feedback with respect to their educational and vocational goals.

The educational program should be structured so that inmates can enter at any time, and proceed through the various grades at their own pace. Progress through the program should not be defined by grade-level attainment, academic marks, or scores; individualized instruction is essential. Programmed instruction including computerized courses, correspondence courses, and educational television may be used, in addition to traditional teaching methods. In some institutions, the education department also provides courses in consumer activities, life skills, and family life.

Education programs should not compete with work assignments, visitation, counseling, and other activities, but should be offered at nonpeak program hours, and should be available in the evenings and on weekends. Participation can be encouraged by limiting the barriers to attendance; some systems even use a reward system.

Recognition of academic and vocational achievements, in the form of certification or graduation ceremonies, is helpful to individual inmates, and enhances the general support for educational programs. The ceremonies also can be used to good effect in a public information program to highlight the institution's successes.

Vocational Training

The primary goal of vocational training is to provide inmates with marketable skills so they are better

There is a close correlation between education level and recidivism—the more education an inmate has the less likely he or she is to return to prison.

Since most inmates eventually will be released, they need to know how to survive in the outside world and life skills education enables them to manage their affairs more competently.

equipped to earn a living for themselves and their dependents when they are released to the community. Traditional trades, such as carpentry, plumbing, welding, painting, automotive repair, and electrical work usually are taught in the facility's maintenance shops and supplemented by classroom instruction. Separate vocational training space may be used to teach other trades such as computer programming, computer-related equipment operation and repair, and repair of small engines, office equipment, refrigerators, air conditioners, and televisions.

The vocational training program usually is supervised by the education department. The number of full-time instructors varies according to the number of shop areas. Part-time contract employees from a local vocational school often can be hired to help the regular staff. Using contract employees also allows greater flexibility when program modifications are needed in response to changes in the job market.

Vocational training programs should relate to the job market. The community's employment needs can be assessed through contacts with local labor and industry representatives. Equipment and curricula for the vocational training programs should be updated periodically to ensure compatibility with training developments in the community.

Existing community resources and community involvement should be used where appropriate. A variety of programs should be linked to outside trades through formal apprenticeship programs in which the inmates complete a very long, detailed course of training and participate in on-the-job experience. The best of these programs prepare inmates to start well-paying jobs upon release. Other, less formal programs can be used as a springboard to entry-level jobs in the community, because they provide the necessary fundamental training and experience needed to break into the field.

Life Skills

- Identify the steps necessary for the individual to start up a utility such as telephone service, gas, and others; to follow billing procedures; and to access resources for an emergency

- Analyze different types of housing loans and key aspects of homeowners'/renters' insurance

- Recognize requirements for keeping the home safe and preventing fires and theft

- Demonstrate familiarity with local, state, and federal government agencies to access information for employment, housing, and health

- Locate medical and health facilities in the community

- Recognize and use the telephone and other special directories

- Identify the various educational opportunities available in the community

- Analyze the value and importance of planning a vacation

- Demonstrate how to select a restaurant appropriate to a situation

- Analyze the importance of using a safety manual and following the policies and procedures in it

- Identify the steps and information needed to process accident reports

- Complete an accident report

- Identify the rights of an injured worker

Work Programs

The mission of work programs in a correctional facility is to employ inmates in constructive activities, foster good work habits, and provide training opportunities in a variety of marketable skills. By providing employment opportunities, a work program also reduces the idleness otherwise inherent in correctional facilities. An institution for 500 inmates often can employ as much as 50 percent of its inmate population in an industrial production program. Good work habits, on-the-job training, and even the satisfaction of a day's work well done are a few intangibles that, in the long run, can help change attitudes and behavior.

In Orange County, Florida, inmates can choose between participating in a rehabilitation program or doing straight jail time. Here, the inmates learn automotive skills that will help them find jobs after their release.

Work activities can include:

- *Day-to-day services* to maintain an institution, such as food service, routine cleaning, and other housekeeping chores, and maintenance and other services. These routine tasks are relatively simple, and can provide employment opportunities for some inmates. Appropriately classified inmates frequently are assigned to maintenance work outside the institution as members of construction or ground details.

- *Vocational training* generally includes the following areas: food preparation such as cooking and baking; meat-cutting; power and filtration plant operations; maintenance and repair; carpentry; plumbing; painting; bricklaying; sheet metal work; installation of electrical equipment; and some assignments in the laundry, dry cleaning, and clothing repair plants.

- *Agricultural work* and other activities related to farming include such activities as dairying, poultry raising, and canning. These assignments also serve to reduce institutional food costs by contributing to the supply of meats and vegetables consumed in the institution. Surplus agricultural and dairy products also may yield a financial profit when sold to other public institutions and eligible agencies.

- *Work camps* may be used for inmates who are approaching the end of their sentences or who have relatively short, nonviolent sentences. They provide opportunities for inmates to live and work in an environment that more nearly resembles conditions existing in free communities. Inmates assigned to work camps often are employed in construction and repair of roads, reforestation, gardening, harvesting, maintenance and improvement of public park areas, and other work concerned with the conservation of natural resources and the upkeep of public properties. Camp programs for properly screened low-risk inmates can provide a relatively inexpensive option for the relief of crowding and idleness in larger institutions.

- *Industrial production.* Correctional industries offers other options. It furnishes jobs for inmates who otherwise might be unassigned, or be assigned to jobs

Some prisons are self-sufficient in that they raise animals and grow food that is eaten in the prison. Here, the inmates work on one of the farms in the North Carolina prison system.

Correctional Officer Resource Guide

Top: During group therapy, inmates learn alternatives to violence and substance abuse and get an opportunity to explore new ways of interacting with others. Bottom: A certain amount of outdoor exercise is required by court order in several places.

that offer no chance to develop marketable skills. Usually, prison industries are limited to selling their goods to other state agencies, so that they do not compete with private production of similar goods in the open market. Private industries that have been introduced in some correctional facilities provide a realistic work environment for inmates to learn and improve work skills and handle many of the same responsibilities as those in the community workforce. Industrial programs offer both economic profit to the institution and specialized vocational training and experience for the individual inmate.

Counseling

While correctional officers may provide common sense advice to inmates and offer a valuable service when they do, most formal counseling programs are conducted by specialized staff. Correctional staff should not attempt to conduct any in-depth counseling but should refer inmates to professional staff members.

Individual sessions with professional staff members can be effective, as can group therapy sessions. In the institutional setting, where staff resources are short, group counseling is far more common. Staff who are qualified to counsel generally include psychiatrists, psychologists, social workers, caseworkers, and trained lay counselors. The type of counseling program available to inmates varies greatly, however. Most prisons have addictions specialists who provide Alcoholics Anonymous and Narcotics Anonymous counseling. Investigate what is available at your institution and learn how to refer inmates to such help (Read 1996).

Recreation and Inmate Activities

A sound recreational program is a crucial element in any correctional facility. By providing inmates with a constructive means for channeling energies and relieving tension, recreation contributes to the facilities' safe and orderly operation. Recreational activities also give inmates an opportunity to use their free time constructively, improve their physical and mental health, and develop good sportsmanship and morale. Many inmates need help in the constructive use of their leisure time. Helping inmates understand their options and choosing constructive options is the role of the recreational therapist.

Typically, the recreation program consists of a wide variety of organized group and individual activities, including various sports, music, drama, movies, arts and crafts, and table games. Some prisons employ art and music therapists who teach skills in these areas and by offering constructive options and outlets, as well as instilling self-pride, hold down the tension level. The recreation specialist must develop programs for a wide variety of inmate needs including those for inmates more than fifty years old, the paraplegic who is wheelchair bound, the vision and hearing impaired, the mentally disabled, and others. Full-time recreation specialists usually coordinate the program, with assistance from security staff and carefully selected inmates. In addition, many community groups and individual volunteers contribute substantial time and effort to help coordinate programs and increase the variety of activities for inmates.

No particular recreational program can be a standard for all institutions; each differs in size, programs, type of population, locale, and physical characteristics. A program that meets the needs of one institution may be a far cry from those in other institutions. Many institutions are limited in the recreational activities they can provide due to lack of facilities or absence of necessary funds.

However, whatever the recreation activity, the resources available must be used to meet the needs of as many inmates as possible. Qualified volunteers can be very helpful in developing and delivering programs, even with limited resources.

Typical Recreation Facilities

Typical recreation facilities include an outdoor recreation area, or yard; an auditorium with stage equipment; game rooms and games such as table tennis, shuffleboard, chess, checkers, and cards; weight lifting and other body-conditioning equipment and space for their use; a music room; and space for the pursuit of arts, crafts, and hobbies. Locker rooms, showers, and dressing rooms also should be available. Provision should be made for the regular inspection of all equipment. The National Recreation and Park Association provides guidelines for facilities and equipment, and American Correctional Association standards provide an excellent set of guidelines for the types of recreation that should be available.

Recreation should be available during nonworking hours. This affords each inmate an opportunity to participate on a voluntary basis. Some provision should be made for inmates with odd work schedules, such as morning watch powerhouse workers, so that they have access to the recreation facilities during their off-duty hours.

Community interaction can include bringing in volunteers to provide instruction, and inviting local teams to compete with institution teams. It also may include taking low-security inmates into the community for recreational activities.

Movies are provided in most institutions; some provide one or two movies a week, with a special program on holidays. Institutions which do not have room for large groups to assemble for a movie can provide movies on video to all recreation hall television sets. These often are made available through the profits of the canteen or institution store.

The library also rates high among recreational outlets for the institution. American Correctional Association standards set requirements for institutional library operations. The materials selected must meet inmates' educational, informational, and recreational needs. They should be easily accessible and regulated by a system that prevents abuse.

The institution's library service generally should be comparable to that of a public library, providing logical organization of materials for convenient circulation to satisfy users' needs. Many libraries go so far as to offer information services to locate facts, as needed; some have supervised inmate access to the "information super highway;" others offer a reader's advisory service; and some even promote library materials through publicity, book lists, special programs, book and film discussion groups, music programs, contests, and other appropriate services. The reference collection is very important, particularly when inmates need specialized prerelease, vocational, and educational information.

The chaplain for the institution helps not only with religious issues but with inmates' concerns over family issues.

Hobby and craft work is encouraged in most correctional institutions. Approved projects may include various types of weaving, sewing, leather work, stamp collecting, watch repairing, woodworking, and the making of plaster figurines. In many locations, this type of activity offers inmates the opportunity to earn money through the sale of products at the institutional store.

Other recreation activities may include:

- playing musical instruments
- seeing entertainment performed by outside groups
- performing in variety programs
- preparing institutional publications
- seeing holiday events
- listening to the radio
- watching television
- using computers

Religious Services

Most administrators and wardens in the correctional field understand the importance of religious programs in correctional institutions. American Correctional Association standards and the Religious Freedom and Restoration Act (RFRA) address the religious issue by emphasizing that all inmates have the right to the voluntary exercise of their religious beliefs, when those practices do not interfere with or create a clear and present danger to the order and security of the institution.

In most facilities, either a full-time chaplain or representative of a faith group from the community should be available to provide regular religious services, individual and group counseling, family contacts, and other

The chaplain plays a vital role in the correctional community. With the passage of the Religious Freedom and Restoration Act, the chaplain has to explain to the administration what the core elements are of many religions, including nontraditional ones, that must be upheld.

Courtesy Capitol Communication Systems, Inc.

services. The chaplain or staff religious program coordinator should be responsible for keeping the door open between the institution and religious groups in the community, and to receive, investigate, clear, and schedule all requests for programs, services, and Bible study from volunteer religious groups in the community. The volunteer religious group leader or coordinator personally should contact the chaplain or the staff religious program coordinator when submitting program requests. Inmates should be kept informed about opportunities to participate in religious programs on a continuing basis, such as through weekly inmate newsletters.

Correctional staff must be sensitive to the increase in the number of less-traditional religions found in prison. Many correctional staff have not had the experience of dealing with Islam or other religions that are less well known in the United States. Nevertheless, the right of a Muslim inmate to have a kufi (a particular type of headpiece) is just as well established as that of a Jewish inmate to have a yarmulke, a Muslim inmate to have the Koran (the sacred scripture of Islam), or a Baptist to have a Bible. The right of a Native American to worship in a sweat lodge or smoke sweet grass is becoming just as well recognized as that of a Catholic to attend mass.

Correctional agencies are dealing with more of these situations every day. It is the agency's responsibility to make very clear the policy on how these groups are to be permitted to worship. For the line officer, when in doubt, ask for advice from a supervisor.

Chaplain's Functions

In most institutions, one or more chaplains coordinate religious services and develop community resources to meet the religious needs of all inmates. In most systems, the chaplains have the endorsement of a recognized religious organization. The chaplain's various functions, common to all denominations, include:

- Offering sacramental ministries, including regular religious services and special services connected with baptisms, confessions, communion, and so forth

- Coordinating ministries to other faith groups through the use of contracts, lay ministers, and volunteers

- Providing religious instruction to inmates in the fundamentals of the denomination of which they are a part, and providing instructional resources for other denominations

- Providing private and personal counseling. An essential part of the chaplain's work includes interviews in the chaplain's offices and visits to inmates in the hospital and locked units.

- Ministering to inmates' families and other concerned people. Many of the tensions in an institution stem from inmates' worries about the welfare of loved ones, or from the fear that they are being forgotten by people on the outside. A good portion of the chaplain's counseling time addresses these problems.

- Serving as a pastor, guide, and counselor to the institution's employees, as well as the inmates

- Providing an interpretative ministry to the community

Too often, society views correctional institutions as merely a place to confine people who have violated the law. Chaplains uniquely are equipped to explain the purposes of modern correctional institutions to the community at large, and to enlist the community's cooperation in the objectives of current correctional procedures.

In their work, chaplains try to help inmates deal with personal problems and the issues of confinement that may lead to positive personal change. Chaplains of all denominations enjoy the confidence of inmates to a degree possessed by no official of the institution, and they try to use this confidence to promote the best interests of the individual and of the institution. This confidentiality is sometimes difficult for other staff to understand; often, it is a burden to the chaplain, but it is an essential part of their role, and staff and inmates should respect it.

Officers' Relation to Religious Programs

Where do correctional officers stand in relation to the chaplain and religious programs?

- Correctional officers should encourage inmates to take advantage of the religious opportunities offered to them.

- When supervising religious services, officers should keep supervision activity to the respectful minimum necessary to ensure order.

- When speaking about a chaplain, officers always should use the chaplain's proper title, such as Father (for a Catholic chaplain), Reverend (for a Protestant chaplain), or Rabbi (for a Jewish chaplain).

- Officers never should make any derogatory statements about an inmate consulting a chaplain or attending services.

- Officers should call the chaplain's attention to inmates who seem to have personal or family problems.

Religion can play an important part in the institutional experience for an inmate. It is important that officers realize the significance of religious programs, and the chaplain's essential place in the institution.

Drug Abuse Programs

Given the increasing number of drug offenders coming into our prisons, the need for treatment programs has never been greater. The war on drugs has succeeded in packing the nation's prisons with drug offenders. The number of persons sentenced to prison for drug offenses has increased steadily. In 1980, only 6.8 percent (8,900 individuals) of new court commitments to state prisons were for drug offenses; by 1992, this percentage had risen to 30.5 percent (102,000) of prison-bound offenders. It is even higher in the federal system, where drug-related commitments nearly reached 60 percent of inmates (U.S. Department of Justice 1995).

Alcoholics Anonymous (AA) and Narcotics Anonymous (NA) programs are beneficial and replicate well-known programs in the community. Other treatment programs and groups exist. For the correctional officer, there are a few general points that are worth noting.

First, many drug offenders already have been through many treatment programs; they know the ropes, and they often use the program for their own purposes. Correctional staff should give proper respect to the professional opinions of counselors and other staff regarding inmate change and program guidelines, but they should not relax security or supervision rules appropriate to that institution. Inmates involved in a program of any type must be required to obey the institution's rules, and staff must enforce those rules.

Second, in some past drug treatment programs, professional staff have let the inmates enforce the rules of the group or unit. This can lead to inmate control of the program, a totally unacceptable practice.

Third, no areas are off-limits to staff or free from staff searches. Correctional officers must continue to make sure that weapons, escape paraphernalia, and drugs are not hidden in the program areas.

Finally, staff always should be aware of the need to devote additional supervision and search activity to a group of drug offenders. It is never safe to assume that inmates in a drug treatment program genuinely want to quit using drugs. Regular procedures always should apply, and additional attention to these procedures often is advisable.

Visiting

A sound visiting program is essential to the successful operation of any correctional institution. Frequent visits by family members and friends help maintain family and community ties, lessen the "prisonization process," and the negative psychological consequences of confinement, and in some cases, generate attitudes that are important for successful reentry into the community following confinement.

In addition, visiting strengthens inmate morale and eases tensions and management problems. Other than family or friends, visitors can include lawyers, parole advisors who assist in release planning, and members of the clergy who may provide counseling to help resolve family problems.

In recognizing these issues, courts consistently have upheld inmates' right to receive visitors, while granting wide discretion to correctional administrators as to how the visitation program should be conducted. However, certain features or practices are common to most visiting programs.

As a general policy, contact visiting is preferred, that is, visiting in an area where inmates actually can be in contact with their visitors without any physical barriers. The use of noncontact visiting for high-security and

Visits of inmates with their children help reestablish the bonds that may have been severed during incarceration.

some jail cases is still a valid strategy, but it is far less common.

Visiting Hours

Visiting hours should not be overly restrictive. The number of visitors an inmate may receive, and the length of visits, should be limited only to the institution's schedule, the available visiting space, and staffing limitations. Most institutions permit visiting on Saturdays, Sundays, and holidays. Because restrictions may be a hardship to some families and other visitors, more generous, flexible visiting hours are encouraged. This means maximizing visiting opportunities and accommodating visitors who are unable to schedule their visits during the institution's regular visiting hours. Ordinarily, the caseworker or some other staff member, not the visiting room officer, approves these exceptions, but exceptions must be coordinated with the security shift commander who must staff the visiting area beyond normal visiting hours.

Because family members are the most frequent visitors, the institution's policy should permit visits by children. This further strengthens family ties, which can be strained during confinement, and reduces any child care problems associated with visits. This practice can make visiting more frequent, convenient, and less expensive.

Processing Procedures

Visitors should be received in a waiting room or lobby area that has a hospitable, nonthreatening atmosphere. Their arrival should be recorded in the necessary records. (The computer is a real asset in this area). All first-time visitors should be given a copy of the institutions' visiting policy, hours of operation, and public transportation schedules to the institution. Other processing typically includes checking identities, advising visitors of contraband regulations, searching them, and then notifying the inmate of their arrival. Provision must be made to securely store a visitor's prohibited personal belongings. Visitors who refuse to follow these procedures, who are under the influence of alcohol or some other substance, or who are not properly dressed may be refused access to the institution under applicable local procedures. Visiting rules should be clearly posted for all visitors to read when entering the institution.

Body searches of inmates, and a search of all clothing worn into the visiting room, is conducted both before and after visits to ensure that no contraband has been passed during the visit. A record of jewelry worn into the visiting room should be taken to ensure it is the same when the visitor leaves. Special care should be taken with inmates who are suspected of passing or receiving contraband (this can be a flag in the computer or on the visiting record). These searches should be conducted in a suitable private area. Most institutions limit the items that may go into the visiting room, and others issue special visiting room clothing, or jumpsuits, to reduce the possibility of concealing contraband.

Private rooms are provided, whenever possible, for visits with attorneys. This permits the free exchange of confidential information and documents necessary in privileged communications between attorneys and their clients. In attorney-client visiting, no supervision is permitted that would allow overhearing any conversations. These areas also may serve as secure visiting rooms for inmates who present serious escape risks or whose behavior may be disruptive, although in those cases, direct staff supervision is mandatory.

Visiting Program Staff

Visiting programs usually are supervised by two or three full-time members of the correctional staff, and should be carried out in the least intrusive manner possible. Although some surveillance can be provided by moving about the visiting room and the use of K-9 drug dogs, there also should be a fixed staff post in the visiting room that affords good visibility of the entire area. Surveillance of the visiting room should not be carried out solely through the use of closed-circuit television or audio monitors, but these devices can help in providing additional surveillance capability.

Special Arrangements

Some visits require special arrangements. For example, visitors for inmates in segregation units or the infirmary can be escorted to these areas where the visits can be held in appropriately supervised rooms or existing multiuse space. In the case of inmates in segregation, the administration also may choose to use the private visiting rooms in the main visiting area. Whatever arrangements are made, these inmates should be properly restrained while being moved, and in some cases, the restraints may have to be left on for the visit. Special search procedures also may be necessary for any visitors moving into the secure compound for a visit of this type.

Issues in Program Supervision

In addition to alcohol and drug treatment groups, all program activities require supervision. Every institution will have its own layout and procedures, which will create unique supervision issues. However, a few tips are applicable to most situations:

- No program area is off-limits to staff supervision or searches.

- Officers assigned to supervise inmate spectators of recreational activities should not become so engrossed in the game as to neglect their job of custodial supervision of all inmates.

- If outside visitors or players are present, officers should take care to prevent unnecessary contact between inmates and visitors.

- Officers should ensure that program activity is carried out only during the time specified.

- Staff should be careful not to give too much authority to inmate clerks or assistants in program areas (Inmates should never supervise other inmates).

The visiting room of the Roxbury Correctional Institution in Hagerstown, Maryland, is inspected by Sergeant Randy Mishcer and K-9 Goldie.

- Except for open yard time and similar activities, most programs will have approved participant lists, which can be checked against call out sheets or other tally systems; correctional staff assigned to posts that control traffic into program areas need to be aware of those systems and be ready to stop unauthorized inmates.

- Officers need to be aware of unusual traffic into or out of an area; large numbers of a minority group at unusual times; or the mass exit of many inmates. All these things can signal a potential problem. These types of subtle signs should be reported to supervisors immediately.

- Program areas can be used as "stashes" for contraband, escape paraphernalia, or weapons. Searches of inmates moving in and out of program areas are important, as are regular searches of the area itself.

- Staff offices periodically should be searched, particularly when they are shared by inmate clerks.

- Some programs have mail and packages delivered to them from outside organizations; these items should go through the regular institution search process, and inmates never should be sent to pick up

By getting in shape physically, inmates are better prepared to follow the demands of the boot camp schedules and stay healthy both in prison and afterwards in the community.

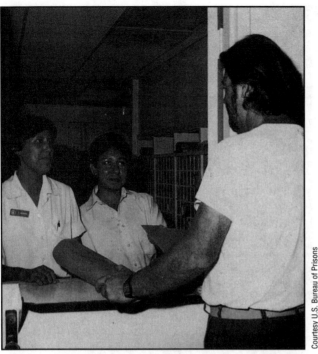
Mail for prisons must be inspected for contraband before it is delivered.

packages of this type. Similarly, any outgoing correspondence for a program should be controlled by staff and subjected to normal institution mail processing.

Segregation (Special Housing)

Delivery of program services to segregated or special housing units is an important issue. Staff working these units often do not understand that there are important management and legal reasons for offering medical, recreational, educational, and sometimes even vocational programs to inmates in segregated status.

The operation of these programs is always a security concern. The movement of inmates to the program, or program materials to inmates' cells, is a time-consuming activity. Searches and application of restraints are necessary if an inmate is moved out of a cell, and the additional materials in inmate cells demand that more time be spent in cell searches. These are, however, necessary programs, and correctional officers should carry them out in accordance with institution policy.

One absolute rule for all segregated-unit programs is that inmates participating in them receive no extra privileges, nor are they relieved from the necessary security precautions that apply to all inmates in the unit. Program participation is commendable, and in most systems there are ways for inmates to be recognized for it eventually. However, the risks of relaxing procedures in the high-security setting are far too great. Even if inmates were not personally inclined to take advantage of a staff member's relaxation of procedure, they would quickly come under pressure from other inmates to do so.

Special Issues in Camp Operations

Camp programs are often very similar to those operated inside secure facilities; the delivery of basic services to inmates differs very little. The trap that correctional staff easily can fall into in camp operations is to begin to believe that the inmates do not need the same kind of supervision that those inside the secure compound require.

In fact, in some respects, the lack of a wall or fence means that more personal supervision actually may be required. In the program area, it is just as important at a camp to supervise groups, search areas, and be alert for unhealthy interactions. Since it is so much easier to introduce drugs, alcohol, and other contraband, the need for searches of all areas, including program departments, is greater.

Mail

While not a program in the strict sense, the importance of inmates' correspondence with relatives and friends becomes greatly magnified in a correctional setting. Frequent visiting by inmates' families is not always feasible because of such factors as cost and location. Thus, correspondence should be encouraged between inmates and their families, friends, and other associates. Moreover, correspondence between inmates and their attorneys and the courts must be assured. This usually requires special handling, adding to the complexities of the mail operation.

The mail room is the area through which all incoming and outgoing mail passes. A major part of the mail room staff's work is opening, inspecting, and sorting incoming inmate mail. There usually are comprehensive rules and regulations governing incoming correspondence, based on the need to maintain security. The control of contraband entering the institution is a major concern. Unless incoming inmate mail is opened and inspected, staff lose control of contraband entering through the mail.

Incoming and outgoing legal mail and other privileged correspondence usually requires special handling. Such mail must be logged, and frequently must be opened in the mail room in the inmate's presence.

Catalog orders and packages delivered under approved programs also require special handling. This includes removing the contents from all packaging, searching the incoming material thoroughly (including

X-ray, if available), inventorying and recording all received property, and giving only those items authorized by directive to the inmate (inmates should sign that they have received the property, and indicate disposition of unauthorized property). The wrapping material is a prime location for contraband, and should be disposed of outside the institution. Unsearched packages never should be brought inside the compound, and for that reason, the package area should not be deep inside the compound. Staff packages should receive special attention as well, with only the designated staff member permitted to pick up and search the package in the package area.

Inmates generally drop outgoing mail in a box in their housing unit, where it is collected daily and brought to the mail room. In most institutions today, inmates are allowed to seal outgoing mail. However, certain inmates suspected of illegal activities using the mail may receive special attention. Usually, inmate mail is no longer censored, and is just spot-checked for codes or other obvious attempts to breach security. Many institutions date and stamp (with the name of the institution) all outgoing inmate mail.

To the degree possible, administrative mail should be kept separate from inmate mail. This usually can be arranged with the postal authorities. Staff members should be assigned individual locked mailboxes.

Summary

The constructive use of an inmate's time should be an integral part of every correctional program. Participation in worthwhile programs can offer inmates a feeling of achievement, and aid them in acquiring skills that can help them live lawfully in the community.

Programs and security must not be viewed as separate systems, but as two important parts of the institutional structure. Correctional officers can assist inmates in their program activities by providing proper supervision, and by advising other staff when inmate conduct may require special attention.

APPLICABLE ACA STANDARDS

Academic and Vocational Education: 3-4410 - 3-4422

Mail, Telephone, Visiting: 3-4429 - 3-4446

Recreation and Activities: 3-4423 - 3-4428

At the Federal Intensive Confinement Center at Lewisburg, Pennsylvania, boot camp trainees listen to volunteer instructor, Anne Smith, discuss aspects of the restorative justice program that concerns victim awareness.

Religious Programs: 3-4454 - 3-4463

Social Services: 3-4344-1, 3-4380 - 3-4388, 3-4388-1, 3-4388-4

Special Management Housing: 3-4254, 3-4255, 3-4258 - 3-4261

Work and Correctional Industries Programs: 3-4394 - 3-4409

BIBLIOGRAPHY

Bayse, Daniel J. 1993. *Helping Hands: A Handbook for Volunteers in Prisons and Jails.* Lanham, Maryland: American Correctional Association.

Glick, B. and A. Goldstein. 1995. *Managing Delinquency Programs that Work.* Lanham, Maryland: American Correctional Association. (Though a book on juvenile issues, the sections on programs offer valuable lessons for correctional officers and administrators.)

Lauen, Roger. 1997. *Positive Approaches to Corrections: Research, Policy, and Practice.* Lanham, Maryland: American Correctional Association.

Read, Edward M. 1996. *Partners in Change: The Twelve-Step Referral Handbook for Probation, Parole and Community Corrections.* Lanham, Maryland: American Correctional Association.

Roberts, John. 1997. *Reform and Retribution: An Illustrated History of American Prisons.* Lanham, Maryland: American Correctional Association.

U.S. Department of Justice. 1995. *Bulletin.* Washington, D.C.

14

Parole and Release

by Edward M. Read, LCSW, NCAC II
United States Parole Officer, Washington, D.C.

Many inmates who serve time in correctional institutions are released early under some form of parole supervision, or are obligated to undergo a period of supervised release following completion of the confinement portion of their sentence. In some states, a parole board or commission decides when to return inmates to the community. In certain states, in addition to parole, inmates may be granted what is called "mandatory release;" they are released automatically after serving their maximum sentence, minus credit for "good time." In most cases, inmates who are released early or who are on supervised release are subject to supervision by a parole officer.

Release to a community is "conditional." It depends on the offender's ability and willingness to comply with a standard set of conditions designed to monitor or control community adjustment. Most conditions stipulate that offenders follow the parole officer's instructions; that they submit monthly "reports" on income and other pertinent household details; that they not travel outside the jurisdiction without permission; that they report as directed; that they refrain from association with known criminals; that they allow the parole officer to notify an employer of their conviction history, if necessary; that they notify the parole officer upon rearrest, address or residence change; that they find gainful employment; that they not be in possession of or use controlled substances, and so forth. Often, there are "special conditions" added as means of assuring cooperation. These may include regular urinalysis, substance abuse and/or mental health counseling, or even financial counseling requirements.

Determinate Sentencing

In many states, there is a move to do away with early release on parole and move entirely toward determinate sentencing, whereby an inmate serves nearly all of the sentence. In other words, an inmate's early release is not contingent on traditional rehabilitative measures. The federal probation and pretrial services system did away with parole around 1986; inmates complete their incarceration and then are placed on supervised release for varying lengths of time. Violations revert back to the sentencing judge, not a parole commission or board. This shift is a result of many complex political and criminal justice decisions, resulting in longer terms being served, making release an even longer-term prospect for many inmates. For staff working in systems with such a sentencing structure, some of this chapter will not apply, but much of it will be good background information on how other correctional systems operate.

The Role of Institutional Staff

Correctional staff in every part of the institution help inmates prepare to return to society. They can try to direct inmates into activities that may help them in lawful functioning on release, including education, vocational training, self-improvement, and especially substance abuse programs, since the majority of offenders usually have trouble with alcohol or other drugs. With the availability of these programs and a properly motivated inmate, preparation for release can begin the day an inmate enters the institution.

Normally, when inmates are committed, institutional staff work with them to identify problem areas in their background, and to encourage them to enter programs that may help them deal with those problems. Probation officers' presentence reports provide the background of case information from which the institution unit teams or classification staff can begin to work to develop this program with the inmate. The unit team or classification staff evaluate other records from custodial, treatment, educational, and industrial areas.

Institutional staff prepare reports about the inmates' program participation that are given to either the paroling authority, sentencing jurisdiction, or parole officer in the community awaiting the inmates' release. Program participation may be one of the factors considered by the paroling authority for early release. And, even for those released to terms of supervised release and not paroled early, such reports are valuable prognosticators of eventual community adjustment.

Prerelease Programs

Prerelease programs take different forms in different states. Most programs are designed to educate inmates about the social and economic realities of life outside the institution, and the agencies and services that can help them adjust. As part of these programs, lectures and discussions address the concerns of soon-to-be-released inmates. Counselors focus on their particular needs, and parole officers may visit them.

Ideally, inmates in prerelease programs gradually receive less supervision as their level of responsibility increases. However, at all times, graduated release must be consistent with public safety and the security level assigned to the inmate. When appropriate, inmates may be released under carefully controlled programs to work, study, and visit their family and community. In many institutions, inmates who are considered minimum-security risks and who are within several months of release are selected carefully to participate in community-based programs, which ease their transition from prison to the community. In some systems, low-risk offenders may be allowed short-term releases through brief furloughs to seek employment commitments or prospective residences. To provide these offenders with a more normal and relaxed living situation shortly before their release, other administrators permit inmates nearing release to live in separate quarters within the institution.

In these programs, inmates' progress is evaluated according to behavior, rather than according to the provisions of their sentences. Officers, though, should be cautious about being overly flexible about rule enforcement when the inmate soon will be released into the community. Disciplinary regulations still apply to all inmates at all times, until their sentences are completed.

The Institutional Parole Officer

Some institutions have institutional parole officers (often classification staff members) who act as liaisons between the classification committee or unit team, the parole authority, and the supervising field staff. Other correctional systems have caseworkers who serve this purpose.

Courtesy ACA

The parole officer should help inmates plan for their release in terms of a job, housing, and other aspects of their life so that they do not repeat the cycle that brought them into the criminal justice system.

Institutional parole officers interpret parole policies for the staff and inmates, help develop preparole training programs, and counsel inmates during their incarceration. Soon after inmates are received in the institution, the parole officer may request additional information from field parole staff, if the probation presentence reports are incomplete. This may result in a field officer visiting an inmate's family or former employer. This effort also can ensure that these important contacts are maintained, and help prepare the inmate's family and community for his or her eventual release.

Most parole authorities require that inmates who are to be released have, at a minimum, a job and a place to live when they are paroled. For that reason, when an inmate is eligible for parole review, the parole officer or caseworker helps develop a parole plan for consideration by the parole authority. This often will involve sending the proposed parole plan to the field parole staff for investigation and approval. The caseworker or parole officer often attends parole hearings, and later may

Parole and Release

explain in some instances why an inmate was denied release. After parole is granted, the officer helps explain the parole conditions to the parolee.

The Parole Officer in the Community

Parole officers supervise offenders once they return to their home community. Their primary objective is to enforce court or parole authority directives and promote community safety through risk assessment, supervision monitoring techniques, and correctional treatment.

Some parole officers begin their work long before an inmate is eligible for release, by investigating and supplementing records received by the institution from the probation department and the court. Ideally, these officers contact the inmate's family to discuss immediate and long-range problems resulting from the commitment, referring them to agencies where they can obtain work. However, most parole officers do not begin their work with inmates until shortly before the inmate's release when called on to investigate and approve release plans that specify proposed living and employment options.

Formal supervision techniques for monitoring and assisting an offender in the community depend on both the resources available and the correctional philosophy of the release jurisdiction. Unfortunately, the reality is that caseloads are often too high, sometimes numbering well over 100 offenders in urban areas, and officers must do their best to isolate and make judgments about those most in need of supervision services and/or surveillance.

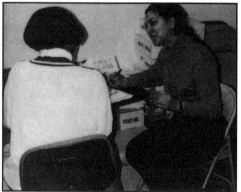

Above: Here a parole officer is showing her credentials when she visits an offender in the community. Right: A probation officer is testing an offender for illicit drug use.

Photos courtesy Edward Read

Parole officers, therefore, must assess the offender and develop a viable supervision plan, taking into account both community risk and correctional treatment needs. A seasoned parole officer will be comfortable in both a law enforcement and counseling approach, depending on the needs of the case.

Standard techniques will involve periodic police checks to determine if someone has reoffended; home and employment contacts to monitor overall compliance with conditions of release; urinalysis testing to determine illicit drug or alcohol abuse; collateral contacts with treatment providers to assess an offenders' compliance in treatment; referral to self-help groups such as Alcoholics Anonymous (AA), Narcotics Anonymous (NA), and Rational Recovery (RA); other community agency referrals designed to assist a person's readjustment; and general counseling efforts. Some parole offices have identified "intensive" supervision caseloads to address the special demands posed by very high-risk offenders.

Parole officers are obligated to expedite the revocation process for offenders who continue to demonstrate threatening behavior, to either themselves or the community. In many (though not all) states, parole officers actually may arrest or cause the arrest of any parolee when there is reason to believe that parole conditions have been violated. In the federal system, United States Marshals apprehend supervised release violators after the sentencing judge signs a warrant prepared by the

Temporary Release Programs

Although this is not a complete list, correctional systems using temporary release programs include many of the following features:

- Written procedures, including those for careful screening and selection procedures that ensure public safety
- Written rules of conduct and sanctions
- A system of supervision to minimize inmate abuse of program privileges
- A complete record-keeping system
- A system for evaluating program effectiveness
- Efforts to obtain community cooperation and support

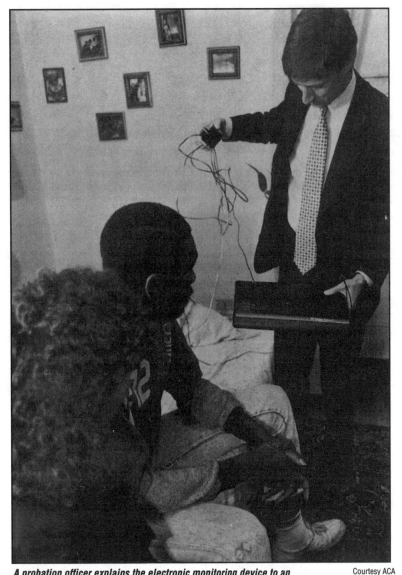

A probation officer explains the electronic monitoring device to an inmate who will be able to work in the community instead of being imprisoned.

An inmate receives his release and some cash. Before leaving the prison, his papers must be checked carefully and his property that was kept in storage returned to him.

parole officer. At some point in the process, regardless of whether the officer actually executes the arrest warrant, detailed reports must be forwarded to either the paroling authority or the sentencing jurisdiction, effectively making the case for revocation. The report is reviewed and a determination made as to whether the individual should be arrested and/or returned to an institution for a formal parole hearing. And, of course, if an offender absconds from supervision, the officer will request that the parole status immediately be suspended and that a warrant be issued for the parolee's arrest.

When an officer believes an individual no longer requires supervision and the paroling authority and/or sentencing jurisdiction concurs, the officer may submit a recommendation for early discharge or termination from supervision. Usually, there are agreed-upon periods of time during which the offender must exhibit continuous law-abiding behavior before such recommendations are considered. In some jurisdictions, the offender must demonstrate an extraordinary response to supervision before being given consideration.

Summary

Correctional officers, as well as other employees, play a major role in preparing inmates for release, whether on parole, supervised release, or straight out the prison door. This is accomplished best by helping inmates develop positive attitudes and behaviors necessary for a law-abiding life within the free community. The correctional officer who proactively works with the community corrections system (including parole offices) even will influence this important aspect of prerelease planning further.

Beginning in the 1970s and continuing today, the concept of parole is being seriously questioned. Some states severely restricted, or even altogether have eliminated discretionary parole release. However, most inmates are released to some form of community supervision. Although it may not be officially titled "parole," some facet of conditional release is likely to remain a part of the overall correctional process.

APPLICABLE ACA STANDARDS

Release Preparation and Temporary Release: 3-4389 - 3-4393

15

Public Relations and Citizen Involvement

Maintaining the public's full confidence and respect are critical if corrections is to receive necessary financial resources. Prisons, reformatories, and other correctional institutions are performing public service functions with public funds. Citizens have a right to know how these institutions are operated and how their tax monies are spent. The level of public support for corrections can decrease rapidly, or even vanish, when headlines recount mismanagement, disturbances, or general inmate discontent. Open relations with the community and the media can aid greatly in achieving public understanding and support.

Paradoxically, when the public understands the concept of low-security inmates, they may push their political leaders and legislators into more use of community corrections and greater use of noninstitutional options. This type of inmate provides little threat to the security of the community. Correctional officers should be informed about various correctional options so that they can be articulate spokespersons with their neighbors and members of community organizations.

By the same token, prison riots in the last several decades also have reflected the inmates' idea that the public knew little or nothing of their plight—real or imagined. As a result, inmates believed that drastic action was needed to alert the public to their demands. A policy of openness regarding public information about the institution may help prevent such potentially disruptive situations.

The Value of Educating the Public

Good institutional public relations is really just public education. If the average citizen had an accurate picture of what corrections is about, what prison staff do, what types of inmates they deal with, and what resources actually are available, there would be far fewer public concerns about prison operations, and probably more resources devoted to program options. The image that most citizens have about prisons is shaped to a large degree by James Cagney and Clint Eastwood movies and the sensationalistic stories that are carried in the press and the electronic media when there is a riot or escape.

Other factors that affect how the public views prisons are within the control of correctional staff. Each correctional officer is a roving ambassador for the correctional institution. For example, telephone contacts and correspondence with the public affect how the institution is regarded; discourteous treatment in the course of a telephone call or the lack of a response to a letter of inquiry can reinforce an already negative image. A taxpayer who is disgruntled because of inconsiderate treatment at the hands of an institutional employee can cause untold damage to the institution's reputation and the professional status of its employees.

To a certain degree, public images about corrections also are shaped by what local citizens see in the public behavior of institutional staff. Careless speech, negative comments about inmates, the improper use of the uniform, impolite and discourteous personal relationships—all of these day-to-day elements can contribute to poor public relations. They certainly can damage or destroy the hard work of many others who are trying to upgrade the public's view of corrections and correctional officers.

Courtesy Capitol Communication Systems, Inc.

Keeping the public informed about the activities of the correctional system can pay big dividends in terms of public support.

The Media

Mass media sources are the most common avenues for information, and yet correctional agencies traditionally have been reluctant to allow the press into institutions, or to allow inmates to have media contacts. However, a series of court cases in the last several decades has reinforced the principle that inmates' First Amendment rights include some form of access to the media. As a result, with the public's increased interest in correctional institutions, it is no surprise that inmates have made more demands to communicate directly to the public, or that the press has sought to report more fully on the activities and conditions of prison life.

Most agencies have a well-developed policy that regulates how and when an inmate can write to the media, receive an in-person media interview, or make telephone calls to media representatives. All employees should familiarize themselves with these regulations to ensure that they do not violate a policy that is based on an important constitutional right.

Allowing the media to have access to correctional institutions should be more than just complying with court decisions. It can be a positive management tool. By permitting media representatives to come into prisons, see the programs and services that are offered, and watch staff do their jobs, correctional administrators easily can neutralize many of the inmates' usually groundless claims of brutality and subhuman living conditions.

When local reporters are familiar with the prison "beat" and know what actual living conditions are in the institution, they are far less likely to sensationalize the raw allegations of a discontented inmate, attorney, or outside support group. If the national media can be convinced of the integrity and humanity of prison operations, fewer negative stories will appear at that level.

The Role of the Correctional Officer

In most cases, the line correctional officer will not have direct contact with the media and will be guided by policies of the institution on what to do if contacted by the media. However, there are some areas which are important to remember.

Public Information Functions

In most states and in the federal prison system, policy and statutes limit who may release information about inmates and institutional operations. These restrictions often are tied to legal limits on information disclosure about individual inmates. As a result, almost all institutions and agencies have a designated public information office, or a public information officer who is the only person authorized to release information about the organization. Line staff should be aware of the limits their particular agency places on employees in this regard, so that if they are approached with a request for information about the institution by a reporter or a member of the public, they should be familiar with what they may and may not say. When in doubt about the appropriate response, it is best to say nothing, and to either refer the person to the public information officer or seek advice from a supervisor.

Media Tours

Media tours can be an excellent way for getting out information about the institution and its programs. There is no question that most reporters, editors, and others in the media are underinformed about corrections. When they receive letters from inmates claiming severe abuses or inhumane living conditions, they have no frame of reference. Tours and regular open house sessions for public leaders help neutralize this factor. Officers who assist in institutional tours can be helpful by responding to questions about institutional routines, but they should refer questions about agency policies or individual inmates to a supervisor or public information officer.

Ethics and Relationships with Ex-inmates and Inmate Families

The entire subject of ethics is an important one, and it is covered in some detail in the ACA Code of Ethics (see page 161). In addition to the topics covered in the Code, several points require additional explanation regarding the specific relationship between inmates and staff.

Most institutions have a clear policy against any type of business dealings between staff and inmates. This is to prevent staff in any way becoming obligated to inmates, and thereby being subject to extortion or pressure to bring in contraband, aid in an escape, or engage in some other improper or illegal activity.

Speaking bluntly, staff need to approach their relationships with inmates with a very healthy dose of skepticism, tempered by extreme caution. While it is perfectly appropriate for employees to give advice to inmates in professional areas in which they are qualified, there are no occasions where staff should approach inmates for advice of any kind, or share with them their personal affairs. Those situations not only can be the start of an obligatory relationship, but can provide the inmate with personal information about the employee which later can be used against him or her and the institution.

The classic example is that of an inmate learning from an officer about financial difficulties, and the inmate offering first financial advice and then direct assistance, if only the officer will do a simple favor. The same strategy can be employed if an inmate learns about an employee's marital problems and attempts to exploit the employee's emotional turmoil. There are many variations on this theme, but in the final analysis, staff members who get too "close" to inmates are at great risk of compromising not only themselves, but institutional security.

Family and community relationships can be just as complicated. In many small towns, the families of inmates, and ex-inmates themselves, may live, work, and, at times, be involved in civic and social functions with institutional staff. These relationships, while not always bad, have a great potential for problems.

In general, most agencies will have a policy that guides staff on the limits on these types of contacts. However, as a rule, business and other financial relationships with even an ex-inmate would be considered a particularly serious concern, as would any personal contact of any kind with the spouse or family of a current inmate.

This is a sensitive area, in which there is not total agreement, primarily because of the increasing use of community correctional programs that keep offenders in or near their home communities. However, the rule of thumb for all of these situations is to follow agency policies and talk to supervisory staff. When in doubt about a particular situation, it is probably best not to be involved.

A volunteer outlines the program and method he will employ in working with inmates.

Photos courtesy Capitol Communication Systems, Inc.

Volunteers play a vital role in the operation of many institutions. It is important that correctional officers understand the role of the volunteers and work with them, whenever possible.

Drug-free Staff

At a time when American society is highly concerned with drug abuse, correctional institutions should be as drug free as modern security can make them. However, in addition to the inmates, staff also must be drug free.

There was a time when such a statement would have been totally unnecessary—when drug use was not a part of middle America or the portion of the workforce that corrections draws on for its staff. Unfortunately, this is no longer the case, as many Americans in all walks of life have experimented with drugs of some type at some point in their lives.

There are several reasons for prison staff members to be drug free. First, in most cases, drug use is illegal, and correctional staff are sworn to uphold the law. Second, in the correctional setting, it is critical that all staff members are fully alert and unimpaired in their ability to act. The lives of inmates and fellow staff members literally depend on it. Third, in institutions where there are armed posts, a drug-impaired person is a risk to not only other staff, but to the public and to inmates.

Next, if inmates detect a person who is drug-dependent (and they very easily can), they will attempt to blackmail that person for personal gain, and ultimately compromise institution security. In most cases, they eventually also turn in the "dirty" staff members when they are done "using" them, often to gain some small

At the Work Ethic Camp, a four-month program at the McNeil Island Corrections Center, youthful offenders learn responsibility through working in an intensive, regimented program.

additional benefit when they finally expose the staff members' cooperation. Finally, the damage to the institution's public image, and to that of corrections as well, is very great when a drug-abusing staff member finally is found out and fired and/or prosecuted.

Personal Conduct and Appearance

The matter of staff members' personal conduct and appearance ties in with the drug issue. If prison employees are involved in disruptive behavior in the community, if they are alcohol abusers, dress disreputably, or otherwise are not good citizens, those impressions inevitably will rub off on the institution. People will say, "Well, if that's the kind of person they have working out there, all those stories I've heard must be true." Every employee is a walking ambassador for corrections, a representative of the institution itself, the agency, and corrections as a profession.

Community involvement on the part of employees is another part of this picture. If employees are contributing to their community in a positive way—managing ball teams or being active in civic organizations or church affairs, for instance—they will reinforce the thought that the institution and its staff are good members of the community, and that corrections is positive.

Citizen Involvement in Prison Activities

Good institutional programming often involves structured inmate contacts with desirable persons from outside the prison. Some jurisdictions have a citizen advisory or community relations board for each institution. These groups can provide information on, and referrals to, community programs that can benefit inmates, such as work and study release, recreation activities, and theater groups. Citizen involvement and volunteer programs can generate a wide variety of services for inmates, both during their confinement and after their release. These activities may include sports programs, volunteer tutoring sessions, and religious counseling.

Security precautions are necessary while permitting these contacts; depending on the institution, staff escorts or supervision may be required. Most locations have a screening and orientation process for those involved, and provide necessary staff escorts or supervision, depending on the activity or area of the institution involved. The institution can contribute to the development of positive community relationships by providing adequate facilities and streamlined procedures for these joint inside-outside activities.

Inmates should be aware of volunteer services and the nature of those services. Attempts should be made to see that inmates understand the volunteers' role and the limits of their authority. Due in part to changing laws, the rate of juveniles incarcerated in adult prisons will require new programs tailored for this age group. It will also require a core of dedicated volunteers to cope with the needs of this age group.

Community and Public Service Activities

Institutions and suitably classified, low-risk inmates have carried out many community and public service programs. These programs not only help the community, but also give inmates a greater sense of self-worth and membership in the outside world. Examples include inmates running marathon races inside institutions to raise money for local charities through community sponsors, Jaycee organizations in prisons assisting outside Jaycee groups in civic activities, institutions providing fire fighting crews for local fire emergencies, and even direct inmate work on civic improvement projects such as improving park and recreation facilities.

Inmates at forestry camps frequently are used for fire fighting and for searching for children or adults lost in the woods. Inmate pharmacists from these camps sometimes give first aid to local residents when regular

Minimum-security inmates can make a major difference during emergencies. Here boot camp members in Illinois build a barricade to prevent further flooding.

Public Relations and Citizen Involvement

The public information officer must learn about all noteworthy situations so that she or he can explain them to the media, the public, and legislators, if necessary.

Courtesy Capitol Communication Systems, Inc.

medical services are not available or during emergencies. Inmates have been released to help communities in snow, flood, and hurricane emergencies.

Inmates from many institutions donate toys they have repaired to needy children during Christmas. They frequently donate products of their craft work, such as ashtrays, lamps, bookends, and custom-made jewelry, to members of the clergy for distribution to various church groups. The inmate stamp club at one correctional institution donated approximately 300 stamp albums with United States cancellations and 300 packets of assorted cancellations to orphanages that sponsor stamp clubs.

Inmates of many institutions have adopted children through organizations devoted to finding suitable homes and sponsors for underprivileged children around the world. The adopting individual or group contributes as little as fifteen dollars a month, out of which the child receives an outright grant. The remainder is used for food and clothing packages, translation of letters, medical services, and education.

Inmates in several state facilities have organized tape-recording programs. Hundreds of books at every level of interest—philosophy, religion, literature, history, mathematics and science—are taped, when requested. In most cases, the sponsoring organization is responsible for supplying the equipment to the correctional institution, and in many cases, the organization receives assistance from such interested groups as service clubs, businesses, and charitable organizations.

Summary

Good public information activity and productive citizen involvement are major factors in the support that a correctional institution receives. Correctional officers have the opportunity to play a role in this function by presenting a professional image of both their work and the correctional institution.

APPLICABLE ACA STANDARDS

Administration and Management: 3-4005

Citizen Involvement and Volunteers: 3-4111 - 3-4119

Media: 3-4021-1

Personnel: 3-4021-1

BIBLIOGRAPHY

Allen, B. and Diana Bosta. 1981. *Games Criminals Play and How You Can Profit by Knowing Them.* Available from American Correctional Association.

Bayse, Daniel. 1993. *Helping Hands: A Handbook for Volunteers in Prisons and Jails.* Lanham, Maryland: American Correctional Association.

Lauen, Roger. 1997. *Positive Approaches to Corrections: Research, Policy, and Practice.* Lanham, Maryland: American Correctional Association.

Job Titles

The following list contains job titles and descriptions of some of the opportunities in the field of corrections. Some of these jobs will require college degrees, and some postgraduate degrees. They are samples of the types of opportunities available in the correctional field. These descriptions are generic, and you should refer to your own facility for a specific federal, state, or local description of a particular position. Remember, advancement within the system is possible with continued education and training.

MANAGERIAL/ADMINISTRATIVE SUPPORT

BUDGET ADMINISTRATOR: This individual plans and coordinates the use of resources for a facility.

COMPUTER SPECIALIST: This individual manages or designs use and maintenance of computer systems. This is an area of great need in the corrections field.

FACILITY MANAGER/PLANT MAINTENANCE MANAGER: This individual manages and maintains buildings, grounds, and other facilities. This position requires that the individual have managerial skills and a broad technical knowledge of operating capabilities and maintenance requirements of various types of physical plants and equipment.

FINANCIAL MANAGER: This person maintains financial services such as audits and credit analysis and coordinates financial policies and procedures.

FOOD SERVICE MANAGER: This person manages and supervises the operation of the institution's or department's food services, including the storeroom, kitchen, dining rooms, and procurement. People in this position often must be certified as a registered dietitians and be familiar with federal, state, and local health codes and sanitary standards.

LIBRARIAN: This person manages and cares for the facility's collection of books, recordings, films, and other materials.

OMBUDSPERSON: This individual acts as an unbiased liaison between inmates and facility administration; investigates inmate complaints, reports findings, and helps achieve equitable settlements of disputes between inmates and the correctional administration. This person also may be called on to achieve equity in staff issues with management.

PERSONNEL/HUMAN RESOURCES MANAGER: This person is responsible for recruiting, advising, hiring, and firing staff; implementing the institution's policies and procedures; providing leadership and supervision; advising and assisting staff with benefits.

PUBLIC INFORMATION OFFICER: This person acts as the institution's representative to the media, funding agency, and the public by providing information and responding to community and legislative requests for information. To maintain media and community relations, the public information officer must be aware of all current issues in corrections generally and the institution specifically.

RESEARCHER: This individual analyzes data for budgets and for projected needs and assists in the evaluation of programs.

SAFETY MANAGER: This individual offers technical advice on or manages occupational safety programs, regulations, and standards. A person in this position must have knowledge of the techniques of safety and pertinent aspects of engineering, psychology, and other factors affecting safety.

SECURITY MANAGER: This individual is responsible for all aspects of an institution's security. This position's responsibilities include reviewing and updating all security policies and procedures. The security manager also is responsible for such things as emergency plans, security inspections, key and lock control, arms and armory control, as well as staff training and discipline.

WARDEN/JAIL MANAGER: This individual oversees all operations and programs within the correctional facility.

COUNSELING/TRAINING

CHAPLAIN: This individual offers religious guidance and spiritual counseling to inmates. This position requires ordination by a recognized ecclesiastical body. Chaplains may be called on to minister to inmates not of their faith.

INDUSTRIAL SPECIALIST: This person assists or manages a prison industry including printshops, carpentry, agriculture, tailor shops, and sign-making programs.

JUVENILE CAREWORKER: This individual supervises the treatment and custody of juvenile offenders in correctional or rehabilitation facilities. This person often provides support and counseling to juvenile offenders and participates in the development and implementation of treatment plans.

PSYCHOLOGIST/COUNSELOR: This person works with inmates and correctional professionals and provides counseling and testing. This position generally requires professional training. Closely allied specialists may include art therapists and drama therapists. Certified drug and alcohol counselors are in great demand.

RECREATION SPECIALIST: This individual plans, organizes, and administers programs that promote inmates' physical, creative, artistic, and social development.

TEACHER: This person leads classes on subjects for both juveniles and adult offenders. This position requires a bachelor's degree plus certification by the state education authority in a specific subject area. People certified in special education are in great demand.

VOCATIONAL COUNSELOR: This person provides educational programs or career training for inmates and determines learning needs, abilities, and other facts about inmates. This individual also may participate in discussions with other staff professionals to aid in inmate rehabilitation.

VOCATIONAL INSTRUCTOR: This person provides both classroom and hands-on training in a variety of trades.

MEDICAL

HEALTH SYSTEM ADMINISTRATOR: This individual is responsible for the administrative management of the health care delivery system and use of outside resources to provide patient care.

MEDICAL OFFICER: This individual performs professional and scientific work in one or more fields of medicine. This position requires, at a minimum, the degree of Doctor of Medicine and, in most states, a current license to practice medicine. Medical support staff may include physicians' assistants, nurses, nurses' assistants, and pharmacists.

GLOSSARY

These are terms used in corrections. Correctional officers should be familiar with them. Not all of these terms are used in this publication.

ACCREDITATION: A process by which facilities or agencies are certified by the American Correctional Association (ACA) or another organization as meeting a set of standards for their physical plant, operations, performance, staffing, programs, and services.

ACQUIRED IMMUNE DEFICIENCY SYNDROME (AIDS): A disease caused by infection with HIV in which the body's immune system is unable to fight illness and disease, making individuals susceptible to a host of infections that otherwise do not affect healthy people.

ADJUDICATION: The process by which a court arrives at a decision regarding a case, also the resulting decision. It is a judgment, acquittal, or dismissal of that case.

ADMINISTRATIVE CONFINEMENT/SEGREGATION: A form of separation from the general population sometimes imposed by classification committees for inmates who pose serious threats to themselves, staff, or other inmates or to institutional security; or for those who are pending investigation for disciplinary violations or hearings for serious rule violations; as well as for those pending transfer.

ADMINISTRATIVE FACILITIES: (Federal Correctional Facility) Administrative facilities are institutions with special missions, such as the detention of noncitizens or pretrial offenders, the treatment of inmates with serious or chronic medical problems, or the containment of extremely dangerous, violent, or escape-prone inmates. Administrative facilities are capable of holding inmates in all security categories.

ADMISSION: The process of entry into a program. During admission processing, the juvenile or adult offender receives an orientation to program goals, rules, and regulations. Assignment to living quarters and to appropriate staff also is completed at this time.

ADULT CORRECTIONAL INSTITUTION: A confinement facility, usually under state or federal auspices, that has custodial authority over adults sentenced to confinement for more than one year.

ADULT LOCAL DETENTION CENTER: *See Jail.*

AFFIRMATIVE ACTION: A concept designed to ensure equal opportunity for all persons regardless of race, religion, age, sex, or ethnic origin. These equal opportunities include all personnel programming, such as selection, retention, rate of pay, demotion, transfer, layoff, termination, and promotion.

AFTERCARE: Postrelease supervision for juveniles, but the term is sometimes used to denote other programs that provide reentry into the community from jails or prisons.

AGENCY: The unit of a governing authority that has direct responsibility for the operations of a corrections program, including the implementation of policy as set by the governing authority. For a community residential center, this would be the administrative headquarters of the facilities. A single community facility that is not a part of a formal consolidation of community facilities is considered to be an agency. In a juvenile correctional organization, this would be the central office responsible for governing the juvenile correctional system for the jurisdiction.

AGENCY ADMINISTRATOR: The administrative officer appointed by the governing authority or designee who is responsible for all operations of the agency, such as the department of corrections or parole, and all related programs under his or her control.

ALCOHOLICS ANONYMOUS (AA): An independent organization that uses a twelve-step program to help members overcome addiction to alcohol.

ALTERNATIVE MEAL SERVICE: Special foods provided to comply with the medical, religious, or security requirements. Alternative meals always must be designed to ensure that basic health needs are met and are provided in strict compliance with the policies signed by the chief executive officer, the chief medical officer, and for the religious diets, by the appropriate religious leader.

AMERICAN CORRECTIONAL ASSOCIATION (ACA): A professional organization, founded in 1870, for correctional personnel and others interested in corrections. It is heavily involved in research, accreditation, and training. People seeking greater professionalization should join this organization.

AMERICAN PRISON ASSOCIATION: Created in 1870, it was the forerunner of the American Correctional Association.

AMERICANS WITH DISABILITIES ACT OF 1990 (ADA): A federal law which prohibits government agencies, including correctional institutions, from denying disabled persons—staff, visitors, and inmates—access to programs and services.

ANTIPSYCHOTIC DRUG: Any drug, such as thorazine, used to relieve or control the symptoms of psychosis (such as delusions or hallucinations). So far, there is no cure for psychotic disorders.

ANTISOCIAL PERSONALITY DISORDER: A disorder characterized by callousness, impulsiveness, lack of loyalty, and a chronic indifference to and violation of the rights of others. Individuals with this disorder are often in trouble with the law.

ASYMPTOMATIC: HIV-infected individual not showing any signs or symptoms of Acquired Immune Deficiency Syndrome (AIDS).

AUBURN SYSTEM, THE: The approach to imprisonment, also called the congregate system, developed in New York in the Auburn penitentiary between 1816-1825. It was designed to reform inmates through congregate labor, a strict rule of silence, harsh discipline, and isolation.

AUDIT: An examination of agency or facility records or accounts to check their accuracy. It is conducted by a person or persons not directly involved in the creation and maintenance of these records or accounts. An independent audit results in an opinion that either affirms or disaffirms the accuracy of records or accounts. An operational or internal audit usually results in a report to management that is not shared with those outside the agency.

BODY CAVITY SEARCHES: Searches conducted of body orifices (such as the anus) for contraband. It should only be performed by qualified medical personnel in private.

BOOKING: Both a law enforcement process and a detention facility procedure. As a police administrative action, it is an official recording of an arrest and the identification of the person, place, time, arresting authority, and reason for the arrest. In a detention facility, it is a procedure for the admission of a person charged with or convicted for an offense, which includes searching, fingerprinting, photographing, medical screening, and collecting personal history data. Booking also includes the inventory and storage of the individual's personal property.

BOOT CAMP: A short-term correctional unit designed to combine elements of basic military training programs, correctional components, and sometimes other elements. These shock incarceration programs allow inmates to shorten the length of their sentence in return for the intensified program. Newer programs often deemphasize the military regimen and put more stress on treatment programs such as education, work, substance-abuse treatment, and developing a prosocial lifestyle. Often, it is followed by some form of community aftercare and supervision.

BURNOUT: A state of emotional exhaustion and cynicism that frequently occurs among individuals who are involved in "people work." This is particularly true for those who work closely with others under conditions of chronic tension and stress. It frequently is characterized by emotional exhaustion, depersonalization, decreased competence, and detachment from the job caused by stress.

CAREER DEVELOPMENT PLAN: The planned sequence of promotions within an agency that contains provision for (1) vertical movement throughout the entire range of a particular discipline, (2) horizontal movement encouraging lateral and promotional movement among disciplines, and (3) opportunity for all to compete for the position of head of the agency. Progression along these three dimensions can occur as long as the candidate has the ambition, ability, and required qualifications.

CASE CONFERENCE: A conference between individuals working with the juvenile or adult offender to see that court-ordered services are being provided.

CASEWORK: The function of the caseworker, social worker, or other professional who provides coordination of social services, such as counseling, credit counseling, and job search help to individuals in custody and on probation or parole.

CELLBLOCK: A group or cluster of single and/or multiple occupancy cells or detention rooms immediately adjacent and directly accessible to a day or activity room.

CHAIN OF COMMAND: A hierarchical structure that indicates levels of supervision. To maintain control of a large organization, a leader delegates oversight of its many workers and activities to executive managers who in turn delegate authority to middle managers who give authority to first-line supervisors, who authorize correctional officers to perform specific duties.

Glossary

CHEMICAL AGENT: An active substance, such as tear gas, used to defer activities that might cause personal injury or property damage.

CIVIL RIGHTS ACT OF 1871: An act passed by the federal legislature that attempted to protect the rights of blacks following the Civil War.

CIVIL RIGHTS ACT OF 1964: A federal law that prohibits discrimination in the workplace.

CIVIL RIGHTS OF INSTITUTIONALIZED PERSONS (CRIPA): This federal law allows the Justice Department to sue a facility on behalf of inmates' civil rights and encourages development of grievance programs, 42 USC 1997.

CIVIL RIGHTS (SECTION 1983) ACTIONS: See Section 1983 of the Civil Rights Act.

CLASSIFICATION: A process for determining the needs and requirements of those for whom confinement has been ordered and for assigning them to housing units and programs according to their needs and existing resources.

CLEAR AND PRESENT DANGER: Doctrine in constitutional law providing that governmental restrictions on freedoms of speech and press will be upheld if necessary to prevent grave and immediate danger to interests which the government may lawfully protect.

CLOSE-CUSTODY INMATES: Classification status reserved for inmates with past assaultive and/or escape histories. Constant supervision and full restraints are required when leaving the facility. During the day, inmates are permitted to leave their cells and go to other parts of the institution on a check-out/check-in basis under staff observation.

CLOSE-SECURITY FACILITIES/LEVEL V: In these institutions, perimeter security is the same as for maximum-security prisons, but with single, outside cells. When not in their cells, inmates are normally under direct supervision, usually with inmates of different custody categories.

CODE OF ETHICS: A set of rules describing acceptable standards of conduct for all employees. The American Correctional Association also issues a code of ethics (see last page in this book).

COMMISSARY: The prison "store" where inmates can buy items such as cigarettes, shampoo, candy, and other items.

COMMITMENT: A judicial action placing an individual in a particular type of confinement as authorized by law.

COMMUNITY CORRECTIONS: Programs that deal with offenders in the community. They may include: work release, home detention, probation/parole, diversion, pretrial release, fine options, community services, and restitution.

COMMUNITY RESOURCES: Human services agencies, service clubs, citizen interest groups, self-help groups, and individual citizen volunteers that offer services, facilities, or other functions that can meet the needs of the facility or have the potential to assist residents. These various resources, which may be public or private and national or local, may assist with material and financial support, guidance, counseling, and supportive services.

COMMUNITY SECURITY FACILITIES/LEVEL I: These are nonsecure facilities that include prerelease centers (such as work release or educational release), halfway houses, and other nonsecure settings.

COMPELLING GOVERNMENT INTEREST: For correctional facilities, this means anything representing a serious threat to a prison's security, order, or discipline.

COMPENSATORY DAMAGES: Money to compensate the injured party for the injury sustained.

CONCURRENT SENTENCE: A sentence that is one of two or more sentences imposed at the same time. After conviction, all or part of each term is served simultaneously. Contrast with Consecutive Sentence.

CONDITIONAL RELEASES: Releases in which the correctional system maintains some supervision over the releasee for a specified period of time. Typically, it includes parole, supervised mandatory release, and supervised work furloughs.

CONSECUTIVE SENTENCE: A sentence that is one of two or more sentences imposed at the same time, after conviction. The sentences are served in sequence. Contrast with Concurrent Sentence.

CONSENT DECREE: A court judgment in which both parties agree to work out the terms of the settlement subject to court approval.

CONTACT VISITS: Prison visitation that permits visitors and inmates to have a limited degree of nonsexual physical contact.

CONTRABAND: Items that are declared illegal or off-limits to inmates by prison authorities. This includes homemade weapons and illegal drugs.

CONTRACTOR: A person or organization that agrees to furnish materials or services at a specified price. Contractors operating in correctional facilities are subject to all applicable rules and regulations for the facility.

CONTROL CENTER: A very secure, self-contained unit designed to maintain the security of the facility. Policies governing the design, staffing, and accessibility of the control center ensure it cannot be commandeered by unauthorized persons.

CONVICT: A name given to inmates, also known as hogs, wise guys, bad dudes, outlaws, or other terms. Inmates with this status are the most respected figures in contemporary prisons and dominate the inmate world in violent prisons; emphasis is on toughness and willingness to use violence to maintain one's status.

CONVICT CODE: The dominant value system in the Big House, heavily influenced by the thieves' code, which included the following values: do your own time, don't rat or snitch on another prisoner; maintain your dignity and respect; help other thieves; leave most other inmates alone; and manifest no weakness.

CORRECTIONAL FACILITY: A single facility or group of buildings used for the incarceration of individuals accused or convicted of criminal activity. A correctional facility is managed by a single chief executive officer with broad authority for the operation of the facility. This authority typically includes the final authority for decisions concerning (1) the employment or termination of staff members, and (2) the facility operation and programming within guidelines established by the parent agency or governing body.

A correctional facility also must have (1) a separate perimeter that precludes the regular commingling of inmates from other facilities, (2) a separate facility budget managed by a chief executive officer within guidelines established by the parent agency or governing authority, and (3) staff that are permanently assigned to the facility.

CORRECTIONAL INSTITUTIONS: This name came into widespread use during the rehabilitation era to connote changes in the focus of prisons from punishment to treatment. Today, it continues to be a method of referring to prisons, state systems, the federal system, and even local systems that deal with detainees and offenders.

CORRECTIONAL OFFICERS (COs): Custodial personnel who directly supervise inmates.

CORRECTIONS: Corrections has at least two definitions: (1) the official response taken by criminal justice agencies to the punishment of convicted offenders in the United States; (2) the agencies, programs, and organizations on the local, state, and federal levels that detain those accused of crimes and those convicted of them.

CORRECTIONS TODAY: Magazine published by the American Correctional Association (ACA); it deals with corrections and other related criminal justice issues. It comes free with ACA membership.

COUNSELING: Planned use of interpersonal relationships to promote social adjustment. Counseling programs provide opportunities to express feelings verbally with the goal of resolving the individual's problems. At least three types of counseling may be provided: individual (a one-to-one relationship), small-group counseling, and large-group counseling in a living unit.

COUNTS: Process for determining the whereabouts of every inmate in a prison/jail by physically counting them. Counts are conducted several times each day and all prison activities usually stop until all inmates are counted. (Counts occur at the beginning and end of each shift of operations, and after any mass movement. Usually there is one formal count each twenty-four hours).

CRUEL AND UNUSUAL PUNISHMENT: Conditions and practices in prisons such as solitary confinement, corporal punishment, use of force by correctional officers, and other conditions of confinement that go beyond the limits allowed by the U.S. Constitution.

CUSTODY: Legal or physical control of or responsibility for a person or thing.

DEADLY FORCE: Force that is considered likely to or intended to cause death or great bodily harm.

DELIBERATE INDIFFERENCE: The meaning of this concept from a legal standpoint is far from clear. However, court cases suggest deliberate indifference occurs if prison officials know or should have known, because the condition is obvious, that what they are doing or not doing is a risk to inmate health and safety but take no action.

DEPARTMENT OF CORRECTIONS: A government agency that is headed by a politically appointed director who develops policy and oversees the operation of mandated correctional facilities and programs.

DETAINER: A warrant placed against a person incarcerated in a correctional facility, notifying the holding authority of the intention of another jurisdiction to take custody of that individual when he or she is released.

DEVELOPMENTALLY DISABLED INMATES: Those inmates who have markedly lower intellectual capacity (IQ), lack social/life skills or who are functionally illiterate, have learning disabilities, organic brain disorders, or who are mildly retarded.

DIRECT SUPERVISION: A method of inmate management that ensures continuing direct contact between inmates and staff by posting an officer(s) inside each housing unit. Officers in general housing units are not separated from inmates by a physical barrier. Officers provide frequent, nonscheduled observation of and personal interaction with inmates.

DISCIPLINARY CONFINEMENT/DETENTION: The punishment given to some inmates found guilty of a serious rule violation. Inmates usually are placed in more secure units and their privileges are restricted.

DISCIPLINARY HEARING: A nonjudicial administrative procedure to determine if substantial evidence exists to find an inmate guilty of a rule violation.

Glossary

DISCIPLINARY REPORT (DR, or TICKET): A written report citing an inmate involved in a relatively serious rule violation. An investigation and/or hearing is held to determine the validity of the complaint and to impose punishment, where appropriate.

DISCIPLINARY SEGREGATION: Condition that results when an inmate is isolated as a result of serious violation of institutional rules and a finding of guilt after a due process hearing. Privileges such as personal visiting, commissary, television, and programs may be suspended. The purpose is to punish wrongdoers and to isolate them from the general inmate population.

DUE PROCESS CLAUSE, FOURTEENTH AMENDMENT: This clause protects persons from state actions. There are two aspects: procedural, in which a person is guaranteed fair procedures, and substantive, which protects a person's property from unfair governmental interference or taking.

DUE PROCESS SAFEGUARDS: Those procedures that ensure just, equal, and lawful treatment of an individual involved in all stages of the juvenile or criminal justice system, such as a notice of allegations, impartial and objective fact finding, the right to counsel, a written record of proceedings, a statement of any disposition ordered with the reasons for it, and the right to confront accusers, call witnesses, and present evidence.

EARLY-RELEASE PROGRAMS: These are inmate release processes that include early parole or sentence reduction for certain offenders (such as early release of usually nonviolent offenders within a few months of sentence completion) to cope with crowding in accordance with court-imposed population caps.

EDUCATION PROGRAM: A program of formal academic education or a vocational training activity designed to improve employment capability.

EIGHTH AMENDMENT, THE: Constitutional amendment that prohibits excessive bail, excessive fines, and cruel and unusual punishment.

ELECTRIFIED FENCES: Fences used in prison perimeter security that are topped with razor wire and carry several thousand volts and at over 70 milliamperes may kill someone who comes in contact with it.

ELECTRONIC MONITORING: Elaborate electronic telemetry devices designed to verify that an offender is at a given location during specified times. Used as an option in community corrections.

EMERGENCY: Any significant disruption of normal facility or agency procedure, policy, or activity caused by riot, escape, fire, natural disaster, employee action, or other serious incident.

EMERGENCY CARE: Care of an acute illness or unexpected health care need that cannot be deferred until the next scheduled sick call. Emergency care shall be provided to the resident population by the medical director or other staff, local ambulance services, and/or outside hospital emergency rooms. This care shall be expedited by following specific written procedures for medical emergencies.

EMERGENCY RESPONSE TEAM (ERT): Selected correctional officers who are specially trained to handle emergencies—including riots, assaultive inmates, large-scale searches, and other concerns.

ENVIRONMENTAL HEALTH: All conditions, circumstances, and surrounding influences that affect the health of individuals or groups in the area.

EXCESS FORCE: Force used beyond the need and circumstances of the particular event, which means it was unnecessary or was used to inflict punishment.

FACILITY: A place, institution, building (or part thereof), set of buildings, or area (whether or not enclosing a building or a set of buildings) that is used for the lawful custody and/or treatment of individuals. It may be owned and/or operated by public or private agencies and includes the staff and services as well as the buildings and grounds.

FACILITY ADMINISTRATOR: Any official, regardless of local title (such as warden/superintendent, chief of police, administrator, or sheriff) who has the ultimate responsibility for managing and operating the facility.

FACILITY SECURITY LEVEL: The nature and number of physical design barriers available to prevent escape and to control inmate behavior.

FEDERAL BUREAU OF PRISONS (BOP): Organization created by Congress in 1930 that is responsible for incarcerating those individuals convicted of violating federal laws.

FELONY: A criminal offense that is punishable by death or by incarceration in a state or federal prison, generally for one year or more. Violent felonies include: murder, rape, abduction, and robbery.

FIRST AMENDMENT, THE: Constitutional guarantee that no laws will be enacted that restrict or abridge our freedom of religion, speech, and the press.

FIRST-LINE SUPERVISORS: Lowest level of administration within the prison (such as corporals, unit managers) who supervise line personnel.

FISH: A newcomer to prison.

FLEX CUFFS: See Handcuffs.

FOURTH AMENDMENT, THE: Constitutional amendment that protects against unreasonable searches and seizures of property by government officials.

FURLOUGH OR TEMPORARY LEAVE: A period of time during which a resident is allowed to leave the facility and go into the community unsuperised.

GANG COLORS: A color or pattern of colors that identifies a particular gang. The color is worn by gang members as part of their clothing.

GENDER BIAS: Bias toward or discrimination against an individual on the basis of his or her sex.

GOOD TIME: A statutory provision for the reduction of time served on a sentence through the accumulation of credits that are either automatic (such as one day for every two days served) and/or earned (such as given for participation in programs or exceptional conduct).

GRIEVANCE/GRIEVANCE PROCESS: A circumstance or action considered to be unjust and grounds for complaint or resentment and/or a response to the circumstance in the form of a written complaint filed with the appropriate body.

HANDCUFFS: Temporary restraints that help control inmates in situations where they might escape, injure themselves or others, or become unruly or dangerous.

HEALTH CARE: The sum of all action taken, preventative and therapeutic, to provide for the physical and mental well-being of a population. Includes medical and dental services, mental health services, nursing, personal hygiene, dietary services, and environmental conditions.

HEARING: A proceeding to determine a course of action, such as the placement of a juvenile or adult offender, or to determine guilt or innocence in a disciplinary matter. Argument, witnesses, or evidence are heard by a judicial officer or administrative body in making the determination.

HILTON-HOTEL SYNDROME: This mistaken idea expresses the concern that inmate living conditions are better than those enjoyed by the majority of free-world Americans.

HONOR BLOCKS OR HONOR TIERS: A dormitory or area within a prison reserved for inmates who have maintained good behavior over relatively long periods of time. Inmates there usually have more privileges.

INDETERMINATE SENTENCE: Under strict indeterminate sentencing, judges assign custody of the offender to the department of corrections, and the offender's release is dependent on the offender's readiness to function prosocially in society. In most cases, it is used in a modified form which consists of a range of time, such as three-to-five years, that is defined in terms of a minimum period to be served before release can be considered, and a maximum period after which the inmate must be released. Usually, it is associated with rehabilitation and parole.

INDIGENT: An individual with no funds or source of income.

INDUSTRIES: An activity existing in a correctional system that uses inmate labor to produce goods and/or services for sale. These goods and/or services are sold at prices calculated to recover all or a substantial portion of costs associated with their production and may include a margin of profit. Sale of the products and/or services is not limited to the institution where the industries' activity is located.

INFIRMARIES: The most common type of medical facility in correctional settings; generally found in jails and prisons with populations of 500 or more inmates. They provide bed care for inmates and thus have round-the-clock nursing care.

INFORMATION SYSTEM: The concepts, personnel, and supporting technology for the collection, organization, and delivery of information for administrative use. There are two such types of information: (1) standard information, consisting of the data required for operations control, such as the daily count, payroll data in a personnel office, probation/parole success rates, referral sources, and caseload levels; (2) demand information, consisting of information that can be generated when a report is required, such as information on the number of residents in educational and training programs, duration of residence, or the number of residents eligible for discharge during a twelve-month period by offense, sentence, and month of release. (Also referred to as a management information system.)

INFORMED CONSENT: The agreement by a patient to a treatment, examination, or procedure after the patient receives the material facts regarding the nature, consequences, risks, and alternatives concerning the proposed treatment, examination, or procedure.

INMATE: Any individual, whether in pretrial, unsentenced, or sentenced status, who is confined in a correctional facility.

INMATE-CUSTODY CATEGORY: The degree of staff supervision necessary to ensure adequate control of the inmate.

INMATE HANDBOOK: A booklet containing information regarding the rules, regulations, programs, and procedures within the prison with which the inmate should become familiar.

INSERVICE TRAINING: Any form of specialized training to enhance the job skills of an individual occurring after the individual has assumed the day-to-day responsibilities of that job. This includes outside workshops, seminars and training programs, and participation in specially developed correspondence courses.

JAIL: 1. A confinement facility usually administered by a local law enforcement agency, intended for adults but sometimes also containing juveniles, which holds persons pending adjudication and/or persons committed after adjudication for sentences of a year or less. 2. The penalty of commitment to the jurisdiction of a confinement facility system for adults, of which the custodial authority is limited to persons sentenced to a year or less of confinement.

Glossary

JAILHOUSE LAWYERS (JHL): Inmates who, without formal training, become proficient in writing writs and briefs and who help other inmates in dealing with appeals, violations of inmate rights, and other legal matters.

JITTERBUGS: The term used to describe many youthful inmates by adult or older inmates.

JOCKERS: Sexual aggressors who take the traditional masculine role in oral or anal intercourse during a homosexual encounter.

JUSTIFIABLE USE OF FORCE: Correctional officers can use force in self-defense and in defense of others; to prevent a crime; to detain or arrest inmates; to enforce prison rules and discipline; and to protect property and prevent inmates from harming themselves.

KEISTERING: A prison term referring to the concealment of such items as hacksaw blades, handcuff keys, and drugs by inmates in their rectums to bring these items into the prison.

LEAST RESTRICTIVE MEANS TEST FOR RFRA CASES: See Religious Freedom Restoration Act (RFRA). Prison officials only can ban legitimate practices that are an important part of pursuing a religion if they show the restriction is based on a compelling government test and there is no alternative means of allowing inmates to engage in this practice that does not comprise a compelling government interest.

LEG IRONS: Cuffs placed on inmates' legs.

LESS THAN LETHAL WEAPONS: These are weapons that are not likely to be lethal if properly used. They include impact weapons (batons), chemical agents, and electrical disablers used to temporarily disable the inmate and not to inflict permanent injury.

LIBERTY INTERESTS: Interests that require due process protection and are defined by the Constitution, court orders, statutes, regulations, or standard practice policies or customs. In the case of statutes or regulations, liberty interests exist only if these rules have in them mandatory language and substantive predicates, in other words, that stipulate specific conditions or requirements.

LIFE SAFETY CODE: A manual published and updated by the National Fire Protection Association specifying minimum standards for fire safety necessary for the public interest. Two chapters are devoted to correctional facilities.

LIFE SKILLS PROGRAMS: Educational programs that provide inmates with practical knowledge on employability/job search skills, consumer skills, the use of community resources, health and safety skills, parenting and family skills, and civic skills.

LINEAR DESIGN FACILITIES: Jail and prison facilities in which the cells are constructed in long straight rows aligned with corridors where correctional staff walk from cell to cell to intermittently supervise inmate activities.

LINE PERSONNEL: These are the workers who directly perform the activities that accomplish the goals and objectives of the organization (especially correctional officers).

LITIGIOUS: Overly inclined to litigate. (We have a litigious inmate population).

LOCKDOWN: An action taken by prison administrators consisting of keeping inmates locked in their cells when a breakdown of order appears imminent.

MACE: A type of tear gas that is the least incapacitating of the gasses currently in use.

MAJOR INFRACTION: A rule violation involving a grievous loss and requiring imposition of due process procedures. Major infractions include (1) violations that may result in disciplinary detention or administrative segregation; (2) violations for which punishment may tend to increase an inmate's sentence, such as extending time until parole eligibility; (3) violations that may result in a forfeiture, such as loss of good-time or work time; and (4) violations that may be referred for criminal prosecution.

MANDATORY RELEASE: Under this form of release from incarceration, inmates are placed under the supervision of a parole officer after they have served their original sentences minus earned or administratively awarded good time.

MAXIMUM-CUSTODY INMATES: They pose the most serious threats to other inmates or staff, or may be high-escape risks. They are confined in single cells; only removed for authorized activities when escorted by at least one staff member; involved only in programs conducted in their cells; eat in their cells; and are allowed only noncontact visits.

MAXIMUM SECURITY/LEVEL V: A prison with the highest level of security generally in an end-of-the-line facility. Inmates here require secure housing in the most secure perimeter, and separate management for activities such as work, exercise, and food service. Inmate housing is normally in single inside cells. In correctional systems with super-max facilities, they represent the highest security level.

MEDICAL RECORDS: Separate records of medical examinations and diagnoses maintained by the responsible physician. The date and time of all medical examinations and copies of standing or direct medical orders from the physician to the facility staff should be transferred to the resident's record.

MEDICAL RESTRAINTS: Either chemical restraints, such as sedatives, or physical restraints, such as straitjackets, applied only for medical or psychiatric purposes.

MEDICAL SCREENING: A system of structured observation/initial health assessment to identify newly arrived juvenile or adult offenders who pose a health or safety threat to themselves or others.

MEDIUM-CUSTODY INMATES: These types of inmates move about the institution during the day within sight of a correctional officer. They are eligible for all programs and activities within the main perimeter. Indoor contact visits are permitted.

MEDIUM-SECURITY PRISONS/LEVEL III: They usually have external perimeter security that is similar to level IV and V. Housing is in single cells, rooms, or dormitories. People at this level are allowed a wide variety of programs and activities and greater freedom of movement within the facility than higher levels of security.

MENTALLY RETARDED: Individual who functions at a subaverage general intellectual level and is deficient in adaptive behavior.

MERCHANTS: Inmates who obtain or manufacture scarce luxury items, both legal and illegal (such as cigarettes, "hooch," or weapons) to be sold or traded in the inmate economy.

MINIMAL NECESSITIES OF CIVILIZED LIFE, THE: The factors considered by the courts in making decisions regarding the constitutionality of the totality of prison living conditions. These include food, shelter, sanitation, health care, and personal safety.

MINIMUM-CUSTODY INMATES: These individuals do not pose risks associated with those in the higher-custody levels. They can move about the facility without being directly within the view of staff. They are eligible for all inside jobs and supervised assignments outside the prison's perimeter. They have access to all programs and activities.

MINIMUM SECURITY PRISON/LEVEL II: This prison is of open design with perimeters consisting of a single fence or clearly designated unarmed "posts." It has no detection devices and no intermittent external mobile patrols. Housing is in open units varying from dormitory style to single or multiple occupancy rooms. Heavy emphasis is on programs and activities.

MISSION STATEMENT: A policy statement that delineates the purpose, goals, and objectives of the organization. This statement sets the tone for the activities of the institution or organization.

MOBILE PATROLS: These are vehicles staffed by armed correctional officers that are used to patrol the perimeter of the prison compound.

NARCOTICS ANONYMOUS (NA): This self-help organization supports recovering addicts. It follows the twelve-step program originated by AA. This is a worldwide organization with groups operating almost everywhere. Groups hold open meetings, at which anyone is welcome, and closed meetings exclusively for members at which personal problems or interpretations of the twelve steps are discussed.

NATIONAL INSTITUTE OF CORRECTIONS (NIC): This agency of the Department of Justice provides technical assistance, training, information, and grants to state and local correctional agencies throughout the country. NIC has four divisions: Jails, Prisons, Community Corrections, and Academy. It operates a clearinghouse known as the NIC Information Center. NIC provides training to state and local correctional personnel as well as Bureau of Prison employees at its Academy in Longmont, Colorado.

NATIONAL COMMISSION ON CORRECTIONAL HEALTH CARE (NCCHC): An organization composed of representatives from thirty-six organizations that have an interest in correctional health care, and who set standards for prison medical services. It also conducts site visits to evaluate jails and prisons to see that they meet certain minimum standards and may achieve accredited status.

NATIONAL PRISON CONGRESS: At this conference held in 1870, the leading reform ideas of the era were discussed and incorporated into a declaration of principles that advocated a philosophy of reformation as opposed to the adoption of punishment. This was the first meeting of what today is called the American Correctional Association.

NOLLE PROSEQUI: A formal decision by the prosecutor not to prosecute further.

NOLO CONTENDERE: A plea in court in answer to a charge stating that the defendant will not contest the charges, but neither admits guilt nor claims innocence. It is tantamount to a guilty plea.

NOMINAL DAMAGES: A trifling sum awarded to a plaintiff where there is no substantial loss or injury.

NONCONTACT VISITATION: A condition of prison visitation in which visitors and inmates are denied physical contact either by being separated by glass partitions and communicating through telephones or separated by mesh screens.

NONVIOLENT FELONY: A criminal offense that did not involve injury or death to the victim nor violence in its commission. Nonviolent felonies include: burglary, grand larceny, embezzlement, and drug possession.

OCCUPATIONAL/JOB STRESS: Factors associated with the job itself, such as negative inmate behavior, crowding, and those which are part of the organizational environment (such as lack of administrative support) that make people feel uncomfortable, overwhelmed, unhappy, fearful, or anxious. These emotional responses to stimuli may have dysfunctional psychological or physiological consequences (such as depression, heart attacks, and hypertension).

OFFENDER: An individual convicted or adjudicated of a criminal offense.

Glossary

OFFENDER PERSONNEL FILE: A current and accurate record of the inmate's job history, including all pertinent information relating to that history.

PAROLE: The process of releasing inmates from incarceration before the end of their sentence, on conditions of supervision by a parole officer and their maintenance of good behavior. If conditions are violated, the inmate may be reincarcerated.

PERIMETER SECURITY: The structures and processes, consisting of secure walls, protected windows, and controlled access to the points of entrance and exit, that protect against escape from a prison or jail.

PERMANENT STATUS: A personnel status for employees that provides due process protection prior to dismissal.

PODULAR DIRECT FACILITIES: Jail or prison facilities with a direct supervision design. Staff is permanently situated among the inmates within each housing unit, thus allowing the most continuous supervision.

PRESERVICE TRAINING: Any form of training occurring before the individual assumes the day-to-day responsibilities of a job.

PRINCIPLE OF LEAST ELIGIBILITY: The notion that prisoners should not be given programs and services nor live under conditions that are better than those of the lowest classes of the noncriminal population in the society.

PRISON: Adult confinement facility administered by the state or federal government.

PRISON CHAPLAINS: Ministers of a particular faith who are typically employed and paid by a jurisdiction to administer, supervise, and plan all religious activities and services at a particular facility and are responsible for ministering to inmates, staff, and families regardless of their religious beliefs or affiliation.

PRISONIZATION: The process by which an offender adapts to the culture of the inmate—how to get along, what inmates to avoid, which officers are helpful.

PROACTIVE: A term that means to act in anticipation of an event. In corrections, this refers to dealing with and correcting conditions that are known to cause problems before the problems can manifest themselves.

PROBATION: A court-ordered disposition alternative through which a convicted adult offender or an adjudicated delinquent is placed under the control, supervision, and care of a probation field staff member.

PROFESSIONAL STAFF: Social workers, probation officers, and other staff assigned to juvenile and adult offender cases. These individuals generally possess bachelor's degrees and advanced training in the social or behavioral sciences.

PROTECTIVE CUSTODY: A form of separation from the general population for inmates requesting or requiring protection from other inmates for reasons of health or safety. Inmates may be witnesses, informants, or others. The inmate's status is reviewed periodically by the classification committee or other designated group.

PUNITIVE DAMAGES: In a correctional setting, those damages awarded over and above what would barely compensate inmates for their losses when the wrongful act was done intentionally and maliciously or with reckless disregard for the rights of the inmate. The intent is to punish the wrongdoer.

REASONABLE FORCE: Refers to the legally justifiable amount of force that may be used in a given situation, which is determined by the amount and type of resistance displayed.

REASONABLENESS TEST: A judicial criterion that mandates that there be a valid rational connection between a prison rule restricting inmate rights and the legitimate government interests put forth to justify it or that there be alternative means of exercising this right.

RECORDS (JUVENILE AND ADULT OFFENDERS): Information concerning the individual's delinquent or criminal, personal, medical history, behavior, and activities while in custody, including but not limited to commitment papers, court order, detainers, personal property receipts, visitor lists, photographs, fingerprints, type of custody, disciplinary infractions and actions taken, grievance reports, work assignments, program participation, and miscellaneous correspondence.

RELIGIOUS FREEDOM RESTORATION ACT (RFRA), 42USC 200bbb: Federal law requiring that the government show a compelling interest in the restriction of religious expression and employ the least restrictive measurements available when curtailing it.

SAFETY EQUIPMENT: Primarily firefighting equipment, such as chemical extinguishers, hoses, nozzles, water supplies, alarm systems, sprinkler systems, portable breathing devices, gas masks, fans, first aid kits, stretchers, and emergency alarms.

SAFETY VESTIBULE: In a correctional facility, a grille cage that divides the inmate areas from the remainder of the institution. They must have two doors or gates, only one of which opens at a time, to permit entry or exit from inmate areas in a safe and controlled manner.

SALLY PORTS: Vehicle/personnel entrances into prison compounds that consist of double gates, only one of which is open at any time. At high-security facilities, a pit or inspection well is used to allow correctional officers to look at the undercarriage of the vehicle or mirrors or creepers can be used for this purpose. After the search is completed, the second gate is opened allowing the vehicle to enter the prison proper.

SECTION 1983, 42 USC 1983 OF THE CIVIL RIGHTS ACT: A part of the Civil Rights Act of 1871 that allowed individuals who were deprived of their rights by any federal, state, county, or city officer, acting under color of law, irrespective of the official's actual authority to engage in the behavior in question, to sue them in federal court.

SECURE INSTITUTION: Any facility that is designed and operated to ensure that all entrances and exits are under the exclusive control of the facility's staff, thereby not allowing an inmate/resident to leave the facility unsupervised or without permission.

SECURITY OR CUSTODY: The degree of restriction of inmate movement within a detention/correctional facility, usually divided into maximum-, medium-, and minimum-risk levels.

SECURITY DEVICES: Locks, gates, doors, bars, fences, screens, ceilings, floors, walls, and barriers used to confine and control detained individuals. Also included are electronic monitoring equipment, security alarm systems, security lights, auxiliary power supplies, and other equipment used to maintain facility security.

SEGREGATION: The confinement of an inmate to an individual cell that is separated from the general population. There are three forms of segregation: administrative segregation, disciplinary detention, and protective custody.

SERIOUS INCIDENT: A situation in which injury serious enough to warrant medical attention occurs involving a resident, employee, or visitor on the grounds of the institution. Also, a situation containing an imminent threat to the security of the institution and/or to the safety of residents, employees, or visitors on the grounds of the institution.

SEVERE MENTAL DISTURBANCE: A condition in which an individual is a danger to self or others or is incapable of attending to basic physiological needs.

SHADOW BOARD: A board on which tools can be hung that has an outline of each item in order to visually know when an item is missing at inventory.

SHAKEDOWNS: Searches of inmates, their cells, common areas, and all other areas of the prison or jail, at frequent, irregular intervals to discover contraband.

SHIVS/SHANKS: Knives made from materials available in the prison, including kitchen utensils, metal from the shops, beds, lockers, and even from seemingly harmless items such as toothbrushes.

SPECIAL DIETS: These fulfill therapeutic/medical requirements and generally accommodate the special dietary restrictions of legitimate religious groups.

STRIP SEARCH: An examination of an inmate/resident's naked body for weapons, contraband, and physical abnormalities. This also includes a thorough search of all the individual's clothing while it is not being worn.

SUPER-MAX INSTITUTIONS: These provide the highest level of custody and security. Inmates assigned to these facilities have demonstrated an inability to adjust satisfactorily to general population units at other secure facilities. Inmates are all housed in single secure units. They typically spend twenty-three hours per day in their cells with one hour for recreation. All programming involving staff is through the cell doors, such as religious and casework services. Other programs are provided by correspondence courses or by closed-circuit TV. When inmates are removed from their cells, they often are strip searched, always placed in full restraints, and accompanied by more than one correctional officer.

THREE-PIECE SUIT: Restraints that include handcuffs, belly or waist chain, and leg irons.

TRAINING: An organized, planned, and evaluated activity designed to achieve specific learning objectives and enhance the job performance of personnel. Training may occur onsite, at an academy or training center, an institution of higher learning, at professional meetings, or through contract service or closely supervised on-the-job training. It includes a formal agenda and instruction by a teacher, manager, or official; physical training; or other instruction programs that include a trainer/trainee relationship. Meetings of professional associations are considered training where there is clear evidence of this. Whether it occurs onsite, at an academy or training center, through contract services, or at professional meetings, the activity must be part of an overall training program.

TYPE I MINIMUM SECURITY FACILITIES: These are designated for inmates who have a short period before release. They help ease reintegration into the community. They have little or no programming.

TYPE II MINIMUM SECURITY FACILITIES: These are designed for inmates, posing no security risk, with release or parole dates of eighteen months or less. They help serve the labor needs of the institution.

UNIT MANAGEMENT: This is a form of correctional management in which a team of correctional workers, including correctional officers, counselors, and others, takes responsibility for managing a particular wing or cell block of a prison. The unit management system has several basic requirements:

1. Each unit holds a relatively small number of inmates. Ideally, there should be fewer than 150 but not more than 500 inmates.
2. Inmates are housed in the same unit for a major portion of their confinement.
3. Inmates assigned to a unit work in a close relationship with a multidisciplinary team of staff who are regularly assigned to the unit and whose officers are located within the unit.

4. Staff members have decision-making authority for the institutional programming and living conditions for the inmates assigned to the unit with broad rules, policies, and guidelines established by the agency and/or facility administrator.
5. Inmate assignments to a unit are based on the inmate's need for control, security, and programs offered.

Unit management increases contact between staff and inmates, fosters increased interpersonal relationships, and leads to more knowledgeable decision making as a direct result of staff dealing with a smaller, more permanent group. At the same time, the facility benefits from the economies inherent in centralized service facilities, such as utilities, food service, health care, educational systems, vocational programs, and recreational facilities.

UNITY OF COMMAND: Refers to the view that workers only should have to report directly to one boss.

UNIVERSAL PRECAUTIONS: These are basic medical standards of safety and care to reduce the spread of infectious diseases.

URINE SURVEILLANCE PROGRAM: A program whereby urine samples are collected on an irregular basis from offenders suspected of having a history of drug use to determine current or recent use.

VOLUNTEER: An individual who donates his or her time and effort to enhance the activities and programs of the agency. They are selected on the basis of their skills or personal qualities to provide services in recreation, counseling, education, religion, and other areas.

WARDEN/SUPERINTENDENT: The individual in charge of the institution; the chief executive or administrative officer. This position is sometimes referred to by other titles, but "warden" and "superintendent" are the most commonly used terms.

WORK RELEASE: This is a formal arrangement sanctioned by law whereby an inmate/resident is released into the community to maintain approved and regular employment.

Note: Some of the definitions of these terms and concepts are adapted from U.S. Department of Justice, Federal Bureau of Prisons; American Correctional Association, Standards Supplement 1996; and other ACA publications.

Index

A

AA. *See Alcoholics Anonymous*
ACA. *See American Correctional Association (ACA)*
ACFSA. *See American Correctional Food Service Association (ACFSA)*
Acquired Immune Deficiency Syndrome (AIDS)
 AIDS Related Complex, 95
 diagnosis, 95
 duty to protect inmates, 17
 effect on immune system, 94–95
 needle hazard, 45
 orientation for inmates with, 113
 transmission of HIV, 95
 treatment, 95
ADA. *See Americans with Disabilities Act (ADA)*
Administrative segregation. *See Special management*
Admission, 111–15
AIDS. *See Acquired Immune Deficiency Syndrome (AIDS)*
AJA. *See American Jail Association (AJA)*
Alcoholics Anonymous (AA), 122, 125, 133
Alcoholism, 102
AMA. *See American Medical Association (AMA)*
American Correctional Association (ACA)
 professional development, 5, 13
 standards, viii–ix, 4
  acceptance by criminal justice system, 32
  emergency plans, 61
  fire prevention, 67
  firearms, 58
  food service, 75, 77
  health care, 89
  library operations, 123
  perimeter construction, 37
  programming, 118
  recreation, 123
  religious practice, 123
  rule book for inmates, 31
  searches, 43
  segregated unit, 33
  training, 10
  use of force, 56
 survey regarding juveniles, ix–x
American Correctional Food Service Association (ACFSA), 81

American Jail Association (AJA), 5
American Medical Association (AMA), ix
Americans with Disabilities Act (ADA), ix, xi–xii
Ankle shackles. *See Restraining devices*
Armed supervision, 52
Armory, 85
Asthma, 99
Attica prison, 4
Attorney, visits of, 46

B

Barbershop. *See Hair care*
Bath. *See Shower*
Bombs, 45, 61, 68–69
BOP. *See United States, Bureau of Prisons (BOP)*

C

CAC. *See Commission on Accreditation for Corrections (CAC)*
Cardiopulmonary resuscitation (CPR), 93
Careworkers, 4
Case law, 16
Case management, 118
Chaplain, 123–25
Chemical agents. *See Gas*
Civil disturbances, 61, 70–71
Classification
 approaches to, 114
 committees, 115, 132
 objectives of, 113–14
 pending, 33
 policies, 114–15
 unit teams, 115, 132
Cleaning
 contaminated areas, 87
 control center, 85
 living quarters, 83, 84
 shops, 85
 yards, 85
Clothing, 85, 86–87
 intake processing, 111
Co-correctional institutions, 30

Index

Commission on Accreditation for Corrections (CAC), ix
Communication, xi, 28, 50
    training, 11
Community corrections, vii, 135. *See also Parole and Parole officer; Probation*
Confidentiality, 87, 118
Contraband
    control of, 43, 44
    disposal, 45
    in mail, 128–29
    marking of, 111
Control center, cleaning of, 85
Cooper v. Pate, 4
Corporal punishment, 17
Correctional officers
    conduct and appearance, 138
    drug-free, 137–38
    education, 5
    employment opportunities, 4–5
    ethics, 137
    in correctional setting, 4–7
    legal representation of, 7
    pay, 5
    public relations skills, 135–36
    public understanding of, 9
    responsibilities, x, 6–7, 12
    role in security, x
    skills needed by, 9, 10
    training needed by, x–xi
Corrections
    cost, 3
    funding, lack of, 9, 61
    history of, 3
    mission of, 9–10
    public goals for, 9
    role in criminal justice, 2
    women in, 5–6
Corrections Corporation of America, 5
Counseling, 122
    cognitive therapy, 118
    in segregated units, 36
    mental illness, 109
Counts, 42–43
Courts, 1–2. *See also Supreme Court*
CPR. *See Cardiopulmonary resuscitation (CPR)*
Crime
    institutional offenses, 32
    public sentiments against, 3, 9
Crowding, vii–viii, 61, 83
Cruel and unusual punishment, 17-89. *See also Inmates, rights of, Eighth Amendment*

D

Death penalty, 17
    inmates under, 50
Dental care, 111
Design issues, 41
Determinate sentencing, 131
Diabetes, 99–100
Disabled, xi–xii
Disasters, 72–73

Disciplinary detention. *See Special management*
Disciplinary procedures for inmates, 31–32, 40
Disciplinary segregation. *See Special management*
Dormitories, inspection of, 83
Dothard v. Rawlinson, 29
Drug abuse, 100–02, 125
    in camp operations, 128
    of staff, 137–38
Drugs. *See Medications*
Due process. *See Inmates, rights of*

E

Education programs. *See Programs, education programs*
Education staff, 119
Eighth Amendment. *See Inmates, rights of*
Emergency plans
    ACA standards for, 61
    bombs, 68–69
    civil disturbances, 70–71
    contents, 62–63
    disasters, 72–73
    employee job action, 71–72
    escapes, 62, 66–67
    fires, 67–68
    hostages, 69–70
    importance of, 61
    preparedness checklist, 63
    recall, 73
    riots, 62, 64–66
    strike (inmates), 71
    training for, 11, 62–63
Emergency release programs, ix
Emergency response teams, 58
Employee job actions, 61, 71–72
Enemies, 111
Entrances, 42
Epilepsy, 98–99
Escapes/escape attempts, 39–40, 61, 62, 66–67
    in trash, 86
Ethics, 137

F

Federal Civil Rights Act of 1871, 19
Federal Tort Claims Act of 1946, 19
Fingerprint, 111
Fire, 61, 67–68
    hazard, 84
    training for, 11
Firearms. *See Weapons*
First aid. *See Health care, first aid*
First Amendment. *See Inmates, rights of*
Flood, 61
Floors, 85
Fog, 61, 71
Food
    ACA standards, 75, 77
    American Correctional Food Service Association (ACFSA), 81
    commissary, 79
    Food Service Manual (Bureau of Prisons), 76
    menus, 75
    preparation, 76

Index

riots and, 75
storage, 75–76
strike, 61, 71
supervision, 47, 79–81
tools, 47
U.S. Navy system, 76
and vermin, 84
Force. *See also Restraining devices*
ACA standards for, 56
deadly, 52–53, 57–58
justifiable circumstances, 56
policy, 51
post orders, 38
training in, 10
Forced cell moves, 59
Ford Foundation, ix
Fourteenth Amendment. *See Inmates, rights of, Fourteenth amendment*
Fourth Amendment. *See Inmates, rights of, Fourth amendment*

G

Games criminals play, 11
Gangs, viii
Gas, 55–56
Grievances of inmates, 21

H

Hair care, 87
Halfway houses, 2
Handcuffs. *See Restraining devices*
Handguns, 55
Hawk, Kathleen, M., 5
Hazardous material spills, 61
Health authority, 89
Health care
ACA standards, 89
cardiopulmonary resuscitation (CPR), 93
emergencies, 92
first aid, 11, 92–93
medical isolation, 113
medical screening, 89–90, 111
medical trips, 91
medication, 90–91
National Commission on Correctional Health Care (NCCHC), 89
needles, 90–91
sick call, 90
suicide, 92
training, 11
Helicopters for escape, 40
Hepatitis, 93–94
HIV infection. *See Acquired Immune Deficiency Syndrome (AIDS)*
Hospital tools and supplies, 47–48
Hostage, 69–70
policy, 39
situation, 38, 61
Housing units
security in, 41
supervision, 25–26
Hurricanes, 61

I

IACO. *See International Association of Correctional Officers (IACO)*
Identification, 27
Immunity, 20
Infirmary, 91–92
Informal resolutions, 32
Information gathering on inmates, 27–28
Inmate accountability, 42
Inmates
AIDS and, 17, 113
behavior, 24–25
civil death statutes, 15
court intervention, 4
death sentenced, 50
description of population, viii
family of, 111
hands-off approach to, 4, 15
hands-on approach to, 4, 15
high-security, 50
identification of, 27
intake processing, 111–12, 113
medical records of, 89
money of, 109
movement of, 43
orientation, 112
population growth of, vii–viii
rights of, xi, 10, 15
due process, 16
Eighth Amendment, 17
First Amendment, 17, 19, 136
Fourteenth Amendment, 17, 18
Fourth Amendment, 17, 18
Sixth Amendment, 17
treatment, 17
rule book for, 31
sexual activity, 29–31
strike, 71
supervision, 10
transfers, 26
Inspection, 36
International Association of Correctional Officers (IACO), 5
Interpersonal relations training, 11

J

Justice Department. *See United States, Department of Justice*
Juveniles
crimes of, ix–x
in adult institutions, ix–x

K

Key control, 11, 48–49
cleaning area of, 85
Kinney v. Indiana Youth Center, 58

L

Laundry programs, 86–87
Law enforcement, 1
Law Enforcement Assistance Administration, ix
Lawsuits. *See Litigation*

Index

Legal reference service, 36
Library access, 36
Lighting, 39
    fixture inspection, 83
Linens, 87
Litigation, 7, 16, 18, 21
    inmate age and, 17
Lock shop, 85
Locked units. *See Special management*
Lombardo, Lucien X., 6

M

Mail, 128–29
Maintenance, 86
Media, 136
Medical care decisions, 89
Medications, 47–48
    drug storage, 91
    intake processing, 109
    in segregated units, 90–91
Mental health, 109
Mental illness
    cyclothymic personality, 107–08
    depression, 106
    increase in inmates with, 103
    mania, 106–07
    mood disorders, 106–07
    neuroses, 103–04
    paranoid personality, 108
    passive-aggressive personalities, 107
    personality disorders, 107–08
    psychoses, 105–06
    schizoid personality, 108
    screening for, 111
    suicide, 104–05
    treatment, 109
Mentally retarded, 108–09
Midnight shift, 7
Minorities, xi, 5

N

NA. *See Narcotics Anonymous (NA)*
Narcotics Anonymous (NA), 122, 125, 133
National Commission on Correctional Health Care (NCCHC), 89
National Recreation and Park Association, 123
NCCHC. *See National Commission on Correctional Health Care (NCCHC)*

O

Orientation, 111–12
OSHA. *See United States, Occupational Safety and Health Administration (OSHA)*
Outcounts, 42

P

Parole and parole officer. *See also Community corrections*
    absconder, 134
    community parole officer, 133–34
    elimination of, 131
    institutional parole officer, 132–33
    orientation for violators, 113
    role in criminal justice, 2, 131
    special conditions of, 131
Patrol duty, 38
Personal property
    in segregation, 35
    limits on, 84
Pest control, 86
Pistols. *See Handguns*
PLRA. *See Prison Litigation Reform Act (PLRA)*
Policies, 27
Post orders, 26–27, 38
Prerelease programs, 132
Prison Litigation Reform Act (PLRA), 18, 21
Privacy, 6
Probation. *See also Community corrections*
    role in criminal justice, 2
Programs
    ACA standards for programming, 118
    balanced model, 117
    case management, 118
    counseling. *See Counseling*
    drug abuse programs, 125
    early development of, 3
    education programs, 36, 118–19
    group therapy, 118
    life skills, 120
    medical model, 3, 117
    prerelease. *See Prerelease programs*
    supervision, 127–28
    vocational training, 119–20, 121
    women, equal program opportunities for, 117–18
    work camps, 128
    work programs, 121–22
Prosecutors, 1
Protective custody. *See Special management*
Psychiatrist, 109
Psychologist, 109
Public relations
    importance of, 135
    media and, 136
    public information officer, 136
    riots and, 135
Public service programs, 138–39

R

Rational Recovery, 133
Reception. *See Inmates, intake processing*
Records, 34–35
Recreation, 122–23
    in segregated units, 36
Reformatories, 3
Rehabilitation. *See Programs*
Release of inmates, 112, 118
    planning for, 131–32
    temporary release programs, 133
Religious Freedom Restoration Act (RFRA), 19, 123
Religious services, 123–25
    in segregated units, 36
Reno, Janet, 5
Report writing, 10
Restitution centers, 2

Restraining devices, 36, 56–57
Restrooms, 46
RFRA. *See Religious Freedom Restoration Act (RFRA)*
Rifles, 54–55
Riots, 64–66
    call-up procedures, 64
    emergency plans, 61, 62, 64–66
    food and, 75
    notification, 64
    public knowledge and, 135
    Santa Fe, New Mexico, 28
    warning signs, 25
Ruffin v. Commonwealth, 4
Rumors, 28

S

Safety hazards, 84
Sanitation
    cell, 84
    contaminated areas, 87
    crowding and, 83
    hair care, 87
    importance of, 83
    inspection, 83
    laundry, 86–87
    maintenance staff, 83
    personal property and, 84
    pest control, 86
    unit upkeep, 84
    waste disposal, 86
Searches
    body searches, 44
    food service and, 79
    housing unit, 44–45
    patdowns, 44
    purpose of, 43
    segregated units, 36
    vehicles, 45
    visitors, 44–45, 126
Security
    consciousness of, 10
    food service, 77
    inspections, 49, 63–64
    internal design features, 40–42
    key control, 48–49
    manual, 41
    perimeter features, 37–39, 58
    in segregation, 34–36
    tool control, 46–47
    training, 11
Segregation units. *See Special management*
Self-defense, 57
Sexual assault, 31
Sexual behavior, 29–31
Sharpshooters, 53
Shift logs, 26–27
Shop areas, 85
Shotguns, 55
Shower
    at intake, 111
    inspection of, 83
    supervision of, 31

Sick call. *See Health care, sick call*
Sinks, inspection of, 83, 84
Snowstorm, 61
Social service staff, 118
Social workers, role of, 118
Special management
    medication in, 90–91
    orientation, 113
    programs, 128
    protective custody, 113
    searches, 45
    segregation, 33–36, 128
    supervision, 50
    tracking inmates in, 26
Standards, definition, viii–ix. *See also American Correctional Association, standards*
Strikes, 61
Suicide, 92, 104–05, 113
Supervision
    activities involved in, 23
    armed, 52
    design philosophies' effect on, 24
    during job assignments, 28
    food preparation and service, 79–81
    inmate behavior, observing, 25
    program activities, 127–28
    segregating inmates, 32–36, 128
    visibility, 40–41
Supreme Court
    access to courts and, 15, 18
    cruel and unusual punishment and, 17
    First Amendment rights and, 19
    intervention of, 4
    refusal of treatment and, 17
Surveillance, 38

T

Temporary release programs. *See Release, temporary release programs*
Tennessee v. Garner, 57
Toilets, inspection of, 83, 84
Tools
    control, 11, 46–47
    hair care, 87
    storage, 47
Tornadoes, 61
Torts, 19–20
Towers, cleaning of, 85
Traffic control, 38–39
Training
    American Correctional Association standards for, 10
    consequences of poor training, 10
    correspondence courses from ACA, 13
    courses, subjects covered in, xi, 10–11
    emergency plans, 62–63
    firearms, 54
    importance of, x–xi, 10
    inservice, 31–32
    security, 41
Trash. *See Waste disposal*
Treatment. *See Programs*
Tuberculosis, 96–98

U

Unit management
    classification, 115
    team, 118
United Nations, ix
United States
    Bureau of Labor Statistics, 5
    Bureau of Prisons (BOP)
      Food Service Manual, 76
      operation of federal prisons, 2
    Department of Justice, ix, 2
    Federal Bureau of Investigation, 6
    Immigration and Naturalization Service, 6
    Marshal's Service, 6, 133
    Occupational Safety and Health Administration (OSHA), 94
Use of force. *See Force*

V

Vehicle searches. *See Searches, vehicle*
Ventilators, inspection of, 83
Visitors and visiting
    importance of, 125
    procedures, 126–127
    searches of, 44–45, 126
    in segregated units, 36, 127
Vocational training. *See Programs, vocational training*
Volunteers, 138

W

Waste disposal, 86
Weapons
    ACA firearms standards, 58
    authority for, 51
    firearms training, 11, 54
    firing, 54–55
    personal ones, 52
    procedures for, 51
    storage and maintenance, 38, 51–52
***Wolff v. McDonnell*,** 34
Women
    equal program opportunities for, 117–18
    in corrections, 5–6, 29
    institutions for, 31
Work camps, 121
Work of inmates, 121–22
    strike, 71
    supervision, 28–29

Y

Yard workers, 85

Z

Zimmer, Lynn, 5

ACA Code of Ethics

Preamble

The American Correctional Association expects of its members unfailing honesty, respect for the dignity and individuality of human beings and a commitment to professional and compassionate service. To this end, we subscribe to the following principles.

1. Members shall respect and protect the civil and legal rights of all individuals.

2. Members shall treat every professional situation with concern for the welfare of the individuals involved and with no intent of personal gain.

3. Members shall maintain relationships with colleagues to promote mutual respect within the profession and improve the quality of service.

4. Members shall make public criticism of their colleagues or their agencies only when warranted, verifiable, and constructive.

5. Members shall respect the importance of all disciplines within the criminal justice system and work to improve cooperation with each segment.

6. Members shall honor the public's right to information and share information with the public to the extent permitted by law subject to individuals' right to privacy.

7. Members shall respect and protect the right of the public to be safeguarded from criminal activity.

8. Members shall refrain from using their positions to secure personal privileges or advantages.

9. Members shall refrain from allowing personal interest to impair objectivity in the performance of duty while acting in an official capacity.

10. Members shall refrain from entering into any formal or informal activity or agreement which presents a conflict of interest or is inconsistent with the conscientious performance of duties.

11. Members shall refrain from accepting any gifts, service, or favor that is or appears to be improper or implies an obligation inconsistent with the free and objective exercise of professional duties.

12. Members shall clearly differentiate between personal views/statements and views/statements/positions made on behalf of the agency or Association.

13. Members shall report to appropriate authorities any corrupt or unethical behaviors in which there is sufficient evidence to justify review.

14. Members shall refrain from discriminating against any individual because of race, gender, creed, national origin, religious affiliation, age, disability, or any other type of prohibited discrimination.

15. Members shall preserve the integrity of private information; they shall refrain from seeking information on individuals beyond that which is necessary to implement responsibilities and perform their duties; members shall refrain from revealing nonpublic information unless expressly authorized to do so.

16. Members shall make all appointments, promotions, and dismissals in accordance with established civil service rules, applicable contract agreements, and individual merit, rather than furtherance of personal interests.

17. Members shall respect, promote, and contribute to a work place that is safe, healthy, and free of harassment in any form.

Adopted August 1975 at the 105th Congress of Correction
Revised August 1990 at the 120th Congress of Correction
Revised August 1994 at the 124th Congress of Correction